flesh

This book contains themes of sexual abuse, eating disorders and suicide, as well as abusive relationships. Reader discretion is advised.

flesh

decentering the male gaze and reclaiming the objectified body

Charli Howard

First published in Great Britain in 2026 by Trapeze,
an imprint of The Orion Publishing Group Ltd
Carmelite House, 50 Victoria Embankment
London EC4Y 0DZ

An Hachette UK Company

The authorised representative in the EEA is Hachette Ireland,
8 Castlecourt Centre, Dublin 15, D15 XTP3, Ireland
(email: info@hbgi.ie)

1 3 5 7 9 10 8 6 4 2

Copyright © Charli Howard 2026

The moral right of Charli Howard to be identified as
the author of this work has been asserted in accordance
with the Copyright, Designs and Patents Act of 1988.

All rights reserved. No part of this publication may be
reproduced, stored in a retrieval system, or transmitted
in any form or by any means, electronic, mechanical,
photocopying, recording, or otherwise, without the
prior permission of both the copyright owner and the
above publisher of this book.

A CIP catalogue record for this book is
available from the British Library.

ISBN (Hardback) 978 1 3987 2808 0
ISBN (Ebook) 978 1 3987 2810 3
ISBN (Audio) 978 1 3987 2811 0

Typeset by Input Data Services Ltd, Bridgwater, Somerset

Printed in Great Britain by Clays Ltd, Elcograf, S.p.A.

www.orionbooks.co.uk

To all the women and girls who have ever felt reduced to their body parts, and who know they are worthy of more.

contents

preface   1

vagina.   15
breasts.   46
skin.   88
stomach.   126
thighs.   159
brain.   179
heart.   211
whole.   234

notes   240
references   245
acknowledgements   247

preface

I have been a body many times in my life. I have rarely been a person.

I have been sexualised since I was a child, and I'm sure most women reading this will have been, too. Sexualisation starts as early as we can remember; thrust in our faces before we have a chance of understanding our bodies, or who we are by ourselves.

For much of my life, I have felt unsafe in my body, and nobody could tell me why. I was aware of my body at all times: the way it may or may not elicit attention from men; the ways I should posture myself to make it appear more attractive and 'flattering'; how the way I dress may or may not be considered 'suggestive' or lead to unwarranted comments or behaviour. If I wasn't constantly analysing my behaviour, my dress sense or how my body looked, then by God, other people would be.

I know I am worth more than my body – or that's what society tells me, anyway – and yet that's what I, like so many women, have often been diminished to. *A body*. Nothing but flesh: used, abused and dissected for the pleasure of others.

Flesh will explore how women's entire identities are reduced to their body parts by society throughout their lives: that, despite our other achievements and capabilities, we will ultimately be valued for, and defined by, our appearance.

Being sexualised is embedded within the female experience; a by-product of being born. Men have shaped the entire way I view myself and my body, and even in some of the most fleeting of encounters, their actions have had a profound impact on the way I see myself.

As a self-proclaimed feminist who genuinely wants the best for women and girls, I feel embarrassed admitting their actions have had such a prominent influence on the way I live my life, the way I view myself and the ways I've needed to prove my worth throughout my relationships. Yet they have. Repeatedly.

Our adolescence is filled with stories of inappropriate behaviour – of men leering at us in our school uniforms; of being told to cover up around weird 'uncles' or family friends; being catcalled from cars; being groped or forced into things we're not sexually comfortable with. It's never our fault, yet it always is. Even on the most mundane of days, undertaking the simplest of tasks, the persistent threat of violence from men requires us to stay vigilant and alert. As women, it's impossible to *just be*.

It doesn't take a lot to be sexualised as a woman, and therefore for our levels of confidence, body image, self-love and self-esteem to be impacted. It is not only our physical bodies that are objectified and fetishised, but our personalities, cultures, ethnicities and ages, too. *Shyness* is sexualised. *Anger* is sexualised. *Intelligence* is sexualised. *Stupidity* is sexualised. *Youthfulness* is sexualised. *Mothering* is sexualised. Should a woman dare act upon or own her sexuality, she will be judged and chastised for it. Therefore, the only 'acceptable' form of female sexualisation is when a man is in control of it.

The patriarchy, racism and capitalism have worked together to transform female bodies into objects. Like most women, I grew up learning that my desirability and worth lay in how men viewed me. I learnt to take their comments or actions as a measure of said worth. A comment, no matter how seedy or disgusting, meant you were wanted – which, ultimately, meant you were fuckable and therefore desirable. It didn't matter whether what they said or did made *me* feel good. It was their words, behaviour and attention that dictated how I would view myself at any given time.

When you're reduced to nothing more than your appearance or body throughout your life, you start to believe that's all you're good for. You're an object. A sex object. Objects do not do anything. They don't speak or move, have feelings or opinions. They just *sit* there, readily available when needed or when they're deemed useful enough. Their sole purpose is for the use, efficiency and enjoyment of others.

When men treated me like a sexual object, that's all I felt I was good for. When they made negative comments about the way I looked or noted the things I should change to become more attractive, I added them to an ever-growing internal list of things that were wrong with me. Rarely did I step back and question the discomfort I felt; whether these men were, in fact, deserving of me. The worse I felt about myself, the more I gravitated towards men who treated me appallingly.

I may have spent my life feeling like nothing more than a body, but I have often treated myself as nothing more than one, too. It turns out that I am far from being alone.

Doctor Caroline Heldman has studied the way women often willingly – and unknowingly – view and use their own bodies as sex objects; something known as 'self-objectification'.

Men, she explains, are sold the idea that they are sexual subjects. They live their lives in the driver's seat, where seeing images of objectified women everywhere makes them feel 'powerful'. Women, however, are the *objects*, sold the idea that being sexy and attractive are means of measuring their worth.

All women, according to Heldman, objectify themselves and others to an extent: a result of learning that their value lies in the way they look, from a lifetime of external messages in a patriarchal society, where women are seen as nothing more than 'things'. In other words, women learn to view themselves as an object first and as a person second.

As we grow older and become even more exposed to daily images of beautiful, semi-naked women selling us anything and everything, we learn to focus on our sexuality and appearance over our character. We learn we are *things* before *human beings*. As Heldman notes: 'We see men's magazines with scantily clad women, and we see women's magazines with scantily clad women.' Regardless of how you sexually identify as a woman, there is no escaping this messaging. The same society that tells us we are worth more than our bodies also reduces us to nothing *but* our body parts.

Gradually, women start to place greater importance on the way they look over how they feel. They end up closely checking their actions and behaviour using something psychologists call 'habitual body monitoring'. This means we use valuable, cognitive energy on the ways we appear to the outside world aesthetically – or, more specifically, the ways we appear to men. You may have found yourself doing this already today: angling your face in a certain direction while speaking to someone, which you believe presents your 'best' or 'favourite' side; 'mewing' – the action of placing your tongue against the roof of your mouth so your jawline appears tauter; positioning your body in photos to appear less 'fat'; wearing clothes that are more 'flattering' (or, in other words, clothing which makes you seem less fat); checking your hair is coiffed or sitting in the 'correct' place; sucking your stomach in when taking a photograph. We learn to concern ourselves with the way we look and how we're perceived by others before knowing how our bodies act or behave naturally.

When beauty becomes a woman's social currency, over time we

learn not just to accept the perspective of the male gaze but also to objectify *other* women, critiquing their bodies and comparing them to our own. Without realising, women begin mimicking the sexist and misogynistic ideals long placed upon them by men – the very behaviours that have made them feel uncomfortable and unworthy – and use beauty as a tool to measure their value against each other. Society teaches us that to be chosen by a man sexually or romantically is considered the ultimate form of female validation, so women compete with other women aesthetically for the attention of men.

But what is this constant self-objectification and pressure to be perfect doing to us as people? A 2006 study examined self-objectification and how it leads to a lack of internal awareness, which in turn leads to self-harming and restrictive behaviours such as bulimia, anxiety, loneliness and depressive symptoms. A further study found correlation between misogyny towards women and how it causes them psychological distress. This constant sexualisation and the impossible standards women are held to are having a huge impact on our overall body image and mental health. Rather than living, many of us are simply existing.

This pressure, or stress, doesn't just affect us mentally, but also takes a toll physically. Research shows how our emotions are stored and expressed through the body. Repressed anger, for example, can build up in the liver, leading to headaches, PMS symptoms and toxin build-up. Stress can show itself on the outside, through dark circles under the eyes or acne on the skin. Chronic fear can impact the kidneys, leading to adrenal fatigue, back pain or bladder stones. Feeling unheard can show up as thyroid imbalances and hormonal issues; grief as shallow breathing, asthma, chronic fatigue or colds; heartbreak as chest palpitations, chest tightness or issues with blood pressure; worry as tension, urgency or urinary issues in the bladder.

How could the pressures and violence we face, simply for being women, *not* have a profound impact on our bodies? Instead of ignoring these issues or avoiding them through using food, sex, drugs or other forms of escapism, we must listen to what our bodies are telling us to truly know ourselves.

If there was ever a reason to denounce the patriarchy, the sake of our health is surely good enough.

Stress is part of the female existence. Male supremacy pushes us into impossible choices and then holds us accountable for the results of those choices. It's no wonder, then, that the stress from the patriarchy, misogyny and beauty standards forces our bodies to exist constantly in survival mode. When I take a step back, I can see how so many women – many of whom I know and witness personally – act out self-objectification from a place of deep unhappiness, insecurity and worthlessness. Discrimination and threats of gendered violence towards us are so routine, so normalised, that we've accepted our constant need to monitor our bodies as our fate. We have learnt to endure this behaviour and, with the knowledge of men being both our saviours and predators, try to find ways to make our lives easier.

'Easier', it turns out, can be achieved by becoming sexually desirable. But by choosing this route we are doing ourselves and the women around us a huge disservice because we're worthy and capable of so much more.

Nowadays, much of female empowerment and beauty is linked to a woman's sexual allure and desirability. Choice feminism has managed to convince many of us that showing our bodies and sexualising ourselves is an act of empowerment – a belief that I, especially, long equated with my power as a woman. Throughout *Flesh*, I will frequently refer back to how choice and the versions of pseudo-empowerment – often linked to how sexy we appear – encouraged by both men and women alike are a means to benefit the patriarchy. I think a lot about this perception of 'choice' because the choices we make individually, no matter how empowering they feel to us, can often impact other women's rights and livelihoods on a bigger scale. I say this having worked in the fashion industry myself, which profits off women, creating an unrealistic expectation of beauty standards and exploiting their insecurities and vulnerabilities. I actively fought to work in and be accepted by this industry, while simultaneously being exploited by it.

While many feminists and women celebrate this hypersexual culture as 'empowerment', I now view it as a poor substitute for what *true* empowerment looks like: social, economic, political and sexual equality that will give women meaningful power over their own – and hopefully other women's – lives. Real collective change can only happen when we think outside of what empowers us individually. Empowerment does not, however, lie solely in our sexual choices.

Some choices really aren't our own at all. Many women make choices and decisions to their own detriment. Your choices will be heavily influenced by the culture, society and ideas around you. Things like your social environment, your culture or your bank balance can influence how you perceive your immediate world and the choices you make. Our *true* choices as women are still very limited.

I was speaking to a man recently who asked me whether I felt I had overshared my life online.

I asked what he was specifically referring to. He mentioned an Instagram post where I'd opened up about how I'd suffered in a relationship with an ex. He brought up the post where I showed before and after photos of my anorexia and bulimia recovery, where I'd tried explaining how I spent my youth trying to mould myself into what society said was beautiful, all in the hope of being loved. He mentioned the article I'd published in the summer of 2023 about how oversexualised modern dating had become, how women face horrifically sexual comments and sexualised treatment on dates.

I knew what he was trying to say. *HE* felt I had overshared these personal parts of my life. What he hadn't yet realised is that those stories are universal.

To a heterosexual man, these occurrences might sound like rarities and perhaps they even made him feel uncomfortable. But in the eyes of women, many of these occurrences *are* our normal.

This man did not like hearing about these issues, and it's hard not to feel like you're offending a man you're speaking to by talking about male behaviour in either specific or generalised ways. But an average female existence is scattered with a series of 'small' incidents we're expected to just brush off or forget about.

Perhaps this man and many others like him didn't like hearing about my experiences because I was too honest? Perhaps I may have shed light on some of their own behaviours? Or maybe turning a blind eye to my stories makes them feel better about their own shortcomings and the women they've failed? After all, why is it that nearly every woman I've spoken to knows someone who has been sexually assaulted but men never seem to know a rapist?

The idea that a female can have traumatic experiences and talk openly about them and without shame means society will finally need to view us as what we are: not just bodies, but *real human beings*. I doubt this man would have considered any of these experiences an overshare had I been a man. I'd be considered brave or strong.

To see the world through the *female gaze* we must first acknowledge the realities of the female experience. We must be open in sharing our stories and the incidents that have defined us as people to show men what we deal with on a regular basis and to show women they are not alone.

Flesh aims to explain how the systemic pressures women experience every day – culturally, societally, romantically – impact the most important relationship of all: the one we have with ourselves.

For years, I built a career around showcasing my body: first, through modelling, where I battled debilitating eating disorders; later, as a 'curve' model, encouraging women to love the skin they're in through unretouched images and encouraging other women to do the same. While I still stand firmly behind the importance of representation and showing authentic, unretouched female bodies, it took this deeply dark time to question the image I've presented of myself and the role I've played not only in my own objectification but in celebrating the objectification of others too.

My messaging may have come from a place of wanting to help empower women, but by repeatedly showing my body off I was still putting it at the forefront of everything I did. I realised that even after all the lengths I'd gone to in recovering from my eating disorders, there were still unresolved traumas that were impacting the way I viewed and presented myself, let alone how I *felt* about myself. I may have no longer been fixated on calories or how much I weighed on a scale, but I was still aware of my body in other ways: the way it took up space, the correct and incorrect ways I was performing womanhood.

I wanted to let go of the way my body looked or at least relax about it somewhat. I realised I wanted more: more for myself, more from my relationships, more for the women around me. I wanted to be the main character of my own story, where men weren't defining the narrative.

I wanted to be more than my body, wanted more *from* my body. I wanted to be more than a vessel for men to project their unresolved emotions and trauma on to; more than a body someone uses and disregards once they've had their fix. I wanted more than the pseudo-feminism promised to me from self-sexualisation. I wanted more from life itself.

What I've often considered an act of self-love hasn't been as radical or feminist as I'd perhaps hoped. As I will explore in this book, I'm beginning to question my feminism and everything I believed modern-day female empowerment to be. Perhaps by the end of this book you will, too.

Adolescence, a four-part television drama created by Jack Thorne and Stephen Graham, became an instant global hit when it launched on Netflix in 2025. Shot in real time, it tells the story of thirteen-year-old Jamie, who is arrested for the murder of a female fellow student, Katie, after she rejects him romantically, his motive seemingly influenced by a mixture of manosphere forums, online incel culture and misogynistic ideas learnt in the playground. It aims to show that no matter how much a parent monitors their child's internet usage, the manosphere's ability to radicalise young men is profound: its hateful messaging and ideologies oozing from the depths of the online world and out into the everyday.

Part of the reason *Adolescence* resonated in the way it did is because Jamie is from a nice, 'normal', relatable family. He is cute-looking, baby-faced and white. We watch how Jamie's actions affected the people around him; how one 'mistake', one outburst, altered the course of his life and that of his family's. It was tragic.

A waste. A life destroyed. We mourn the future Jamie could have had, had he not been radicalised by the content he'd read and seen online. But while the show was undoubtedly important to the bigger conversation, it does not tell Katie's side of the story. We do not know anything about Katie herself: her dreams, her goals, her background. We do not see how her murder impacted her family; the trail of devastation her death at such a young age leaves behind.

Later in the show, a female detective sergeant makes a point about how women and girls involved in these violent cases are rarely discussed or remembered. 'Katie isn't important. Jamie is,' she tells her detective inspector. 'Everyone will remember Jamie. No one will remember her.' And she is right. If Katie's story were real, she would become yet another young woman buried beneath news story after news story of male on female violence.

Stories like the one featured in *Adolescence*, while shocking and thought-provoking, are now an unfortunate regular reality. It is not a coincidence that since the rise of vile, extreme misogynists such as Andrew Tate, violence against women and girls is becoming increasingly worse worldwide. In 2024, Home Secretary Yvette Cooper announced that extreme misogyny and male supremacist ideology will be treated as a form of extremism.

In Britain, stories of misogynistic extremism are repeatedly making the news. In 2021, twelve-year-old Ava White was stabbed by a fourteen-year-old boy in Liverpool. In 2023, fifteen-year-old Elianne Andam was attacked with a kitchen knife by a seventeen-year-old boy in Croydon. In July 2024, Louise Hunt was raped and murdered with a crossbow and butcher's knife alongside her mother, Carol, and sister, Hannah, by Louise's ex-boyfriend. Louise had broken up with him two weeks prior, due to his increasingly extremist views and behaviour. The Femicide Census shows that a woman has been killed by a man, on average, once every three days.

Within a couple of weeks of *Adolescence* being aired, Prime Minister Keir Starmer held a roundtable with the show's creators to discuss the issue of extreme misogyny. He called misogyny a 'cultural issue' and said it is something that society will need to work on collectively to help resolve. He also welcomed Netflix's move to make the series available for free within British secondary schools.

But when campaigner and writer Laura Bates's book *Men Who Hate Women* was published in 2020, there was no government intervention or roundtables, despite Bates's extensive research into misogyny, the then-underground manosphere and incel forums. Governments barely listen when charities speak out about male on female violence. Police often victim-blame when women come forward about their stalkers, abusers or rapists. Taught that 'boys will be boys', women consistently downplay sexist and misogynistic behaviour, believing they are overreacting.

A 2025 report from the National Audit Office called violence against women and girls (VAWG) an epidemic that is a 'significant and growing problem' affecting one in twelve women in England and Wales, and an issue that causes 'physical, mental, social and financial harm' to survivors. VAWG accounted for 20 per cent of all police-recorded crime in the UK from 2022–23. Keir Starmer promised to halve VAWG in a decade, which campaigners said was 'laudable' but 'impossible' without the commitment of every government department and without combating the deep-rooted sexism and misogyny in the UK.

But while political will is a step in the right direction and *finally* we are starting to take note of the severe effect that misogyny is having on men and teenage boys, we are still continuously turning a blind eye to the women and girls dealing with misogyny from birth and the impact it has on them and their development. The manosphere is one form of misogyny – an extreme form – but *every* woman on this planet has experienced misogyny and sexism in some way, from microaggressions to abuse. The high-profile murder cases we read about may be the most violent and extreme cases against women, but let's not assume misogyny is rare or limited to a few men. Every woman and girl I know has experienced misogyny more than once, and each and every one of us carries it within our bodies and psyches.

So, how do we stop objectifying ourselves? This is what I am exploring in the essays throughout this book. When we break our body parts down into individual pieces, which is how I've chosen to structure *Flesh*, we can clearly see how our lives as women have been eroded via sexism and misogyny over time. Every part of us is sexualised, objectified and fetishised in ways I don't even think we're necessarily conscious of.

I will touch on my own stories and experiences with misogyny and my body, but will also explore the wider social and historical context around each of these individual body parts: how our perception of them has changed over the years and what these body parts mean to women – and society – now. While I don't have all the answers on how to decenter men, I do hope that through observing and understanding the effect that misogyny has on us, we can start reclaiming our bodies as our own.

I want to understand how the cumulative and ongoing sexism and misogyny women face throughout our lives not only impact the way we experience the world but also the way we experience ourselves – from the way we view our bodies, the effect they have on our mental health, to our experiences of dating, sex and relationships. You will notice how much of this messaging is rooted in racism and sexism and how many women uphold these beliefs generationally, believing they are undeserving of more. Through these essays I aim to understand the connection between my sexualised self-image and my psychological self-image, piecing together the way society has had a damaging effect on my identity. This is about piecing bits of my life together, facing some uncomfortable truths and wondering whether it's truly possible to un-objectify and unlearn what I've been taught about myself.

I hope to bridge the connection between my true self versus my objectified self; between the person I really am versus the version of myself I've tried to run away from, the version I've been shaped into or, more specifically, the woman I've shaped *myself* into. I hope that by showing how incredible our bodies are internally, we can find a new respect for them outside our externalised gaze. I hope sharing my own stories of abuse, trauma and objectification may help you feel seen, less alone and to want more for yourself, too.

It is only when we become knowledgeable about our bodies and understand what our bodies do for us outside of their objectified, sexualised selves that we can start appreciating ourselves as *people*. Only then will women experience the revolution we need.

vagina.

During the months I spent forming in my mother's womb, slowly morphing from a cluster of cells into something more human, my future as a woman was already predetermined.

Like all humans, the very probability of my existence was pretty low. It took a certain time of the month, a certain body temperature, a certain environment, for that particular egg and sperm to fertilise. After that, another small chance at being conceived successfully, and even *then*, there was a 10–20 per cent chance of my mother miscarrying whatever I was back then within the first twelve weeks.

Once my mother's pregnancy became viable, naturally, there was a 50 per cent chance of me becoming a boy. Had I *actually* been born male, my life's experience would've been very different indeed.

I don't need to tell you why. I don't need to tell you how. You already know. You've witnessed it first-hand.

I was born to parents who didn't care what sex I was. When the midwife asked if they'd like to know my sex, they said they didn't care to know. Clothes were bought in 'neutral' colours – yellows, greens, purples – and my parents prepared for my arrival, safe in the knowledge they would love me regardless.

But even with that in mind, had I been born a boy I would've undoubtedly been treated differently because of the way society treats boys versus girls. Regardless of how much I was loved by my parents, regardless of how special *they* thought I was, being female made me lesser.

Parental love could only protect me so much. Having a vagina set the standard of how I'd be treated by the world: by society, by culture, by family, by employers, by boys and then by men. My genitals dictated who I was before *I* knew who I was; defining my future before I had a chance of experiencing life first-hand.

In another country, or another life, once I'd been born, the grand unveiling of my vulva may have been met with disappointment, possibly even dread or regret. The initial joy of giving birth to a healthy, newborn daughter may suddenly have been clouded by reality: the realisation of their daughter existing in a world where she'll mean very little; where life happens *to* her, *at* her and not *for* her. Some mothers would feel nervous for my future, thinking back to the life they'd experienced as girls and/or as women: a life where their existence had minimal worth, status or meaning. Like many loving mothers, they may have wished, or hoped, for more: more for me and my future, knowing my sex would automatically hold me back.

Elsewhere in the world, my birth would have been disappointing for other reasons. Despite having zero influence over the development of my sex, my mother may have felt she'd somehow let her family or partner down for giving birth to a girl, having herself been raised in a culture where being male gave you instantaneous rights, stature and power. She may have internalised misogyny so much that she, too, viewed her existence through the lens of men, viewing herself with the same low level of worth and respect as the society and culture around her. She may have never thought to challenge the possibility that she, or her daughter, were destined for more, for the very idea of women with opportunities was – *is* – unfathomable.

As a baby, I obviously had no idea that being female would

make me more prone to domestic abuse, something which, according to the World Health Organization, will be experienced by one in three women worldwide. I had no idea that every ten minutes, a woman or girl is killed by a family member or an intimate partner. I didn't know the fear of sexual violence would linger above my day-to-day existence – that even basic tasks or activities, like popping to a corner shop or going on a date or going for a walk or taking public transport, would always come with precautions. I didn't yet realise that it wasn't being killed I feared most at the hands of a man but the things he could possibly do to me beforehand.

And yet, despite all that was destined for me, my life came with privileges unawarded to others. For one, I am white. I am in good physical health. Despite not finishing university, I am educated. I have physical features that deem me conventionally attractive in the Western world, and capitalising on my looks has contributed to me earning more than most women (and men) of my age. I own a property. I can vote, drive a car, take public transport, educate myself, use social media, access safe abortion, wear whatever I want, date whoever I want, be gay, live alone, have my own bank account. All it took was a fluke, really, the genetic lottery, for me to have been born at that exact time, in this exact part of the world, in this specific culture, to the parents I had.

Had I been born in, say, Afghanistan – a country the UN deems the most repressive in the world for women – I would have fewer rights than an animal. Being female under current Taliban rule would make me unable to receive an education past the age of twelve. It would see me banned from most public places, including parks, and from participating in sports. On the rare occasion I *was* allowed to go outside, I would be expected to wear a full veil so as not to attract male attention and I could be flogged in public if I did. A contraception ban was introduced in 2023, despite Afghanistan having one of the highest maternal mortality rates in the world. The UN estimates that every two hours, an Afghan woman dies during pregnancy or in childbirth.

The one bit of my anatomy I had left – my voice – would also be taken from me. Women are currently banned from singing, speaking too loudly or even laughing in public. With such little meaning or reason to exist, it is probably not surprising to hear widespread reports of women in Afghanistan experiencing severe depression and suicidal thoughts and tendencies.

Had I been born in Iraq, I could have easily become one of the 28 per cent of girls married before the age of eighteen. In 2024, the Iraqi government proposed to amend its personal status law, allowing girls as young as nine to marry under certain religious interpretations.

According to the charity Girls Not Brides, 12 million girls worldwide marry before the age of eighteen and over 650 million women alive today were married as children. In communities already facing conflict and instability, child marriage puts girls at risk of physical and sexual violence, exploitation and cycles of poverty. Child pregnancy contributes to many health risks – the leading one being death.

If I were born in Sierra Leone, I would have most likely been a victim of female genital mutilation (FGM), which according to the charity ActionAid, is common among 90 per cent of women and girls in the country aged between fifteen and forty-nine. FGM involves partially or fully removing a female's external genitals for non-medical reasons. While FGM is classified into four major types, the most common practised in Sierra Leone involves removal of part or all of the clitoris and the labia minora.

If I were to give birth in Sudan, I would be at huge risk of dying in childbirth, where more than one out of every hundred

Sudanese women will die from either childbirth or complications from pregnancy, giving it the highest maternal mortality rate in the world. As I write this, Sudan is experiencing civil war, and according to the UN, women and girls are being disproportionately impacted by the lack of safe, easily accessible and affordable water, sanitation and hygiene.

In the UK, misogyny is a bigger threat to women than terrorism and organised crime but is not yet considered a criminal offence. Each week, a British woman dies at the hands of a violent partner. In 2024, the National Police Chiefs' Council described violence against women as a 'national emergency'.

The charity Rape Crisis reports that 798,000 British women are raped per year. Between 2013 and 2022, child sexual abuse and exploitation increased by more than 400 per cent.

British women are more likely to find themselves in low-paid and unstable work and are more likely to live in poverty than men, a risk that is higher if you are Black or from an ethnic minority background. The average British woman earns 13.1 per cent less per hour than a man.

In the USA, the overturning of *Roe v. Wade* in June 2022 saw fourteen states enact near total abortion bans, leaving millions of women in danger, at risk of severe health complications or death. Eighteen states have now either completely banned or significantly restricted abortion. One in three American women now live in a state where abortion is inaccessible. Illegal abortions in states such as Texas or Alabama can result in lifetime imprisonment. At present, some right-wing activists are working to pass restrictions on contraception, considering them a 'potential abortifacient'.

The abortion ban disproportionately affects marginalised groups, especially women who already have limited access to reproductive health services (like contraception or abortion), lower rates of employment and who are less likely to have health insurance. It just so happens that the states with the highest population of Black, Hispanic or Indigenous women (Southern and Midwestern states) happen to be the states that have banned abortion completely.

A 2018 report by the FBI broke down the percentages of crimes committed by men, against women, in the US: 96.8 per cent of rape cases were committed by men; 93.1 per cent of sex offences were committed by men; 96 per cent of paedophilia cases were committed by men; 87.8 per cent of murders and manslaughters were committed by men. It is naive to downplay or underestimate misogyny or to see these attacks as anything other than a gender-based issue.

So although my sex makes me second-class, although the fear of sexual assault impacts my day-to-day life, although my sexuality is weaponised against me, although I must stay vigilant at all times, although my gender means I'm perceived as weak, although being female means I am more likely to deal with physical pain than men, I know I must find gratitude for being female within the world and the levels of freedom granted to me simply because of when and where I was born.

My identity, value and life's meaning as a woman are shaped around my vagina. Everything starts here. When I look between my legs, I am reminded of who I am, the way I'm viewed by society and the woman I'm expected to be.

To many, I won't be considered a complete woman until I have a child. Whether *I* actually want a child or not is irrelevant. To many, without my reproductive system, I wouldn't be considered a woman – and, therefore, valuable – at all.

A man is considered separate from his penis; viewed as a complete and whole person away from his genitalia. If a man is promiscuous or sexually driven, we laugh about how his brain is in his trousers; how he 'thinks with his dick', as though his penis has a mind of its own and cannot be controlled. The emphasis of his urges is placed entirely on his dick, separating him from his thoughts, actions or behaviour; removing him from any responsibility in his treatment of women.

A woman cannot be separated from her vagina. Her gender and sexuality define her. It is used to measure her fertility; her fuckability; her virtue. Unlike a man, my sexual organs do not hang outside my body like some sort of extra limb. My vagina, and entire reproductive system, is inside me. It *is* me. It's hard to separate emotionally from your vagina, when it's not only the center point of your reproductive and sexual health, but it is also constantly being used as a way of defining you, your status and your worth as a person. If the vagina isn't being pornified or being eyed up as something to fuck, then it is seen as something to impregnate, demean or control.

We know a woman only by what she provides and not for *who* she is. Before I am allowed to *be me*, I am expected to be somebody's partner; somebody's wife; somebody's mother. If I am not any of those things, I will be expected to fulfil those roles – and quickly. Marriage and motherhood come with a time frame: not just biologically but societally. If I choose *not* to become a mother or somebody's wife, then who am I? I *am* somebody's daughter, but 'belonging' to my parents hasn't made men treat me any better or helped them see me as a human being or grant me respect in the past.

When my desires or choices don't include or involve traditional female roles – specifically reproduction, nurturing or marriage – there is judgement; the belief that I am anti-men. If I take ownership of my life or control over my own freedom I am somehow heartless and emotionless. For putting my needs first, I am void of soul.

With the level of focus and attention put on women's bodies, one would assume our health and well-being would be taken seriously. If society *truly* views human life as important or hierarchical, then by default, a woman's ability to bring life into the world should put her at the top of the pecking order. But we know that not to be true. A woman's body is a constant reminder of where she sits on the social scale. She is her sexual organs and, therefore, is her sexuality. If her body isn't being bred with/from, then it is being sexualised. Her body – and existence – is for everyone else's use or enjoyment but her own.

It's not enough to simply exist. It's not enough to live for myself. As a woman, my body must always provide something – arousal, pleasure, therapy, home-cooked dishes, a baby – otherwise my entire existence has been in vain. My vagina holds more importance than the rest of my body: more than my brain and my intellect, my soul and its kindness, my heart and its love. I must bleed, stretch, tear, birth to be considered a full woman, and *even then*, society has strict ideas of the ways in which women should be, act or behave to be considered 'whole'.

If we're asked to picture a vagina, we will likely visualise a hairless, smooth vulva: the types of vulvas we've seen in porn, on Barbie dolls or even in historic art. Very rarely would we think to picture our own: our pubic mound dotted in stubble rash from the use of a cheap razor; a pair of asymmetrical labial lips; a string hanging out from a tampon.

The vagina manages to elicit a mixture of reactions: arousal, confusion, interest, fear. It's somewhat paradoxical. Vaginas, and the women attached to them, are seen as either wild or holy; the creator of humankind (Madonna) or the temptation of desire (whore). A woman, and her vagina, apparently cannot be all of these.

The media rarely portrays the vagina in a positive light. We've come to see the vagina as something seen in porn videos, something hairless, something upskirted, wet, gushing, bloody, slutty, grabbed, pounded, ripped, destroyed. We see the vagina – and female body – as something sex *happens to*, rather than being a wilful participant.

Vaginas glare at us from the pages of our brothers' lads' mags; from the phone screen or a laptop; but *actual* vaginas, with *real* health problems, *real* scents and attached to *real* female bodies are kept out of conversations altogether. Without their sexual function, they're rarely considered at all.

Nowadays, easy access to porn and trends in hair removal have left us even more confused when it comes to our own vulvas. We view anything less than hairless, symmetrical vulvas as some sort of medical abnormality. Labiaplasty surgeries, which change the size, shape or appearance of the labia, are on the rise. In 2023, a report by the International Society of Aesthetic Plastic Surgery revealed that labiaplasty surgeries had increased by 65.64 per cent worldwide since the procedure was first recorded in 2013.

Society has objectified women's bodies so much that we have come to see our own vaginas as naughty or pornographic, even when it's doing nothing except exist. We live our lives through how our bodies may appear to the outside world or, perhaps more specifically, how they appear to men. Despite being part of our genetic make-up, we see things like menstruation and even menopause as gross or shameful.

In many religions, it is widely assumed that a woman has the ability to tempt a man to stray from God using her vagina's sexual prowess. In certain religions, many girls and women undergo humiliating hymen tests to check they are still 'intact' – her value depleted to nothing, deemed unmarriable, if it is torn. In some religious sects, such as Hasidic Judaism, the woman is seen as impure during her period, meaning her husband cannot touch her, pass anything directly into her hands or say anything to her that may incite arousal, and she must sleep in a separate bed.

Even basic tasks relating to our vaginal health, such as inserting a tampon or going for a cervical screening, can often be associated with a sexual undertone. 'Does it turn you on, having one in?' I recall one (fully grown adult) man asking me about using tampons.

Regardless of geography or religion, the predominant stigma around vaginas is hygiene: that vaginas are dirty. Although the vagina is an amazing self-cleaning organ, full of incredible bacteria that help it self-clean without the use of soaps or gels, there is a reason feminine hygiene products sell in the millions: to make us believe our natural scents are 'wrong'. Our vulvas are rooted in shame, not only in the way they smell or because they bleed but for having *actual* purpose and function beyond the way they look or for their sexual use.

It's remarkable how amid our own pain and discomfort, we still try to keep our vaginas as desirable and alluring as possible. The unfortunate truth is real vaginas aren't all that sexy. Periods are not sexy. Vaginal hygiene isn't sexy. Ruining your PH balance by spreading hair-removal cream all over your labia before a date is not sexy. Vaginal dryness, discharge, spotting, endometriosis, adenomyosis, thrush, bacterial vaginosis and pelvic-floor exercises are not sexy. When the vagina is associated with anything less than flowery, cutesy, sweet-smelling metaphors or imagery, it is not only seen as disgusting, but a reflection on us as people. Admitting this scares us. We must remain feminine and alluring so as not to ruin our vagina's sexual mystique. We mustn't dare be seen as human.

This shame around our bodies is, quite literally, killing us. Shame around what we deem aesthetically abnormal (such as dangling, visible inner labia, rarely shown in porn, yet present in over 50 per cent of vaginas) is stopping women from visiting doctors or gynaecologists, from having cervical screenings, from getting STD tests, asking for contraception or buying condoms. A woman being sexually active, let alone taking ownership of her sexual health, is still heavily associated with shame or promiscuity.

A study by YouGov of 2,010 British adults showed that nearly half of women (45 per cent) were unsure about the location of the vagina, 55 per cent were unable to explain where the urethra was and 43 per cent failed to correctly label the labia. Another study of 1,000 British women by the charity Eve Appeal showed that 44 per cent couldn't identify the vagina on a medical illustration, 60 per cent couldn't identify the vulva and only a third could correctly place the vulva, vagina, cervix, uterus, fallopian tubes and ovaries. Up until recently, I wouldn't have been able to correctly identify most of these, either. Like many women I, too, saw my vagina as something embarrassing. I lost my virginity before being able to use a tampon, and even when I did try inserting one, finding the correct hole took me an embarrassingly long time to work out. As a teenager, I was happy enough to have sex but not to understand how my vagina might play a part in that.

A 2019 Eve Appeal and YouGov report showed that just one in five (19 per cent) British parents use the word 'vagina' when talking to their daughters. One in three parents believed it was inappropriate to use the words 'vagina' and 'vulva' with a child below the age of fourteen. Only 1 per cent of parents used the word 'vulva' and 22 per cent of parents avoided using the word at all.

According to the report, most parents encourage their daughters to 'cutesify' their vulvas by describing them with euphemisms, such as 'bits', 'private parts', 'kitty' (eurgh) or 'flower' – perhaps as a well-intentioned means of desexualising them and because they believe words like 'vagina' to be vulgar. But in their quest to desexualise their daughter's vagina, they are, ironically, sexualising them instead. There is nothing wrong with being factually correct. Studies show that refusing to call a female's anatomy by the correct names has a detrimental effect on the female's well-being. It not only teaches the child that their genitals are shameful, but the child won't be able to accurately describe or understand sexual abuse if it were to happen to them.

We see the vagina as weak, but I want you to see the vagina as powerful. Ironically, it's believed that fear around the vagina's power is what helped build the patriarchy to begin with. In prehistoric times, women were seen as the stronger sex and it made men feel incredibly inadequate. How could a man possibly compete with a woman, whose body had the power to birth armies of humans, whose nurturing side helped build communities and take care of families, whose love could make a house a home? The woman would take what she was given by a man – sperm, food – and double it, benefiting not only her family but the systems around her. And so ideas within the contexts of religion began to form, around marriage, education and sin, ideas that would ultimately create a power structure where men were in charge and where women were, for whatever reason, seen as the weaker sex.

It is incredible that a bodily organ has the ability to put fear into the so-called manliest of men; how something so soft, so fleshy, has managed to scare the patriarchy for centuries and made a lot of men feel incredibly inadequate in their masculinity.

I am not stupid. I know to a lot of men I am considered a vagina, a pussy, a hole, before I am a human being, and even *that's* a push, if we are to consider a female an actual living, breathing human with her own thoughts, feelings and emotions.

Whenever I meet a man, I feel their eyes quickly scanning my body, analysing what they see, because I know if I am deemed fuckable enough – or at the very least, passable – I have value.

I learnt from a young age that my body is my currency. Respect from men is earnt by what I can offer them via my body. To be treated nicely, or treated with an ounce of respect, comes with a price; a cost; an exchange. The more I perform or become an ideal version of the woman they want me to be, the better chance I have of being chosen – of feeling wanted; of *being* wanted. *If you like what you see, I will be worth something to you. You will be kind to me. You will treat me better. If I am lucky, you may eventually even love me.*

Throughout my teens, twenties and early thirties, I found myself constantly seeking male approval and validation, even when I wasn't conscious of it. Amid my own discomfort at being leered at, I am still told that I should take things like catcalling as a compliment, because one day, when I age and lose my looks, men won't pay me much interest at all.

Men should want to fuck me, even if I don't want to fuck them. If they do not show interest, then I am clearly not attractive enough and may as well be invisible. And if I become invisible . . . then what is the point? Womanhood has taught me I must remain visible but not *too* visible; attractive enough to be chosen and attractive enough for a man to want to show me off but not enough to show him up. If I wear something too revealing or happen to attract other male attention for the way I look, I am a whore. It reflects badly on him. Everything I do is a reflection on him. It is my duty to make him appear the best he can. It is my duty for him to want me, to be proud of me, not for my achievements or my intelligence but for how I look and how I make *him* look to the outside world. My body is not my own and it never has been.

*

I was first knowingly sexualised when I was seven, in what would become the start of a series of incidents involving boys and men throughout my life. I say 'knowingly', as the disturbing reality is that my childish body would've undoubtedly been lusted over before I was even conscious of it.

His name was Sean. He was a neighbour. He was in his thirties. He was a paedophile.

He is not responsible for how other men would treat me over the years – only they can be accountable for their actions – but he was the first person to treat me like a sex object; to make me *feel* like a sex object; the first person to disconnect me from my body, my soul and my sense of self.

Sean was the first person to make me fully aware of who I am, to remind me of what I am: *a girl. A vagina.* He is the reason I learnt grown men are to be feared. He is the core reason I've long believed I wasn't worth anything; the crux of my debilitating childhood anxiety, which would later develop into depression, crippling low self-worth and subsequent eating disorders.

It took me a very long time to make the connection between this internalised shame and years of self-destructive behaviours. Men like Sean are the reason so many women, like myself, choose to abuse our bodies, whether that be through food control, bingeing, drug use, cutting or other forms of self-harm. We punish ourselves for their wrongdoings, treating ourselves with the same unworthiness, revulsion and disrespect that they made us feel.

Deep down, I knew what Sean was doing was wrong, but for some reason, the confusing, tingling sensation in my groin made the guilt feel very much my own. I couldn't understand why my body was reacting in the way it was. What *was* this sensation? I'd never felt it before. Was I scared? Did I want it? Ask for it?

I had no idea that a moment so fleeting, in the grand scheme of things, would change not only the way I interacted with boys and men moving forward, but also the way I viewed myself and treated my body: with disgust, humiliation and shame.

From then on, I didn't just live in fear of Sean coming back or touching me again, but also of what other men like him could do. Every man became an enemy; every man a potential threat. I was pulled out of the protective, shielded cocoon of childhood and saw the world for what it really was – dangerous, scary, where having a vagina meant I'd forever need to be on guard. Creepy men weren't just strangers in trench coats, lurking in the back of vans with the promises of sweets or puppies. They could be married. They were your parents' friends; men in supermarkets; teachers at school. Men like Sean were everywhere.

There was also no way of escaping my body; from ridding myself of these feelings. The shame fell on to me to fix and on me to carry. I had to change *my* behaviour, the way I carried myself or dressed myself, my routes home and even my personality so as not to tempt them, to stop anything like this from happening again.

Shame is rooted in the female existence. Simply existing seems to elicit a reaction. The smallest movements, actions or behaviours can somehow be twisted into being shameful or unladylike: speaking too loudly, wearing something too tight-fitting or low cut, sitting down with your legs too far apart, wearing too much make-up, or for not bothering with your appearance at all. Who made these rules? As a result, we often try to pre-empt the way people may view or perceive us, moulding ourselves into the women we think society (and men) would prefer us to be.

Since time began, women have been blamed and shamed for the results of male lust, the overlying message being that women are to blame for male behaviour. The war on women is not just physical, but ideological and psychological, interwoven among centuries' old texts, myths, cultures and beliefs. In Ancient Greek mythology, sirens lure sailors to their deaths using their beauty and angelic singing voices. Medusa, long viewed as one of the most evil and terrifying mythological figures, turned men into stone, until the brave and oh-so-wonderful Perseus beheaded her, carrying her head as a tool to turn his enemies into stone. (Medusa supposedly didn't like men because she had been raped by one, but this is often left out of her story.) In fact, most Greek female mythological figures were killed, defeated or outsmarted by a man, who naturally was the hero of the story. The same can be seen in the Bible, where Eve encourages Adam to take a bite of the forbidden apple. She is subsequently punished by God with subservience to Adam and pain during childbirth because Adam, of course, couldn't possibly make wrong or selfish decisions of his own accord.

A woman's sex life and sexuality often determine her purity and, therefore, how she is perceived by society. On the one hand, women are seen as a symbol of fertility, maternal and unconditional love and purity. But when she resists, or takes ownership of her own life, body or sexuality, she can be labelled as uncontrollable, hysterical, devious or impure. A woman like this must be controlled, which is where shame – a powerful tool – comes into play.

Shame has long been used as a tool to break a woman's spirit, to destroy her self-confidence, to subjugate her and exclude her from society. Throughout history humiliation, shaming, exposure and accusations have been key to maintaining the patriarchal system.

In the years 1400 to 1775, between forty thousand and sixty thousand 'witches' – the majority of whom were women – were killed across Europe in publicly humiliating witch trials. Rebelling against the status quo could often cause a woman to be accused of being a witch, and once accused, a woman had no chance of proving her innocence. A woman who was not submissive, who disagreed, defended herself, swore, possessed cats, had a strong bond with other women or who was accused of adultery, having illegitimate children, promiscuity or prostitution could be burnt at the stake.

Shame has had a profound impact on women throughout history, especially within medieval witch trials, which is often forgotten in the history of capitalism. In her book *Caliban and the Witch*, Silvia Federici writes how the practice of magic was not compatible with the evolving capitalist order. Witch hunts helped discipline the emerging working class, especially to control women's bodies, their autonomy and reproductive labour. Before witchcraft became prominent, there were widespread beliefs of vivid energies within nature, where many people turned to herbs and plants for their healing and medicinal benefits. Being connected to nature, as well as having wisdom and knowledge of plants, soon became a tell-tale sign of somebody being a witch. Federici explains how nature and spells, which would have then been an important part of women's lives, were destroyed as part of the development of capitalism and the emergence of rationalist science. In other words, if women's beliefs didn't make money or were misaligned with men's thoughts, they were shunned and ignored. If a woman rebelled against the system, she was dangerous. There was no place in society for her.

Federici also notes how the violence of witch hunts was a key part of capitalist development and that similar patterns of violence against women, land and communal resources continue today. We still witness modern-day witch hunts, with acts like revenge porn, public slut-shaming and honour killings, usually tied to a woman's sexuality, free will or free speech. Rarely, if ever, will you see a man being publicly shamed or attacked for the same things.

But wherever there has been war against women's bodies and voices, there is always the counteracting war of female rebellion: the rebelling body, the unsilenced voice, the impenetrable spirit. Whenever a woman rejects social norms or lives a life of her own choosing, she is very threatening indeed. No matter how small an act, decentering the patriarchy, society's norms and living a life that brings you joy is incredibly powerful; a nod to our female ancestors who were humiliated, punished and killed for doing the very same.

I'm convinced that this repeated, ongoing and often lifelong shame around our womanhood rises from the foundations of our sex – our vaginas – and goes deep into the core depths of our being, impacting our overall self-esteem, self-worth and how we see ourselves as people.

Physically, shame manifests itself in the body in many ways: a sinking feeling in the pit of the stomach, a churning in our guts, a tightness in the shoulders or within our chests. So when shame is based on your gender and how you *perform* as that gender, how could it *not* consume you?

Shame is the patriarchy repeatedly whispering in our ear and reminding us of our place. It diminishes our ideas, our thoughts and our ability to think freely. Without shame, there would be nothing to control, nothing to demean, nothing to measure a woman's worth by – nothing for a woman to measure her *own* worth by. It thrives off dismantling a woman's spirit, reminding her that a man's opinion can make or break her, that she will be nothing unless she conforms to society's standards.

Without the power of shame around female sexuality, things like revenge porn or leaking a woman's nudes wouldn't destroy a woman's life or career. Shame thrives on knowing that a woman's entire world can be ruined if she dares take ownership of her own body and sexuality.

To stop shame, a woman believes she must remain within the confines of 'acceptable' female behaviour. The difficulty in this is knowing where the boundaries lie, maintaining a careful balancing act between exhibiting correct 'feminine' behaviours – nurturance, selflessness, compassion, gentleness, and adopting acceptable 'masculine' ones – being protective, assertive, tough, dominant. The truth is, perfection is an impossible guideline. There will always be something to change or better to be considered a 'perfect' woman.

Because physically my vagina and reproductive system lie within me, attacks on my womanhood feel that much more personal. Abuse towards and around my gender feels harder to disconnect from. When we internalise the shame we come to see assaults on our bodies as shameful as well.

Logically, it makes absolutely *zero* sense as to why rape, sexual assault or any other type of abuse should reflect badly on me as a person, let alone be my fault. So why does it feel as though it is from my own wrongdoing? Why does anything unwanted – a sexual comment, a dick pic, a grope or a violent act – feel so *personal*? As though a man's touch can reduce my worth or value? Why have I, do I, consistently allow this shame to become my own?

Over the years, I've confided in a few people about what happened with Sean, and it didn't seem to have much of an impact. One person asked, 'Is that all he did?' as though it wasn't significant enough – *bad* enough – to be considered assault.

Perhaps they were right. Yes, he touched me, but it wasn't like it was full-on *rape* or a level of molestation others speak of. I felt silly for even mentioning it. I came to realise that speaking about Sean wasn't worth it: that if what I went through wasn't considered serious enough in the eyes of others then, clearly, I was just being dramatic.

But if it's not that much of a big deal, why can't I let it go? Why, in my lowest moments, am I brought back there in graphic detail, rewatching his hands rub and squeeze my prepubescent thighs while I fixate on my shiny blonde thigh hairs to distract myself from what is happening? Why, of all the memories my brain has decided to store, do I remember what I was wearing that day; what the weather was like; the texture of the seat I was sitting on? Why do I remember how slimy and wet his finger felt after he sucked it and rubbed it down my arm, telling me to keep it our secret? Why, even now, do I often feel like that scared eight-year-old little girl, glued to my chair, unable to move?

I've lived my entire life around what men may or may not do to me, and nobody seems to question that. Their actions will be because of what I wore; because I didn't give them my phone number; because I put myself in a compromising position; because I took X route instead of my usual Y; because I dared smile at a man and gave him the wrong impression.

Even though I know sexual abuse is not a competition of who has the worst story to tell, I am often made to feel as though it is. My stories are often not violent enough, not scary enough, not humiliating enough, to be taken seriously. And yet, like many women – *most* women – there are many of them.

And so it makes me wonder: how traumatic does an experience with a man need to be in order for it to 'count'? How disturbing, violent or strange does sexual assault need to be in order for it to be considered 'bad'? What will it take for women and girls, like me, to be heard? For our stories of day-to-day sexual abuse to be taken seriously? At what point are we allowed to acknowledge the impact of a man's actions on our overall being and our brain chemistry? Most of all, at what point do we recognise that the sexual violence we come to expect from being born female is not *normal*?

Sean killed himself a few years ago, alone and living a life of solitude. I *revel* in this fact. It is not ladylike to wish death on someone, and society doesn't allow for an angry woman, but I can't help but feel the way I do. Part of healing is allowing yourself to be angry.

I do not want to play judge or jury with forgiveness. I have suppressed my feelings for too long. It is not my duty to forgive those who have hurt me, and I'm not going to pretend that forgiveness will help make me feel better.

I know that men like Sean do not abuse just one little girl, and I have a strong gut feeling that he knew his time was up. Nowadays, I carry shame around what happened for different reasons. I feel shame in my silence. I wish I'd spoken up about what he'd done to me years before, instead of burying it away, just so there weren't any opportunities for him to hurt or destroy another person. I wonder, in my shame of keeping quiet, whether I could have protected another girl.

For years, I have been scared to write his name: scared to make him and what happened 'real'. Acknowledging what he did to me not only means having to revisit it but also confronting my shame head on – both of which feel scary and affronting. I could choose to anonymise him in this book. But like other men I have dealt with in my life, I have carried *his* shame, *his* actions and *his* behaviour around with me for over twenty-five years. To grant him the respect of anonymity would do a huge disservice to myself and to others like me.

I read that to release shame from our bodies, we need to acknowledge and find compassion for our mistakes; to learn to forgive ourselves. But what if the mistakes weren't ours? What is there to forgive if we didn't actively create the shame we were made to feel?

As most women will attest, it is never usually one assault. There might be one, big, defining incident, but usually, it will be a cherry on top of a large, tiered cake of normalised, day-to-day sexist experiences.

Women all have their stories, ongoing lists of sexual assaults that continually grow. Yet despite these experiences, we've somehow managed to convince generations of women that sexual assault and violence are what's to be expected.

The molestation I experienced at the hands of Sean was merely the first of many bad incidents with men. Truly, I have too many sexually abusive stories to count. Some involve obvious physical abuse; other stories lie in the murky, grey waters of the unknown: a secret, hidden truth between me and the abuser himself that I still don't feel comfortable sharing, at least not within these pages.

Because of how many things I've experienced, I've often felt too embarrassed to share them. Over time, I've internalised many of these incidents, convincing myself that I was the cause. Surely – *surely* – it isn't normal to repeatedly be taken advantage of by men? Shame has made me wonder whether women will question what I've done to be repeatedly abused or, even worse, that they'll see me as 'slutty', because any woman who goes through multiple experiences surely must be 'asking for it'.

There is still a lot of confusion around what constitutes consent. Society tends to view sexual assault as black and white: either as violent rape or nothing.

It's really not as simple as saying 'no'. Rape doesn't have to be violent to 'count'. If we are pushed and harassed into sleeping with someone until we finally say yes, does that signify as being a wilful participant? This miscommunication around what constitutes rape tends to make us ignore an entire culture and system that leads to sexual violence to begin with – otherwise known as rape culture. Rather than addressing the root problems of sexism, misogyny and what many men believe is their God-given right to a woman's body, the onus is put entirely on women to come up with solutions and, once again, this breeds a society of women internalising shame.

It's hard to truly explain the way sexual assault makes you feel. How do you explain the feeling of 'nothingness' – the feeling of *becoming* nothing? Other than how I'd assume death feels, there is no other experience or feeling to compare it to. You feel erased. You feel used, unclean . . . but what is there to wash off? You're living in a permanent filth that is impossible to scrub; your body covered in the remnants of their skin, their touch, their sweat, their scent, their memory.

Real-life, consensual sex is fun, sensual and joyful. It is a deeply vulnerable act that also requires us to *show* our vulnerability – to not only bare our bodies, exposing the most *private* parts of them, but also the innermost depths of ourselves. In that moment, we put our entire selves in the trust of someone else. We exchange energies, saliva and bodily fluids, releasing distinctive bonding hormones and scents. Physically, it's the closest we can be to another human. Even in the most casual of sexual encounters, the act of sex really isn't that casual at all.

But rape and sexual assault put you face to face with the depths of human depravity, eye to eye with the worst parts of sex: ego, selfishness, power, violence, control and dominance. It removes all desire and arousal and replaces it with a punch. It removes the humanity from connection – all emotions, all senses, all feeling – reducing you to nothing but the vagina you were born with.

Maybe I am simply unlucky to have experienced so many abusive experiences. Perhaps I am a rarity. Or, maybe, I am not that abnormal at all. How would I know? Shame stops women from talking with one another about their assaults; victims are too often afraid to speak up. Shame thrives in keeping us silent and afraid. Within our current culture, abusers often take advantage of knowing that society will likely blame the victim for their own assault.

The Rape Culture Pyramid, designed by Jaime Chandra and the website 11th Principle: Consent!, explains and demonstrates how rape culture is not about individual actions and behaviours, but rather how it exists within a series of cultural beliefs, relationship dynamics and larger societal systems. Instead of 'measuring' or 'ranking' types of harm, it showcases how behaviours, beliefs and systems are built on, and work in conjunction with one another.

The pyramid is broken up into three sections: *Normalisation*, *Degradation* and *Assault*.

Normalisation sits at the bottom of the pyramid, the day-to-day, normalised behaviours that most of us will have experienced – or, perhaps, maybe even participated in ourselves. They include rape jokes, sexist attitudes, catcalling, unsolicited nude or dick pics, unwanted non-sexual touch, stalking, flashing and exposing. These behaviours are *so* common in a woman's life that we may barely regard or recognise them as being problematic at all.

As we move up the pyramid, we reach *Degradation*: things like revenge porn, manipulation and coercion, victim-blaming and -shaming, groping and threats. Arguably, although more serious, many of us will have experienced these, too.

Finally, at the top of the pyramid is *Assault*: acts like contraception sabotage (piercing a condom), stealthing (the act of removing a condom midway through sex without a person's knowledge), drugging, molestation and rape. We tell ourselves that these incidents are rare but, as most women will attest, they are not. They simply vary in levels of violence.

I'd never had much luck with therapists. The first time I sought therapy was when I was nineteen, on the NHS. I had recently been assaulted by an ex-boyfriend and had just gone through a lengthy – and traumatic – police investigation.

The detective on the case – a man who I assume would've then been in his thirties – began sending me inappropriate, sexually charged text messages. In my naive and traumatised mind, I took this attention as flattering – even as care.

It started off friendly. 'Text me whenever you need to chat,' he said as we left the station. He didn't just hand me his police business card but his personal number as well. 'We'll get this fucker.'

And friendly he was. He texted me regularly to see how I was doing, to see whether my ex had been in touch. It was lovely to have a man want to help me and to help get me justice.

Within a couple of weeks, his texts became more flirty. *'I bet you get all the boys after you,'* he texted me one evening. *'If I wasn't in a relationship, you'd be the exact type of girl I'd go for,'* he wrote in another. He'd tell me about his own personal problems, about how annoying his girlfriend was being and how he was on the brink of breaking up with her.

It felt nice, I suppose, to have someone older and someone with authority giving me attention. I'd reread his texts and smile, wondering whether one day we could possibly have a relationship outside of what was going on.

Deep down, I think I knew what he was texting me was crossing a boundary, but I didn't have the mental maturity, nor intelligence, to understand that a person in authority could possibly take advantage of me. The police were meant to protect you; to keep you safe from the abusers. In my police interview, I'd opened up to him about things I hadn't previously been able to bring myself to say out loud: gory, explicit, intense information about my assault that left me sobbing and made me feel sick with shame. No one would take advantage of someone who'd been through something like that . . . would they?

Suddenly, his flirty texts stopped. In fact, the texts stopped altogether. He became cold and distant. The last text I received was him asking me to hand in my phone at the police station '*for evidence*', which, he said, would help get my abusive ex arrested.

A few months later, my phone was ready to be collected. I'd dressed up especially to go and see him at the police station, wearing clothes that deliberately showed off my figure. In my naivety, I truly hoped that by looking pretty he might suddenly want to talk to me again.

'There wasn't enough evidence,' he said, poking his head around the station door and handing me my phone in a plastic bag. He could barely look me in the eye. Later, when I finally turned my phone back on, his text messages to me had been wiped.

And just like that, the case was done.

At the time I sought therapy I was lost and aggressive. I hated men. I hated the world. I liked picking fights with people, especially physical ones. I could feel the aggression bubbling beneath my skin, trying to push its way to the surface. I wanted people to fight me, to hit me, to make me *feel* something again; to bring me back to life.

My assigned therapist was a tall, handsome man called Steven. Each week he'd wear a tight black T-shirt, showcasing his enormous muscles from hours spent at the gym. He had a smile that lit up his whole face; kind, dark-brown eyes that wrinkled when he laughed. He didn't *look* like a traditional therapist, nor one I'd envisioned in my head, but I guess the fact he didn't look like a shrink helped relax me into opening up.

I began to enjoy the routine of mine and Steven's sessions, which took place every Saturday morning. I started to enjoy peeling back the layers; at better understanding myself. I was telling Steven secrets about myself that I wouldn't even write in my own diary. I liked the fact he listened to me. I liked the fact he believed me.

Part of me, I think, enjoyed the uncertainty of whether Steven wanted me sexually – trying to make sense of the boundaries, trying to read whether his gentle arm touches, or hugs, or laughter at my jokes were because he found me attractive or because he simply liked me as a person. Deep down, I rather hoped it was because he liked who I was. I wanted to converse with a man without the feeling of him wanting to sleep with me.

As the weeks went on and as I continued to bare my soul, Steven began telling me about his *own* problems: the main issue being marital problems with his wife after catching her having an affair. Again, as a nineteen-year-old, I didn't exactly have the maturity or life's experience to deal with such matters – only empathy, which I hoped would suffice.

One day, Steven said he had to tell me something: he'd developed feelings for me and couldn't decipher whether they were romantic or not. As a result, he needed to stop our sessions. It wouldn't be ethical. Besides, he felt I was doing OK now. If it was all right with me, however, he'd like us to become friends on Facebook.

I sat there rather awkwardly in that final session, watching him use an NHS computer to search Facebook for my name and add me as a friend. Perhaps he thought that by adding me as a friend it would put my feelings at ease – that he had viewed our chats as special, in the same ways I had. Or, maybe it wasn't that deep at all. Maybe that's how I want to decipher it – that a man had listened to my innermost secrets, hurt and fears without thinking of what was in it for him.

I felt let down by Steven and once again let down by a system that was supposed to look after me. I felt embarrassed at having opened up to him and at feeling as though I could trust a man. Without taking my clothes off, I once again felt stripped.

Years later, back at a medication check-up with a new therapist, I was cold and closed off in my sessions. I found myself trying to work out this new male therapist; figuring out what his intentions were. I'd sit in the armchair with my arms folded, leaning forward as though to protect my body. While Dr Patil didn't give any impression of wanting to sleep with me, I could never be too sure. If there was anything I'd learnt from men, it was that I could never entirely trust their motives.

'Have you noticed any side effects?' he asks about the antidepressants he'd prescribed me. 'Weight gain? Nausea?'

'There is one . . .' I say. I watch him click his pen, ready to take notes. 'I've noticed I have no sex drive. No sexual feelings whatsoever.'

It was true. Since taking the medication, I'd felt absolutely nothing towards anything or anyone.

'Mmm.' He scribbles in his notepad. 'That can certainly be a side effect, though it's normally more prevalent in men. Have you always had a high sex drive?'

'Yes. Yeah, I guess so,' I reply.

'Are you sleeping with anyone right now?'

'No.' I pause. 'Because I don't feel sexual.'

'Then how are you sure you've lost your sex drive?'

How much more obvious did I need to be? Was he listening to a word I said?

'Because I've *always* been a sexual person and now I don't feel a single thing towards anyone,' I reply. I could feel myself getting annoyed, as though I was having to defend myself and my sexuality. These pills had changed me. *I knew who I was.* I felt different to the person I'd been before taking them. I certainly didn't need *A MAN* questioning me or, worst of all, making me question myself.

Being a woman in tune with her body – certainly in a sexual sense – had always felt powerful. Whether it was how I dressed or how I interacted with men, I wore my sexuality as a badge of honour. Now, without my sexuality, I wasn't sure who I was. It felt as though depression had robbed me of one more thing that made me *me*.

'Have you ever considered that maybe you *weren't* as sexual as you thought you were?' he asks. 'That maybe your high sex drive was a reaction to the way you've been treated by men, and the antidepressants are bringing you back to who you truly are?'

It was as though, at that moment, I had been awoken from a daydream, snapped back to reality and out of the fog I'd been blindly walking through for all these years. I was forced to confront an uncomfortable possibility: that my body and my sexuality have been my shield.

Why does this realisation feel so affronting? What is so wrong with admitting that maybe you're not as sexually confident as you thought you were? What is wrong with admitting that you are, in fact, a victim – not only of men and their abuse, but of society and what we teach women to aim for?

I want, desperately, to believe I have power over men through using my sexuality. I absolutely hate to think the effort I've gone to in performing for men is ultimately for nothing.

But when I look back, time and time again, I force my body into sexual situations I'm not entirely comfortable with in the hope of being 'powerful'. I push past the feelings of unease – the part of me that doesn't want to be treated like a piece of meat – because I want to believe, as I have long believed, that my sexuality will save me. I desperately hope that by becoming some sort of femme fatale – or at least, by pretending to be one – that I will regain control over my body and what has repeatedly been taken.

Yet I rarely feel powerful. Whenever I dress in tight, figure-fitting clothes, I rarely feel sexy, even though I've always been told I will. My body tenses up whenever I post a sexy lingerie picture on Instagram, and I feel like a fraud, because my entire account is about making women feel good about their bodies, encouraging them to love the skin they're in. Part of me isn't sure whether I want to post pictures of my body at all, and sometimes my gut churns with anxiety, but I post it anyway. I'm not sure whether I'm so used to posting sexy pictures of myself that I feel I must keep up the image of a self-assured, sexually confident woman.

I don't *want* to be a sex object, yet I treat myself like one. I mistake empowerment with freedom; desirability with being loved; sex with meaning. I seek partners whose affection I need to chase; where the only form of connection is when we are intimate, and even then, I don't feel seen by them. What will it take for them to notice me, to want me, to love me? What must I do or change for them to treat me right?

Even before the age of social media, I was sold the idea that being sexy was an act of empowerment. I was taught that my low self-esteem could be transformed by sexualising myself and from being desired; that there is power in being a woman that men can ogle at but can't have. So why do I rarely feel empowered? Sure, there are days where I feel sexier than others – normally when I'm ovulating. But why does being provocative often leave me feeling hollow?

And so I embark on a vicious cycle. This time I post, I will feel different. This time I'll wear a bra that makes my chest look massive, and I will finally feel sexy. Because this time, it *has* to be different. *It has to.*

Sometimes, posting sexy photos boosts my self-esteem. But while the likes may validate me for a minute, the feeling never truly stays. I cannot understand what I am doing wrong, why I rarely feel liberated, despite succumbing to what I'm told female liberation is. Most of all, I don't know why I can't stop doing it.

If my identity as a woman starts with my sex, then my journey towards self-discovery involves unlearning and dissembling everything I've believed femininity to be. Healing requires unlearning what is expected from me and my body; questioning the limitations placed on my gender; and seeing my worth beyond my vagina.

My vagina is a powerful organ, more than just a vessel in childbirth, something used to shame or place limits on me. Starting with my vagina, I aim to reclaim my objectified body parts, to treat my vagina as more than just an organ for male pleasure, but as part of the complete, whole woman I know I can be.

breasts.

I was six years old when I first saw a topless model on Page 3. I spotted her in my grandfather's copy of the *Sun*, watching him casually flick past the photo as he sipped tea on our living room couch as though it was totally normal for breasts to be on display to anyone.

I'm sure, to my grandfather, Page 3 *was* normal. He was a mechanic, a working-class man, who likely had these pictures and other topless calendars on the walls where he worked. A topless woman on the third page of a newspaper was not considered questionable or out of the ordinary at this time, not unless you were a feminist hellbent on destroying everyone else's fun and livelihoods. Page 3 was considered *so* normal, such a part of everyday life, that photos like these weren't hidden or kept away from children's prying eyes. It was just one of those things many families accepted: as British an institution as fish and chips.

Still, I had to make sure my eyes weren't deceiving me. Once the adults left the room, leaving the newspaper folded neatly on the coffee table, I quickly snuck a look.

I remember this moment vividly, because I'd never seen a woman so wonderful, let alone *so beautiful* in the entire six years I'd been alive. I was fascinated by her: the way the black, lacy knickers skimmed the tops of her thighs; the goosebumps running across her balloon-like breasts; her silky, shiny, peroxide-blonde hair; the way she half-smiled towards the camera, as though she knew you or wanted to tell you a secret.

There was something confusing – if not thrilling – about spotting a topless woman in your grandfather's newspaper, as well as an uncertainty as to whether I should have been looking at all. I'd grown up believing nudity was something sacred, that there was a time and a place to be naked and that your nude body wasn't for everyone's eyes. This photo challenged all that. What I was seeing *must* have been OK because it was in the family newspaper, in full view of my elderly grandparents, my parents and my baby sister.

My undeveloped brain could appreciate that this was a *real* woman, obviously – that she was as real as you or I – but she seemed . . . well . . . *more* than that, somehow, a fantasy of a woman in comparison to the women I was used to seeing day to day. I didn't know much about beauty standards back then, but I did know she must've been special: special enough to have her photo printed on the page of a newspaper simply for the way she looked.

Her name, according to the text in the little box at the top of the photo, was Caprice. *Caprice!* What an exotic name, the kind of name the princesses in my storybooks had. My fingers traced the curves of her body. I wondered if my flat chest would ever develop into anything as pillowy, whether I'd be as pretty, glamorous or shiny when I finally grew up.

I don't *think* I fancied her. Or perhaps I did. I don't know. It was definitely a crush of some sort. She aroused feelings in me I'd not previously felt. The likelihood was that, like many little girls, I was tantalised by the unknown, fascinated by a body so different to my mother's, which at that stage in life was the only adult female nude body I'd seen.

Realistically, I knew, deep down, that there was a high

probability Caprice was posing for men. I knew there was a certain naughtiness to the image, even though in the grand scheme of things she wasn't *really* doing anything particularly naughty or sexual. But I also knew her femininity – her breasts, her curves, her beauty – gave her a certain power, a sexual kind of power that only women possessed, which could be held above men and used to her advantage. Her body was something you wanted but couldn't have. You could look but not touch.

To thousands, if not millions, of households around the country that night, Caprice became chip paper, her body yesterday's news. To me, she became my first pin-up. Once the paper ended up in the recycling bin, I took some scissors out of the kitchen drawer and carefully cut around the outline of her body, taking her to my room with the idea of putting her up on my wall next to my Spice Girls posters. I planned on cutting more Page 3 women out of newspapers and collecting them like Barbie dolls – the types of women I'd hope to look like someday.

Caprice was mine for approximately two hours. She was rudely confiscated by my dad that evening, who'd found her lying on top of my bedside table when he came to tuck me in. She was returned to me the following morning – from the neck up. I was allowed to keep her, my dad explained, but only her face. It was inappropriate and strange, apparently, for a little girl to want to keep rude pictures of a naked woman.

Most people would probably agree that removing Caprice from my six-year-old clutches was the right thing to do. Like most parents, my father's intentions were good. He wanted to protect my innocence for as long as possible. But decapitating pretty Caprice sent conflicting messages. What was so bad about a topless woman? Why were her boobs considered so rude? *All* women had breasts. Did this mean they were inherently bad? Perhaps most confusing of all, is if they were considered *that* outrageous, why were they on full display for all to see?

I learnt there and then that breasts were powerful: that they not only had the ability to sell but to shock. Bare breasts – these two, measly lumps of flesh cupped to the front of a woman's body – sold newspapers, but could also embarrass, if not frighten, grown men like my military father. There was something amusing, something remarkable, in knowing the female body had this power.

I learnt there and then that a woman's body could not only be beautiful, but illicit, dangerous and exciting.

Until relatively recently I had a complicated relationship with my breasts, something I think I have in common with many other women. Because of how they are represented in the media, I believed that breasts, much like the vagina, were sexual organs. They may have been attached to me, but they didn't feel like my own. I knew 'acceptable' breasts only by how I saw them in the media: big, bouncy and for the enjoyment of men. Their natural biological purpose was heavily outweighed by the sexualised gaze staring at them.

Throughout much of Western history, various efforts by men – husbands, lovers, fathers – and male-dominated institutions – politics, medicine, the Church – have controlled the way we view, appreciate and understand female breasts. Breasts have been subjected to controversy, censure and, like most other body parts belonging to women, erasure.

For the most part, I have only known breasts through the perspective of the male imagination. From the strokes of an artist's paintbrush in medieval paintings, to the pixelated digital images on a computer screen, I know breasts, and the owners of them, as art pieces, fantasies or figurines. I know breasts only as things, not as organs, attached to real human beings with beating hearts and blood pumping around their bodies. While I clearly identify them as women because of the things on their chest, I do not know these women as *people*. I know nothing of their backstories in these images; their history; their struggles; their hopes and desires. These women are frozen in time, existing as flesh but without substance. These images are representations of women and what the artist believes women to be; or, perhaps, what they *hope* women to be. These women are objects, often unidentifiable, encapsulated by the lens of people fascinated by their beauty and allure but who care to know little else.

We now live in a society where breasts are shown in movies, commercials, magazines and advertisements for men to lust over but where mothers are often forced to breastfeed in secret so as not to offend. Breasts are considered fine for men to masturbate to, but if a woman takes ownership of her body – if she breast-feeds in public, wears a low-cut top, takes provocative selfies or sells photos of her breasts on OnlyFans – she is ultimately condemned for it.

It's hard to know exactly where this sexualisation of the breasts developed from. Sigmund Freud, whose theories about sex, relationships and psychosexuality are now generally considered to be outdated and inaccurate, believed our fascination with breasts stemmed from the body needing satisfaction, noting a baby's first experience of being satisfied is often when it's being breastfed by its mother. This was, of course, based on Freud's knowledge of life and the world at the time, a world in which *every* baby had to be breastfed to survive and where formula milk had not yet been invented.

The Freudian breast is not made of flesh; rather, it represents and triggers a series of feelings, memories and emotions evoked from infancy: being taken care of, being held, being indulged and having one's needs met. Freud was one of the first people to write of sexuality being psychological rather than biological. With this framing, it could be argued that most sexual kinks stem from childhood influences or unmet needs. It just so happens that the female breast seems to be one of the most common, if not widely acceptable, fetishes of them all.

Western culture, in particular, seems to have more of a sexual interest in breasts than other cultures around the world, seeing them as some sort of sexual bodily ornament, or a prized, feminine symbol. In Africa and the South Pacific, in certain tribes like the Himba and Nyae Nyae Peoples of Namibia and San People (Bushmen) of Southern Africa, women walk around topless, without shame, sexualisation or erotic connotations. In the West, however, breasts have a popular, and some may say excessive, social and erotic appeal.

Very few women, let alone men, remain unaffected by the media, which presents breasts with both visual and metaphorical narrow-mindedness: the pinnacle of femininity; a commercialised product; an erotic fantasy. Breasts are not presented as something *belonging* to women, but, instead, as separate objects, commercial entities, *attached* to women.

The size and shape of a woman's breasts can determine the way she is treated. Bigger breasts can instantly suggest the woman is sexual, even slutty; flatter, smaller breasts can allude to a woman having no sexuality at all. It's perhaps no wonder that our breasts become things we often feel ashamed of, or things we need to change in order to be accepted by society.

Breasts are physical symbols of how women's bodies are seen in general: sacred or sexual; life-givers or life-destroyers; to feed or to entice. Breasts signify femininity and sexuality; nurturance and life; art and poetry; power and pleasure; virtue and sin. They can arouse feelings and images of both the divine feminine and the sexual temptress. They have a multiplicity of meanings and uses:

babies see food; men, sex; businesses, dollar signs; politicians, a potential threat.

I often find myself viewing my own breasts from an outsider's perspective, judging them as I think others may. Throughout the month when my areolas change colour or shape, or when my breasts swell, or sag more from heat and don't look as firm, they move further away from the image sold to me of 'correct' breasts. I appreciate the ways my breasts react to hormonal changes or other external factors are entirely normal, but I can't help comparing them to the perfectly symmetrical breasts I've seen in images my entire life. I am conscious of the way my breasts jiggle when I walk, so sometimes I walk slower to stop them from bouncing as vigorously. On particularly bad self-image days, I wear baggier tops just to prevent the inevitable male stares. I am conscious about being stared at before I even leave the house. I feel as though I'm catering to male fantasies for simply being.

Generally, the media presents breasts as firm, upright and semi-large, seen often on tiny, petite bodies. Breasts, for the most part, define your sexual desirability to men. Because of this nonstop sexualisation, as well as the impossible ideals set of a perfect female body, many women consider breast augmentations to achieve what they believe to be the feminine ideal. Perhaps also unsurprisingly, because of these unrealistic standards the media has defined as beauty, many women succumb to eating disorders, like anorexia and bulimia, and other forms of harm and self-hatred as a response to not measuring up. Boob jobs continue to be one of the most sought-after forms of plastic surgery: nearly 2.2 million breast augmentation surgeries were undertaken globally in 2022.

Women's nipples are sexualised without our consent; seen as sexual without *being* sexual, aside from the fact they are on the bodies of a gender that is sexualised and objectified. Nipples are not gender specific, although, of course, men aren't banned from social media for posing without a top on. When showing your nipples can lead to your accounts being banned, it becomes difficult to see your body parts for their natural, intended purpose instead of the sexualised image that has been sold to you about them since you were little.

Most of all, breasts mean money. Unlike any other body part on both women and men, they have endless commercial possibilities. A woman capitalising on her breasts is not new, but it has only really been within the last hundred years or so that capitalism has monetised female breasts to help sell pretty much any commercial product you can think of.

Throughout history women have used, sold and commercialised their breasts for erotic purposes, which, in many instances, would help support their survival. Women using their breasts to get ahead dates as far back to the hetairai in Ancient Greece. From the courtesans in Ancient Rome, to royal mistresses and actresses in medieval and Tudor times; from the *demi-mondaines* of the nineteenth century to the actresses, singers and celebrities of today, breasts have helped women reap substantial material rewards. Considering women are still heavily underpaid because of their sex, one cannot blame women for profiting from their body parts that will undoubtedly be sexualised anyway.

Whether women are the *exploiters* or the *exploited* by choosing to make money from their bodies is complicated. It is an argument I have struggled with, having posed topless, nude and in lingerie, both consensually *and* non-consensually, in the past. For every empowered woman capitalising on her sexuality, there are equally as many unempowered women whose breasts and bodies are being used to exploit them. In our valid quest for individual sexual empowerment, it's important not to forget the women whose bodies are dehumanised for profit.

Breasts have not only been used erotically for monetary gain. For centuries, the intimate labour of wet-nursing allowed many women to earn an income through lactation. In the 1800s, wet-nursing became such a viable source of income for working-class women that at times they could out-earn their husbands, which was simply unheard of at the time.

While some wet nurses would be welcomed in and treated as part of the family, the average wet nurse was likely not treated very well at all. In environments characterised by large power indifferences, especially those involving large sums of money and a total lack of legal, psychological and physical protection (as is documented in as recent as 1960s India) it is highly probable that Victorian wet nurses would have been sexually abused by and forced to provide sexual favours for their wealthy male employers – as well as having to abandon their own children in order to prioritise the care of the children they were nursing.

During the horrific slave trade in America, Black enslaved women were essentially treated like cattle, expected to wet-nurse the slave owners' children with little to no pay.

In royal and upper-class families in the 1800s it was seen as unfashionable to breastfeed. Often, it was seen as better for the mother *not* to breastfeed so that her breasts would remain youthful and bountiful for her husband and, possibly, so her body could become pregnant again quickly afterwards, especially if she needed to produce a male heir. Much like today, youth was synonymous with female beauty, and that included maintaining the youthfulness of her breasts. Breasts, which, as we know, naturally droop through gravity and age, were expected even then to remain perky, round and upright. The onus fell on poor and working-class women to sacrifice their bodies for the freedom and vanity of the rich.

Even now, we see women trading their bodies for non-sexual

profit. With the help of modern science, surrogacy has become a privilege for the wealthy in countries like the US, made famous by the likes of the Kardashians. Many women question whether carrying and growing someone else's child is an incredible act of selflessness or whether it is exploitative. When the privileged or affluent can purchase or rent the body parts of the underprivileged, the chances of women being exploited arguably become higher.

And so, if a woman capitalises on her body for monetary gain – whether that's for a man to gawk over or as a 'rent-a-womb' – is she *truly* exercising freedom of choice or are her choices simply driven by financial reward? Where do we draw the line between a woman's *individual* sense of empowerment and the victimisation of women?

The sexual objectification of breasts, and subsequent harassment for having them, is an issue women and girls face the world over. However, in some cultures, people will go to extreme lengths to stop breasts from destroying girls' lives, but in doing so, unknowingly, become abusers themselves.

While women understand how breasts can be used as an asset, to many women and girls, including those in the West, they signify the beginning of male attention and harassment. In some cultures, breasts turn a girl into a woman overnight. In the hope of keeping a girl a child rather than an object of lust, and to help keep her in school and free from forced marriage, families will go to great lengths to help keep her looking as prepubescent as possible for her safety.

According to the National FGM Centre, breast ironing is where 'young pubescent girls' breasts are ironed, massaged, flattened and/or pounded down over a period of time (sometimes years) in order for the breasts to disappear or delay the development of the breasts entirely'. In some cultures, large stones, hammers or spatulas heated over scorching coals are used to compress the breast tissue to stop growth, while others, the charity explains, may opt for an elastic belt or binder to press the breasts.

Although this practice happens worldwide, it is especially prevalent in many African countries, especially Cameroon. Similarly to FGM, more often than not the practice is undertaken by female relatives who believe they are acting in the best interests of the child. They believe that reducing the appearance of the breasts and visible puberty will help protect the girl from rape, harassment, pregnancy, child marriage and abduction, and keep her safely away from unwanted male attention.

Breast ironing can cause many physical issues, including painful abscesses, cysts, tissue damage, infections, fever and breast development problems where they differ in size and composition. Once again, it is the girl, a child, whose body is altered to stop unwanted sexual attention or assault from men, rather than holding adult men accountable.

I often wonder whether I should feel lucky that my breasts have merely elicited catcalls, inappropriate comments and groping, rather than forcing me into a life of physical pain, child marriage, where I am pulled out of school or worse. I am lucky, I suppose, to live in a culture where I can flaunt my breasts for opportunities, instead of them hindering my adult life and destroying my body overall.

Page 3 was my introduction to a world of women's bodies being commodities to men, where the boundaries between female empowerment and female exploitation are murky. As a child, I had no idea of the sheer volume of sexualised, nude, female bodies I would come to see throughout my lifetime, female bodies which pretty much universally conformed to the same, accepted beauty standards.

Since its launch in November 1970, Page 3 was controversial. Many women unsurprisingly viewed it as sexist and degrading. In 1986, MP Clare Short proposed a bill that would ban British newspapers from publishing 'pornographic' images, but it did not garner much support. Over the years, Short became a repeated target of the *Sun* for her views on Page 3. In 2004, the *Sun* put a photo of her head on to the topless body of a Page 3 model and described her as 'Killjoy Clare', as well as 'fat and jealous'.

In 1994, the *Daily Sport* had a countdown to model Linsey Dawn McKenzie's sixteenth birthday, upon which she would be allowed to be topless. The countdown was a feature the paper would run periodically as models approached the age of sixteen. Even as recently as 2003, newspapers were allowed to feature topless sixteen- and seventeen-year-old girls.

Many people wrongfully assume that Page 3 was for working-class men but objectifying women was never, and is never, limited to the working class. Misogyny is a disease that runs throughout the veins of society and, as we are witnessing, is only becoming worse.

In the early noughties, as I moved into my teens, lads' mags – men's magazines defining a new idea of modern, British masculinity – were in their prime. It was hard to avoid them. Topless and nude women stared at you from top shelves in supermarkets, in petrol stations, in newsagents – real-life Barbie dolls who were tight, taut, cellulite-free and airbrushed to perfection.

Magazines like *FHM*, *Loaded*, *Nuts* and *Zoo* were lad culture bibles for men who enjoyed bonding over booze, football, hooliganism and tits. By 2000, *Loaded* was selling 400,000 copies a month, and *FHM* was selling more than 750,000 copies an issue. The more explicit the content, the higher the magazines were on the shelf. Before the accessibility of internet porn, the more high-end men's magazines such as *GQ* and *Esquire* and the 'softness' of Page 3 and lads' mags acted as a middle ground.

Most of the men I've met in my life have been indoctrinated by lad culture to some degree. They come from varying social classes, from the not-so-well-off working class to old money. They've been educated differently. They practise various religions (although the majority encourage women to be benevolent, submissive and in their place). And yet somehow, miraculously, their attitudes towards women tend to be similar. 'Not all men', I should say, but most: the men I've been intimate with, bosses, crushes, strangers on the street, the men I've spoken to online or on dating apps, the men in power.

Unlike *Playboy*, which seemed relatively upmarket by comparison, lads' mags did not attempt to hide their misogyny. In their heyday, their offence became less about the nudity and more about the written content. Many of the magazines featured jokes about incest, trafficking, pornography and rape. In 2010, actor Danny Dyer, who was briefly acting as *Zoo* magazine's celebrity agony aunt, advised one reader who had been recently broken up with to 'cut' his ex's face so 'no one will want her'. Many of the articles also included advice on how to target 'vulnerable women' for 'sexual conquest'. Although the last of the lads' mags ceased publishing in 2015, a lot of the beliefs and sexist attitudes set by these magazines remain embedded within our culture today.

Like Page 3, these articles, jokes and images weren't seen as harmful but a normal part of mainstream culture, where women and girls were secondary to men: props for their amusement, existing in a world designed for and around them. Sexism was cleverly disguised as banter, a joke between lads that women simply wouldn't understand. The women who *could* take the jokes were cool and 'one of the guys'. It became easy to separate boring feminists from the fun ladettes – the women subconsciously competing for male validation.

Being a ladette required you to take on characteristically feminine traits and combine them with the fun parts of masculinity: non-committal casual sex, binge-drinking and partying. Many women learnt that by internalising these misogynistic ideas they would be pseudo-accepted by men. It became a balancing act between maintaining your femininity and sexuality, while acting in a way men could relate to. It was far better to appear fun than it was to be a nag.

Much in the way girls of my generation were impacted mentally by images of frail, size zero bodies and repeatedly sold the notion that thinness was the epitome of beauty, it would be naive to assume that boys weren't impacted by lad culture and misogyny masked as 'jokes'. Andrew Tate, for example, would have been a teenager when lads' mags were in their prime; where article titles such as *'Sex Toys: Keep her quiet while the football's on'*, *'The girls that can't say no'* and *'Win your girlfriend a £4,000 boob job!'* featured on the cover.

A study in 2011 by the *British Journal of Psychology* found that many young men could not tell the difference between quotes from lads' mags and statements by convicted rapists. Some of the quotes, from magazines such as *Zoo, Nuts, Loaded, FHM* and website UniLad.com, included: *'If the girl you've taken for a drink won't spread for your head, think about this mathematical statistic: 85 per cent of rape cases go unreported'*; *'The possibility of murder does bring a certain frisson to the bedroom'*; and *'If your girl is making a face that seems forced during sex, then she's pretending to enjoy you, but if she looks like she's just been punched in the kidneys, she's in the moment.'*

Although in the early noughties social media was still in its infancy and sites like OnlyFans didn't yet exist, lads' mags were one of the first forms of media to bridge the gap between the 'girl next door' and paid, unobtainable glamour models. With devices like digicams now allowing women to take instant, uploadable photos, women (and girls) could now send topless photos of themselves to these magazines in the hope of becoming the next star – or, at least, that week's pin-up.

In 2002, *FHM* launched a competition called 'High Street Honeys', where readers could send in sexy photos of their girlfriends. As the internet progressed, *Nuts* magazine launched an online feature called 'Assess My Breasts', where women could upload topless photos (with their heads cropped out), which readers could rate and vote on. Like millions of women today, there were many women at that time who wanted men to desire them sexually, who wanted to be considered as beautiful as the glamour models that appeared on the covers – and the editors knew that.

In what I now consider a sick psychological ploy, many of these magazines capitalised on knowing that women and teenage girls *wanted* to be sexy and desired by men – and if they didn't, then they could be groomed into eventually behaving a certain way. The newsagent and stationer WHSmith had whole displays dedicated to *Playboy* pencil cases, folders, pens and other types of stationery aimed at impressionable teenage girls. Following the success of *The Girls Next Door* (2005–2010), a reality TV show about Hugh Hefner's main 'girlfriends' at the Playboy Mansion, you could transform your bedroom into a Playboy Mansion of your own with branded duvet covers, lampshades, curtains and bunny-shaped pillows featuring the infamous bunny logo. Argos had an entire jewellery section featuring *Playboy* bunny necklaces, earrings and belly button rings. We all know sex sells, but for the first time, girls could physically buy their own way into the sexiness, beauty and celebrity culture that men's magazines promoted and, ultimately, what they believed the pinnacle of female sex appeal to be.

For a select few, being a glamour model could lead to lucrative opportunities, fame and wealth. Katie Price – then known as Jordan – became one of the first glamour models to create a successful brand from her body and breasts, first appearing as a teenager on Page 3 before fronting the covers of every major lads' mag, including American *Playboy*. From bestselling books and TV shows, to perfumes, lingerie and even equestrian gear, she made millions from capitalising on her surgically enhanced breasts. She even married a pop star! From simply posing topless, Price went from humble beginnings to building a successful empire. It is no wonder that her success and fame inspired millions of girls to save up for boob jobs and follow suit.

After campaign groups including No More Page 3 and Lose the Lads' Mags fought to remove topless models from the shelves, in 2015, the era of lads' mags was finally over.

Of course, topless and nude images of women did not disappear. They simply gravitated online, a Wild West where nothing was too extreme. Lads' mags, as well as the models who featured in them, *loved* to blame boring feminists for their fading popularity. In reality they simply couldn't compete with the highly explicit free content available elsewhere.

Porn, which was once seen as seedy and underground, has now become a fixture within society and mainstream culture. While publications like *Playboy* didn't invent porn, they brought pornography to the masses, not only making it somewhat 'acceptable', but perpetuating a false sense of sexual liberation.

Porn reduces a woman to her body parts: her breasts, her thighs, her bum, her vagina. It doesn't take her brain, her heart or her soul into account – the needs, desires and wants that make her human. It takes the joy out of intimacy, erasing the real human connection. It reduces women to as little of an object as humanly possible.

Porn is now firmly embedded within our identities, structures, self-image and relationships. It shows up in music, in clothing, in the ways we have sex and even in how we date. It has created a culture where everything is fast, non-committal and, unfortunately, women bear the brunt of it. You needn't necessarily be a consumer, or even watcher, of it to become influenced by its messaging.

Since I first saw Page 3 as a child in the nineties, I have watched, in real time, material become more and more explicit. According to US anti-porn charity Fight the New Drug, at least one in three porn videos show sexual violence or aggression. Most children are exposed to porn by the age of thirteen. In a UK study, 39 per cent of eleven- to sixteen-year-old girls thought porn was a realistic depiction of sex.

Porn fetishises female pain and discomfort. It is no wonder that many children and adults believe behaviour like choking and slapping are normal acts during sex. In fact, one council-funded sex education PowerPoint was shown to teenagers in certain schools in the UK explaining how to choke their partner 'safely'. It is not difficult to understand the reason why many men can't reach orgasm unless they see a partner in pain. We are teaching the pleasure part of our brain that sex requires violence.

There is, of course, virtually no way of guaranteeing that the porn we're watching is consensual. Exploitation and trafficking are common experiences in the porn industry, yet something we turn a blind eye to. And yet, as a feminist, when women say they've turned to sex work out of love for the job or as a form of sexual liberation, I am expected to take them at their word. For a long time, I did. Now, I've been forced to challenge the ideas of sexual liberation and female empowerment that I've been taught. I am not anti-sex work. I am, however, anti-violence. I am firmly against pornography as it is today – that so much of it is now consistently violent. I see modern-day pornography as being less about sex and more about brutality. I am against any system that profits from harming women. I might view porn differently if people could separate the fantasy of porn from reality. The truth is that many of us can't and the violent ideologies we see now bleed into everyday life and mindsets.

Sex work will exist for as long as humans remain on this planet. I believe if you want to earn money or help subsidise your income through escorting or sites like OnlyFans then that is your right and choice to make. I believe in creating safe working environments for anyone engaging in sex work or prostitution, where they can access regular healthcare, fair payment and where they can work off the streets and away from pimps and trafficking. I also believe that one way of feeling empowered as a woman can come from becoming sexually empowered – understanding your likes and dislikes in bed, in becoming comfortable in your nude body, at making safe sexual choices and being able to say no. However, I do not believe sex work itself is empowering.

Boys and girls do not grow up viewing porn in the same way. Boys watch porn as though they are in the driver's seat. Women become the car, valued by mileage, age and model. The reality of watching porn as a young girl is not that you grow up with pornified fantasies like boys; rather, you *become* the pornified fantasy. It does not teach girls to enjoy sex or even to give sex. It teaches them to *take* sex – to behave, act and perform like the actresses in the videos – and, perhaps more disturbingly, to take the pain. Boys are taught that the screaming, yelling and over-exaggerated moans are a sign or proof of female pleasure. Whether the actress is *actually* enjoying it, we will never know.

After all, porn is not about human feelings or even real humans. It's simply about reaching orgasm and making men feel like kings. The porn industry would not exist without women but pretending that this has benefited women, or helped us reach sexual equality, is ludicrous. We're simply continuing to feed men what they want.

For a brief period in my early twenties, and at the height of my bulimia, I was dating a man who, many, *many* times throughout our relationship, I caught watching pornography. The type of women he was watching – curvy redheads or BBW Latinas – couldn't have been more opposite to my then-anorexic frame. Knowing he was masturbating to these women whenever he had alone time did not exactly boost my already minuscule confidence. Instead, it made me feel as though I couldn't compete: that these women could clearly arouse my boyfriend better than I could and that they were obviously the type of women he actually wanted to date.

If and when I confronted him about his developing porn obsession, it would ultimately turn into a blazing row. He'd tell me it wasn't a big deal. I said I didn't like it and would get upset. He'd tell me he'd stop. I'd eventually calm down. And then it would happen again.

I remember voicing my concerns about his porn viewing with friends and feeling unheard when they considered me jealous or that I was overreacting. Men watching porn was 'normal'. No, it wasn't that great a feeling, but it was just what they did. Men needed to let off pressure. Their sex drives were different to ours. Just because they repeatedly masturbated to the same type of body shapes did not mean they wanted to actually date women who looked like that. It wasn't like he was *cheating*. And so, ignoring how I truly felt, I convinced myself that they were right.

Just as I would in many of my later romantic relationships, I ignored my own feelings and discomfort and reluctantly turned a blind eye but frequently came across the videos on my laptop, where he often forgot to close the tab once he was finished. His daily porn watching was, allegedly, not a reflection of me or what I could offer him . . . so why did it feel as though it was? Why did I take it so personally? These women were, technically, just pixels on a screen. I'd never meet them. *He'd* never meet them. And yet I felt like I was competing for his attention, his lust, his love, with women more desirable than I'd ever be.

In 2004, feminist icon Andrea Dworkin said: 'If we give up now, younger generations of women will be told porn is good for them and they will believe it.' A little over twenty years later, Dworkin was proved right.

In the last few years, and especially in lockdown during the Covid pandemic, a new type of sex work emerged. As women were struggling to pay their bills, stuck at home with nothing to do, a new platform began to rise in popularity: OnlyFans. Created by British businessman Tim Stokely in 2016, OnlyFans capitalised on the growing demand for amateur (aka homemade) porn. Like most British men of his generation, it is highly likely that Stokely was a reader of lads' mags.

OnlyFans created a bridge between traditional pornography and the everyday woman. It allows all women, essentially, to become an idealised object of someone's lust and to capitalise from it. In industries previously defined by rigid beauty standards, *all* women – regardless of shape, size, nationality, skin colour, disability – can now become pin-ups. For women who may have felt excluded from the male gaze previously, it has allowed them to feel desired.

By 2023, OnlyFans had 305 million registered users and around 3 million creators, predominantly women. To get paid or gain new buyers, creators have to drive traffic to their pages by promoting their OnlyFans accounts on different social media platforms, meaning that sites like Instagram, TikTok, X and Reddit are littered with sexy and provocative selfies and videos.

Many female content creators report a pressure to create more and more explicit content so as to keep subscribers. Not only do they create content they are not comfortable with, but if they refuse requests they can also receive abuse. Content on OnlyFans can be leaked and shared across the internet, especially on other porn sites, and people can exploit and profit off content without the consent of the creator. It is near impossible to track where images end up and if they are found to have them taken down.

If OnlyFans had existed when I was in my late teens, there's a high possibility I would've joined it too. Which insecure teenager *isn't* excited by the possibility of making millions or a legion of male simps paying for the privilege of seeing their body and telling them how beautiful they are? The truth is, despite the allure, the average creator only makes $1,300 annually.

OnlyFans is sex work. It is not social media. Yet it works as though it is, requiring you to promote your account by getting people to sign up using your referral link. Some ask what the difference is between posting a bikini picture for likes on Instagram versus posting a topless photo on OnlyFans for money. With the rise of AI, it is likely that many women will become victims of deepfake porn. Does it make sense for creators to profit off this content while they can and are in control?

Sites like OnlyFans are incredibly clever at manipulating women into believing they are making these decisions of their own accord. OnlyFans *loves* to tell women that creating their own content is a form of empowerment, a form of feminism. You can be your own boss! You can create your own work schedule! You can double your income! Its PR machine will spew out success story after success story, each more appealing than the one before. It picks on women's vulnerabilities – which can often be financial – and tells them that their lives will transform from simply posting some sexy photos.

And women buy into it. You see, we love to read stories about the struggling mother who became an overnight millionaire thanks to her OnlyFans account. We are fascinated by the lifestyles of twenty-something women who show us their huge houses on TikTok, own a handful of sports cars, go on exotic trips and are financially independent.

Yet we repeatedly choose to ignore the stories of other women: the woman working on the street corner who is struggling to feed her children; the woman addicted to hard drugs, risking her safety and life every time she climbs into a stranger's car. We do not like hearing the stories of women who are trafficked into sex work against their will; of women who have been raped and cannot get the video removed from porn sites despite their persistent trying; of women whose husband or boyfriend is forcing them to create explicit OnlyFans content for money. We cannot be empowered through sex work when we ignore the women disempowered by it.

The success of OnlyFans has merely encouraged other websites to follow suit, exploiting women for their own gain. Unsee, an app originally designed to share images discreetly, has been exploited by men as a means of sharing intimate photos of female strangers – and even of their own girlfriends, wives, mothers and daughters – without their knowledge or consent. Their bodies are turned into a catalogue for other men to scroll through, including their names, ages, sexual 'menus' and even notes on whether or not they've been abused. The photos disappear after one view but can also be placed in 'rooms' where users can comment, download and share them. Some photos include pregnant women; others feature very young women, who appear to be underage or children. Unsee makes money through ads and donations while leaving women exposed, humiliated and violated: a system built on exploiting women's bodies for men's entertainment.

Emma Pickering, head of technology-facilitated abuse at Refuge – the British charity for women and children, against domestic abuse – explained to me how many women using sites like OnlyFans are being forced into sex work by their partners; horrific abuse which, like a lot of the sex industry, is often overlooked.

'Unfortunately, platforms like OnlyFans are being weaponised by perpetrators of domestic abuse,' she said. 'This includes survivors whose intimate images have been shared and monetised without their knowledge, often by their abusive partners or ex-partners, in clear violation of laws on the non-consensual sharing of intimate images. It is devastating that abusers can profit from intimate content – whether this is through coercing survivors to create and share content, or by creating content, sometimes secretly, and then distributing it without the survivor's consent.'

She explained how the charity is 'incredibly concerned' by reports of women being compelled to perform sex acts by their coercive and controlling partners. 'This is unacceptable and we urgently need safeguards to prevent platforms like OnlyFans from being used to facilitate abuse,' she told me. 'Among other necessary measures, including tagging flagged content to stop it from being reshared, the platform should implement technology requiring creators to submit recorded proof of consent at the point of upload. OnlyFans must be held accountable for effectively moderating content and preventing the distribution of illegal and non-consensual images.'

The debate of whether sites like OnlyFans can ever be empowering seems to be an issue echoed by the charity, especially with the current rules in place. One of the concerns raised by creators is how blocked users are automatically issued refunds instead of being reported to the authorities, and how they could subsequently perpetuate, or even incentivise, abuse in retaliation.

'While OnlyFans can be a source of empowerment for some creators, there are systemic issues in how the platform is structured, managed and moderated that leaves survivors vulnerable to exploitation and harm,' she explained. 'Perpetrators are increasingly weaponising digital platforms and tools to reinforce patterns of coercion and control. If the government fails to take the threat of this devastating form of abuse seriously, there is no doubt that its pledge to halve violence against women and girls within the next decade will not be met.'

A common statement from OnlyFans models is that men will sexualise them regardless, so they may as well make money from it. But is it empowering to play men at their own game? Because once you make the money by catering to men's desires and bringing them to orgasm, you will still find yourself as unempowered as you were before.

I have seen some of the most awful and degrading content on OnlyFans. I watched one creator make herself vomit at the request of one buyer, before eating it. The same woman fisted her anus with her own hand until she gave herself an anal prolapse, sharing it to X – much to the joy of her male followers. Can you *truly* define this is sexy or empowering? Of course not. It's about violence and degradation on another scale, fuelling sick male appetites under the guise of 'kink'. We are supposed not to sex- or kink-shame the men who enjoy or ask for this content, but . . . really? Is giving yourself a prolapse for cash *really* an act of empowerment? Where do we draw the line? Where do these *creators* draw the line?

Many of the top creators could easily pass as underage

teenagers, and in some cases, even as children. I once genuinely believed I'd accidentally stumbled upon child pornography when I saw photos of a Japanese female dressed in baby clothes and sucking a dummy, though her account made sure to point out she was of legal age.

At this stage, I feel empowerment has lost all meaning. It's become incredibly easy for women to showcase their bodies, wear revealing clothes or strip nude for strangers, but what about addressing the root of why some women choose to do this? While sold to us as an equal form of pleasure, sex work has still not granted us sexual equality. It says a lot that a woman's life and career can still be ruined by having her nudes leaked, while a man accused of numerous rape allegations and sex-trafficking can be the president of the US.

While women may enter the sex industry with financial incentives in mind – a fair reason, I'd say – ultimately, I am unsure who this type of sex work is benefiting in the long run. If you see your body or beauty as the thing that defines you, it will also, ultimately, become the thing that destroys you. Yes, whether we engage in porn or OnlyFans is our choice to make. But oppression, and choice feminism, has a very clever way of gaslighting women into thinking their choices are their own.

On the other hand, a man would be unlikely to think of other men (let alone women) when he makes decisions, so why should we think of others? No matter what we do, the choices we make as women are consistently dissected, debated and dismissed. Why are selflessness and needing to consider others in our decision making expectations of womanhood?

'A sex symbol becomes a thing. I hate being a thing.'

So said arguably the biggest movie star of all time, Marilyn Monroe, a woman who had been abused and taken advantage of by men throughout her life, before her tragic death by suicide at just thirty-six.

Monroe had been a victim of child sex abuse. Her mother was a diagnosed schizophrenic, frequently in and out of psychiatric facilities, and she never met her father. As a result, she spent much of her childhood and early teenage years in foster care, where she was sexually abused many times over and raped at the age of eleven. Her choices were seemingly fuelled by insecurities and feelings of low self-worth, feelings that not only drove her need to be famous and 'seen' but repeatedly revealed themselves within her romantic relationships and the men she married.

Monroe married her first husband, James Dougherty, at just sixteen. He disapproved of her having a modelling career. When she was offered a contract with 20th Century Fox, it stipulated that she must be unmarried so as not to fall pregnant. Due to this opportunity and the opposition Dougherty had towards her career, in 1946 she filed for divorce. By the time she married her second husband, Joe DiMaggio, in 1954, she was now a world-famous movie star, renowned globally for her beauty, body and sex appeal. Monroe divorced him just nine months later citing 'mental cruelty', and where it was claimed DiMaggio was unable to handle the popularity around her sexuality and 'sex goddess' persona. The constant sexualisation of Monroe took its toll on her own mental well-being. 'Men see me as a fantasy and not as a woman with a woman's body and a woman's needs,' she once said.

In December 1953, as she was becoming a Hollywood star, a series of nude photos of Monroe were published both inside as a centerfold and on the front cover of a new men's magazine called *Playboy*, created by businessman Hugh Hefner. Four years earlier in 1949, struggling for money and under the promise of anonymity, Monroe had been paid $50 for a two-hour calendar photo shoot with pin-up photographer Tom Kelley. She signed the release forms under a false name, an indication that these photos were not taken with pride but out of financial desperation. Years later, these were the photos published in *Playboy*.

While the photos undoubtedly helped her become a worldwide sex symbol, Monroe became the world's first celebrity 'leak'. Hefner cited these photos of Monroe as one of the reasons *Playboy* became as successful as it did. However, he failed to mention that Monroe had not been paid for the use of the photos; nor had she signed off on the use of the images. Monroe had to buy a copy of the magazine herself and would later tell a friend that she had not received so much as a 'thank you' from the people who made millions from images of her nude body.

In *Right-Wing Women*, Andrea Dworkin wrote of Monroe: 'She grinned, she posed, she pretended, she had affairs with famous and powerful men. A friend of hers claimed that she had so many illegal abortions performed that her reproductive organs were severely injured. She died alone, possibly acting on her own behalf for the first time . . . Her lovers in both flesh and fantasy had fucked her to death, and her apparent suicide stood at once as accusation and answer: no, Marilyn Monroe, the ideal sexual female, had not liked it.'

In 1992, Hefner purchased the crypt next to Marilyn's for $75,000. Shortly before his death in 2017, he told the *LA Times*: 'I'm a believer in things symbolic. Spending eternity next to Marilyn is too sweet to pass up.' Even in death, she could not escape the man who had violated her. For all she'd unwillingly contributed towards his success, once again, she could not give consent.

Like Monroe, I think of all the women whose sexualised material will outlive them or be used, shared or sold without their consent. No matter how much control you *think* you have of your bodily image and the ways it's perceived, there is always a chance your body will be used in ways you wouldn't consent to.

While I was looking back at my own stories of sexual abuse and assault and the possible links between them and my need to self-objectify, I noticed that many more of my idols, known for their sex appeal, had been victims of sexual assault themselves.

One of the most famous and successful celebrities to capitalise on her sexuality in the early noughties was Paris Hilton, whose sex tape turned her into a household name. The release coincided with the debut of her TV show with Nicole Richie, *The Simple Life*, and it boosted ratings and turned her into a worldwide star. Although Hilton did not have the stereotypical porn star body at the time – she had a flat chest and a model-thin physique – the tape turned her into an automatic sex symbol. Her body became synonymous with the size zero craze of the early noughties: it was a body women wanted to emulate and which men wanted to fuck.

It is alleged that after the release of the sex tape, Hilton was disinherited from the Hilton family fortune. However, the success of the Paris Hilton brand has meant she's amassed her own wealth. Her perfume line alone has made over $2.5 *billion* in revenue. After seeing the fame and success from Hilton's sex tape, other celebrity tapes were soon 'leaked' – most noticeably that of Hilton's previous assistant Kim Kardashian, who is now a billionaire herself and who has become arguably the world's biggest modern-day sex symbol, inspiring an entirely new idea of female beauty.

It was only recently, however, in *Paris: the Memoir* (2023) that Hilton opened up about childhood sexual abuse and her sex tape. While in eighth grade (aged thirteen to fourteen), Hilton explains how she was groomed by her male teacher. She explains how she never felt as though she was being manipulated, because like many young women in a similar situation to hers, why would she? She instead felt as though she was being 'worshipped'. It felt wonderful for all of the attention to be on her, for the attention to be on her 'intoxicating beauty' rather than his inappropriate behaviour.

After driving to her house one evening while her parents were out, the teacher kissed Hilton in his car. During what 'went on for what seemed like a long time and seemed to be evolving into something more', Hilton's parents suddenly pulled into the driveway. She caught her dad's 'stunned face' through the glass, and her teacher sped off with her still in the car. 'Fuck! Fuck! Fuck!' the teacher said. 'My life is over. What am I doing? Why did you make me do this?'

Eventually, her teacher dropped her back home – without kissing her good night, Hilton adds, which she believed to be the ending of all romantic 'dates' – and Hilton snuck back into her bedroom. When her parents burst into her room and began screaming at her, she tried to pretend she'd been sleeping all along. As a result of what happened, Hilton was sent to Palm Springs to live with her maternal grandmother, before eventually attending a series of correctional boarding schools for troublesome teens. While she does not know what happened to the teacher, it seems like Hilton was punished for her own childhood grooming.

At one of these correctional schools, Hilton explains how she was molested and sexually abused by staff in late-night 'gynaecological examinations' and 'drug tests'. She recalled to *Glamour* magazine how groups of adults – both men and women – would regularly hold her and other girls down and put fingers inside of them.

At fifteen, Hilton says that she lost her virginity after being spiked and raped. Later, at nineteen, Hilton met Rick Salomon – the boyfriend who would partake in and release her now infamous sex tape without her permission. Despite claiming she 'hated' sex after the 'abuse and degradation' she'd experienced at these boarding schools, Salomon asked her if they could film them having sex. Eventually, after taking Quaaludes – a powerful sedative and recreational drug – and drinking heavily, she reluctantly agreed as a means to 'prove something' to him and to herself.

When the video was released, she explained how 'shame, loss and stark terror swept over me'. After talking to Salomon over the phone about why he leaked it, Salomon said he 'had every right to sell something that belonged to him – something that had a lot of financial value'.

Salomon eventually went on to have a brief marriage with Pamela Anderson, another icon of mine who, in her self-titled documentary, *Pamela: A Love Story* (2023), revealed she had been sexually abused as a child by her babysitter, as well as raped at the age of twelve. As CJ Parker on *Baywatch*, Anderson became the ultimate sex symbol of the nineties: her body, with her large, inflated breasts and tiny physique, seen as the pinnacle of female sexuality.

After years of dealing with her crippling sexual trauma, Anderson chose to pose nude for *Playboy*, explaining how she gained an 'awakening' of her sexuality afterwards. Like Hilton, she believed that leaning into her sexuality and posing nude on her own terms would help reclaim what was taken from her.

However, after *Playboy* and at the height of her nineties fame, a sex tape of her and then-husband Tommy Lee was stolen from her home. After being offered $5 million to approve publishing rights to the tape, despite turning it down, the tape was released to the public regardless. While Tommy Lee was hailed as some sort of stud after the leak, because she had consented to pose nude for *Playboy* previously, many people assumed her sex tape automatically revoked Anderson's right to privacy, especially around her sex life. The lack of empathy for Anderson seemed to suggest her body was public property. Anderson's sexual public image was used to discredit her right to call herself a victim and led to much slut-shaming for what had been a private, consensual video. In the public's eyes, she lost all credibility and the right to call herself a victim of abuse.

What we rarely discuss is how sexual abuse can lead women into hypersexualising themselves. Anderson's account of the leaked sex tape, lack of control over her own content and the abuse she faced after the tape was non-consensually leaked comes at a time where image-based abuse, such as revenge porn and AI deep fakes, is rapidly developing. Regardless of whether a woman consents to nude photos, sex tapes or OnlyFans content, her face and body can now be taken, morphed and used without her knowledge (so obviously without her consent) to create sexual imagery and pornographic material. It is a modern, technological form of abuse that can affect anyone, even those who have not taken any sexual photographs of themselves. Not using sites like OnlyFans or not sending nudes to a partner no longer protects you from being sexualised against your will. The effect this has and *will* have on women and girls is devastating.

We mustn't ignore the toll that ongoing misogyny and abuse have on the female body and psyche and the impact this has on the choices we make, the relationships we choose, the type of love we seek, even the careers we undertake. While it would be undoubtedly wrong to assume that *all* women who engage in glamour modelling or sex work have been sexually abused, I can't help but notice a familiar pattern among many women who choose to objectify themselves or capitalise off their sexuality.

I believe we're overlooking one of the core reasons women choose to sexualise themselves to begin with: a deep, ravenous need to be 'seen' and, possibly, an even deeper desire to be loved. We speak about self-objectification and the need to be validated by men, but we don't often speak about the inherent human feelings many of us crave: *wanting* to be loved in the ways we can't or don't know how to love ourselves.

In this digital era, we are all, for the most part, screaming for intimacy. We yearn to be seen; for people to see us beneath our personas. A like, follow or heart validates us, even makes us feel special, if only for a second. We are a society of sad people, lonely and longing for touch. We are unaware of how our objectifying culture, both online and offline, has left many of us feeling inadequate, disassociated from our bodies and from who we truly are. After a lifetime of feeling we are never enough, we are unaware of how many women feel desperately unloved and unseen and who use their bodies for a sliver of attention.

When life teaches you that love comes from the way you look or from being sexy, we unknowingly often seek attention from men. Love should be the easiest thing in the world, but often we lose ourselves trying to find it. We do not think to find it within.

While Page 3 and glamour modelling feel relatively tame compared to the content that exists online now, they still propelled a lot of women into work built off their own trauma. In 2017, Katie Price said on the TV show *Loose Women* that being sexually assaulted at the age of seven was related to her decision to become a glamour model. She explained how becoming a glamour model allowed her to be 'all sexy'. Like many women, she believed that objectifying herself would help her to regain control of her body. 'Being a glamour model is a trade for men, so it was like, you can look at me, but you can't touch me,' she said.

She also added on the show: 'I've been abused and raped since [my childhood assault], I'm not going to say [by] who', though in other interviews she states that one rapist was a famous celebrity. Price has also recalled how she was raped at gunpoint by six men during a carjacking incident in 2018.

Although Price provides bait for numerous tabloids, I can't help but feel her turbulent personal life – including her various drink and drug offences, numerous marriages, OnlyFans career trajectory and excessive cosmetic surgery – appears to be a way of filling an unexplainable void; a yearning and longing for love and acceptance that only victims of sexual abuse and trauma can explain. What I will add, however, is that when female celebrities renowned for their power and beauty come forward about these allegations, they make women the world over feel less alone. We feel seen. We feel less like freaks. We may not be as rich, sexy, beautiful or successful, but slowly we let go of the shame that rape and sexual assault hold over us and show abusers that we are no longer fearful of them.

Should I feel privileged in being sexually desired or objectified, when some women never get to experience it at all?

In a 2016 *New York Times* op-ed piece entitled 'Longing for the Male Gaze', writer Jennifer Bartlett, who has cerebral palsy, wrote about how she *wants* to be sexually objectified and seen as a sexual person, as that would make her feel like an actual human being. It was a thought-provoking essay, one which made me question my feelings as a woman who has felt like a sex object her entire life and who experiences disrespectful comments and behaviour fairly frequently.

Was it wrong, ignorant or naive of me to assume *every* woman has experienced sexual leers in the street; to assume that every woman, non-disabled or disabled, experiences disgusting comments and abuse from men over her lifetime?

I spoke to my friend Lottie Jackson, a writer and disability activist, about her experiences with sexual objectification and mentioned the op-ed to her. Lottie has had a generalised muscle weakness disability since birth, a rare, non-progressive condition affecting her physical strength, which along with other severe illnesses (including pneumonia) has required her to use a wheelchair. I mention to Lottie how many women often feel a strange mix of both *wanting* to be desired by men and often wishing they would leave their bodies alone. It is a complicated feeling, full of paradoxes, as more often than not women feel this is where their worth and value lie, stemming from a lifetime of being rewarded for catering to the male gaze.

'It *is* paradoxical,' Lottie agrees. 'On one hand, most disabled women want to be seen as sexual beings with the same desires and romantic goals as the next person. Most people wrongly believe that disabled individuals aren't interested in, or even capable of, sex and intimacy. There's often a painful assumption of asexuality among the disabled community. [So] to feel wanted is like a stamp of validation, it confirms not only our womanhood, but it also asserts our value and humanity in a world that often emphasises our inadequacies. It's the promise of connection, acceptance and pleasure, rather than alienation and avoidance. Some people even view disabled people as childlike, which prevents them from being seen as sexual beings. So when you're desired by someone, it can feel like a sort of victory, a sign that you have successfully overcome all these obstacles and prejudices that are "normal".'

When it comes to Bartlett's op-ed piece in which she wishes for objectification as a means of 'normalcy' or Lottie mentioning how many disabled women feel validated at being chosen by men, I wonder why has sexual objectification become an indicator of female beauty and desirability, as well as becoming the core of what we believe the normal female experience to be? Why is it that objectification has become so normalised that we've come to see it as the status quo?

Lottie tells me how that in the 1980s, a 23-year-old student with paraplegia, Ellen Stohl, posed naked for a *Playboy* pictorial.

This was a decision which puzzled and angered many feminists, who could not understand why she would reduce herself to a sex object or ally herself with a magazine that caters specifically to male desires. Ellen, who was interviewed by Lottie for her book *See Me Rolling* (2023), told Lottie that this response made her feel as though she 'was a child again . . . and people treated me as such. Sexuality is the hardest thing for disabled persons to hold on to. I wasn't taking off my clothes for men. I posed for *Playboy* to discover my own sexuality, to celebrate that part of me that was stripped away by a disability.'

Lottie goes on to explain how women and girls face double discrimination linked to both their gender and disabilities. Statistics show that disabled women are incredibly vulnerable to sexual abuse and, in fact, twice as likely as the general population to experience gender-based violence. 'In a world where disabled bodies are often feared and disparaged, it may seem surprising that disabled women are facing a disproportionate threat of sexual assault, physical invasion, groping and rape,' she adds.

In the past, I have met women who have been fetishised for their disabilities, reduced to nothing more than a porn genre, a conquest, a fetish, a fantasy and whose bodies are treated as though they owe men who sexually desire them. I spoke to another woman about her experiences with sexual objectification, an amputee, who wishes to remain anonymous. She is frequently bombarded with men sliding into her Instagram DMs asking her for sex or nudes, men treating her body as a fetish. She tells me it's as though her page, which is used as a positive means of highlighting her disability and inclusive fashion, has become a slideshow of images for men to masturbate or sexually fantasise over, or a platform to contact her and directly proposition her for sex. Unlike OnlyFans models who choose to post sexually driven content for monetary means, these women are treated as sex workers themselves by simply existing in their bodies – *and* treated as though they should feel grateful for the attention.

Lottie explains there is a disturbing phenomenon called devoteeism, where people with disabilities face extreme objectification and fetishisation. Devotees – roughly defined as people who are sexually aroused by disability – may conceal exploitative and voyeuristic behaviours under a veil of generosity or compassion.

'In many circumstances, the devotee's desire thrives on an imbalance of power, a predatory attempt to take on a caretaker's role,' she tells me. 'There's even a sinister publication called the *Amputee Times*, which encourages readers to report the names and addresses of amputee women for a national (or international) register of attractive amputees. If disabled women continue to be dehumanised and perceived as powerless, they will remain prime targets of sexual abuse.'

I suppose – while not sexually, necessarily – women like Lottie are objectified in other ways, seen as 'useless' objects that aren't valid of feelings, human desire or even basic empathy.

Because that's the thing. Regardless of what you look like, if a man doesn't find you the least bit fuckable, he will barely give you the time of day, let alone respect. Then, of course, you meet the other men who feel that the attention they place on you has the ability to value or devalue you . . . with many of us on the receiving end of it – myself included – believing it.

At some point in our lives, we'll likely all become sexually useless to certain men. It's just a matter of when. When I think of older women I know, who tell me I should feel 'grateful' for catcalls while I still get them, I think about how most of us will eventually morph from one object to another: from a shiny toy to a used toy, covered in dust and out of sight, exchanged for something newer. You needn't necessarily be a *sex* object to be treated as one. But regardless of how you look as a woman, or whether you're non-disabled or disabled, sexy or not, why aren't we worthy of simple human decency?

The ways I was made to feel as a child seemed to grow with every year I did, trailing me wherever I went. I couldn't fully connect with myself because I simply didn't trust myself enough to exist freely. I told myself I was disgusting, because that's how Sean's hands made me feel.

After Sean, I'd begun to be made uncomfortable by other men and boys. Not long after what happened with him, I remember a boy in his mid-teens, a male babysitter, looking after me one afternoon. I must've been eight or so. He had always been strange with me and made me feel uncomfortable in ways I couldn't understand.

He told me to connect to the internet on my family computer – a lengthy process, back then – and search for *sex.com*. The first image I saw was a woman giving a man a blow job. The teenage boy explained to me what a blow job meant, what another photo meant and so forth. Feeling as though I was looking at something illegal, I disconnected the modem from the computer and ran downstairs.

After that, whenever I had to spend time with him, he would try to act out his weird fantasies with me. One 'game', for example, involved stripping to just our underwear, then climbing underneath his bed covers and pretending we were a married couple. A friend at school had told me that babies were made if you slept next to a man. I spent the next few months panicking about whether I could be pregnant and if I were, how I'd possibly explain this to my mother.

Not *all* men were inappropriate with me, but the men who did make me uncomfortable seemed to go out of their way to make me as confused and ashamed as possible. One time, a drunk older man asked nine-year-old me if I fancied a snog. It was as though they relished making me feel less than; reminding me that as men, they had the power to make or break me.

At this age, anything regarding sex made me feel physically ill. The more I tried to avoid the thought of sex or witness anything sex related, the more it seemed to appear in front of me. It was hard to escape it when it appeared in nearly everything I saw. I came to associate it with sin. Sex wasn't just the images and acts I'd seen on *sex.com*, but a feeling; a sensation; a product; a way of being.

Around the age of ten, I began to develop severe intrusive thoughts. I would watch a news report about rape and begin to truly believe that I'd either been raped or had raped someone myself. The thoughts were so realistic that I would vomit or tremble out of fear. I knew, deep down, that these thoughts weren't true, yet I would have to spend days, weeks, months, convincing myself it was all in my head. I felt like a prisoner within my own brain.

Usually, the thoughts would be triggered by seeing or engaging with men or older boys. I could talk to a male teacher or a boy in the street and overanalyse the interaction until I became utterly convinced that they had, or were going to, hurt me sexually in some way. I would watch a film with a sex scene or two adults in the midst of passion, and my brain would spew out disturbing thoughts.

My brain, of course, was not mature enough to connect the dots: that what happened with Sean, as well the onslaught of sexual imagery around me, were having a profound impact on my mental health and manifesting in physical symptoms.

And then, while my brain was still very much stuck in its childlike ways of thinking, my body began to develop. Puberty hit me out of nowhere, my body maturing at a rate my mind had not yet caught up with. The brewing lumps on my chest felt too mature, too womanly, for the mentality of someone who still enjoyed watching silly kids' TV shows and playing on swings.

I had gone from innocently craving the breasts of a glamour model to not wanting them at all. As my breasts continued to develop, so did my desire to shrink.

What was it about my breasts that I instantly equated to sex? Was it the fact that the bigger they became, the more flesh there was to grab – more *woman* to grab – that made me feel so uncomfortable? My breasts were a part of me, built into me, which meant I couldn't escape them. I didn't want to be grabbable. I wanted to be left alone, free to exist as I was, free from prying eyes and unwarranted comments about my changing shape.

There comes a time, of course, where even little lumps need support; where the outline of nipples through clothing, even on a child's body, are suddenly deemed inappropriate or unsightly. Reluctantly, I had to admit defeat. Whether I liked it or not, I'd have to wear a bra.

There was something to me about bras that felt inherently sexual. I knew that the moment I wore a bra, I'd start to be considered a woman, and if I was considered a woman, I wouldn't be able to escape being sexualised. Being a woman meant you'd be touched by men and expected to do things to them. I didn't want to do sexual things, let alone be *seen* as sexual in any way.

Some girls in my class, especially my immediate group of friends, fully leant into the changes in their breasts and the attention they were getting. They'd wear tween bras from Tammy Girl or Marks & Spencer, designed to make you *feel* like you were grown up, but in shape, print and colour they were extremely childlike: two triangle cut-outs of fabric to cover the bee stings and elasticated straps to make you think your boobs were being supported, though, of course, they weren't supporting very much. My friends were excited about becoming women. I wanted to remain a girl.

I stood in the Marks & Spencer changing rooms in embarrassment as the woman held a measuring tape around my chest, noting the centimetres down on a piece of paper. 'Aren't these pretty?' she said, handing me a selection of bras adorned with little girly embellishments like ribbons and diamanté hearts. It was supposed to be one of female life's defining moments, yet the whole experience made me feel uncomfortable and self-conscious.

The bras may have been hidden under my clothing, yet somehow I still felt very much on show. The elastic dug into the skin around my ribcage, the red and purple indents leaving me itchy. I missed my childhood vests, which protected my body by covering my torso and back. Now, with just a small amount of cloth to cover my breasts, I felt practically naked.

Wearing bras ignited an interest in our prepubescent bodies. Girls showcased bra straps almost like a badge of honour. Boys snapped the elastic bands against our skin as a 'joke', but also likely in curious fascination. But perhaps even more bizarrely, disturbingly, our growing bodies suddenly made us noticeable to adult men.

We were the 'in between' girls, no longer children, not yet teenagers, but with the early makings of a woman; mouldable, malleable and impressionable, with infantile, miniature versions of adult female body parts. Although we were visibly still very much adolescents, there were many men – *far too many men* – who were clearly aroused by girls with the onset of a woman's body, yet who had the mindset of children.

Every woman on earth has experienced men like these: grown men who enjoy sniffing out childlike vulnerabilities, who become excited at the thought of virginial, docile and vulnerable girls. We could be innocently sitting in a park on a weekend and grown men would come and talk to us. Men would yell inappropriate comments at us about our bodies from cars or tell us we looked sexy. My body, and especially my breasts, became larger than life characters, bigger than me, separate to me.

There is a certain type of man who relishes reminding young girls of his sexual power, whose warped ideas of masculinity are fuelled by knowing his stature alone can scare girls into submission. He delights in reminding girls that he has the ability to make or break them, whether that's via overpowering them with his physical strength, the intimidating build of his masculine frame or the viciousness of his tongue. He is, more often than not, the type of man who is offended if a girl dares to stand up for herself or put him in his place, the kind of man who will usually respond to female rejection by attacking the way she looks.

In a society that regards female beauty above all other characteristics – a message the patriarchy has taught us to believe will create a life of prosperity, love and adoration – criticising or belittling a woman's looks is considered to be an ultimate attack. These men believe, as the patriarchy has convinced women and girls, that without her beauty or youth, a woman is nothing. If she *thinks* she is nothing, she becomes easier to control, easier to manipulate, easier to keep in her place. And for some reason, no matter how vile these men are to us, we often allow these words and opinions to consume us, because everything we know and everything we're taught is built on the basis of our beauty and sexual desirability.

Out of all my sexualised body parts, I have come to love my breasts the most. I own them with pride, celebrating them as part of me. The parts of myself I tried desperately to strap down and shrink to pry them away from male attention have become those that make me proud to be feminine. I love to cup them in my hands, the flesh spilling over my fingers. I enjoy the ways they add shape to my physique; the ways they make me feel womanly, sexy and unashamed of the femininity I've been encouraged to hate. But most of all, my breasts represent the sexualised parts of myself I've started to reclaim as my own.

skin.

Some women are born with that 'thing' that makes them special or stand out. Their beauty stops you in your tracks. Our voices become giddy around them, our faces bashful, even if we aren't attracted to them sexually. We want to know what make-up they use, what perfume they're wearing, which brand their shoes are, all so we can emulate them, in a hope of feeling just as *pretty*. We analyse their faces meticulously, in the hope of finding a fault to make us feel somewhat better about our own; search for anything, any flaw, to make them more human. We hope that by hanging around with them, perhaps some of their magic, their beauty, will rub off on to us, and we can live just a few moments in their skin. Their lives seem easier than ours, more joyful than ours, simply for winning the genetic lottery.

And by God, I wanted to be one of those women.

As a child, I was fine to look at but I wasn't beautiful and, by the age of ten, I would find every way to cover my body, to hide it from public view, and especially the view of men. I watched their eyes watching me, even then. I hated clothes that were tight against the skin, the way they clung to every curve, making me feel as though someone could grab, touch or squeeze me at any time. On holidays, I would wear oversized T-shirts to cover my body in the pool, telling my family it was to protect my skin from the sun, while secretly wanting to steer men's eyes away from me. I didn't wear a bikini until I was twenty-four.

By my early teens, I could be described as nothing other than categorically plain. My face was round and undefined, my eyebrows far too thick for my face, my body overweight. As a means of clinging on to my childhood, I decided not to shave my legs, providing much entertainment for the bitchy girls who'd point out my leg hair as I went to class.

I knew I was ugly. There are very few photos of me as a teenager because I avoided the camera like the plague. I was disgusted by my own appearance, persistently anxious at the thought of the body I currently was and of it being forever frozen in time within a snapshot.

I had never been aware of beauty until I first saw a second-hand copy of *Elle* magazine. It was the first time I'd picked up a fashion magazine: the women stunningly beautiful and otherworldly thin; the clothes like something out of a storybook.

Fashion was a world so different to my own. My father was in the forces, which required us to move from country to country, house to house, school to school. I have truly lost count of the number of homes I have lived in over the years, but it is more than twenty.

But the fantasy of fashion remained consistent. It transported me to a different place; somewhere I could escape to in my imagination.

The models on the glossy pages clearly had no problems, had no idea how it felt to be unnoticed and mediocre. They would have never been made fun of for their looks; no concept of what it was to be lonely. Judging by their bodies, they clearly didn't overeat as a form of comfort, either.

I became somewhat obsessed with fashion magazines, in creating stories and lives around the fashion editorials. Each week I would head to the newsagent's and buy them, fawning over the beautiful clothes and make-up, as well as the models wearing them. Their life could be in reach, if I simply lost weight.

Becoming beautiful was the solution to all my problems. I was sure of it.

As I began losing weight, I started to daydream about how life may look if I were to become a model. Was this all too far-fetched? On some good days, I'd catch a look at my reflection and think there was *something* to work with. My face drastically improved when I wore make-up. Boys began taking an interest. But I needed *more*. I wanted to change my life drastically; to *totally* transform my life and become better than anything I dreamt possible.

My bulimia, which was at an all-time high, now had meaning. Shrinking myself would make me thin, which would make me beautiful, which would mean I would have a chance at becoming a model. And so, from the age of fourteen, I made becoming a model my ultimate goal.

My insecurity, ego and vanity led me into numerous dangerous situations with men. I physically cringe when I think about them. It was simply so other people – women *and* men – would deem me glamorous, sexy or beautiful. I wanted people to stare at photos of me and think that I was special; to aspire to be me, just as I aspired to be other women.

And believe me, I would've done anything to be told that I was 'beautiful', especially if it happened to come from the lips of seedy, disgusting male photographers. I was too naive, too immature and too awestruck by the fashion industry to believe these men could possibly harm me, place me in uncomfortable situations or use me for their own satisfaction.

Subconsciously, I believed the thin, non-fleshy bodies and smooth skin of fashion models of the time would mean men would leave me alone.

Oh, how wrong I was.

I applied to model agency after model agency, frequently receiving letters of rejection, which meant I clearly wasn't attractive enough.

And so developed my long, and dare I say unhealthy, relationship with outer beauty and the skin I was in. I wanted, desperately, to be beautiful, for other people to see me as beautiful. All I'd ever known was how much better life would become if I were prettier.

Whenever a woman says she looks ugly, we immediately cry, 'No!' even if we don't mean it, because there is nothing worse, nothing more dreadful, than a woman not being pretty – especially in *feeling* not pretty.

Ugliness, much like fatness, is not so much an aesthetic problem, I think, but a means of describing our inner complicated emotions: a feeling of unworthiness beneath the skin, where every negative thought leaves us uncomfortable and exposed. None of us wish to feel ugly, yet all of us have experienced it at least once in our lives, made worse through nasty comments, comparisons to other women and derogatory comments from men. Even the prettiest of women know how it feels to feel ugly; how it feels to be *made* to feel ugly. And it's something we spend our lifetimes trying desperately to avoid, usually at the expense of our own well-being and mental health.

When we believe we're ugly, I think we become more susceptible to outside forces. We start to surround ourselves with people who aren't nice to us. We spend our valuable time obsessing in front of the mirror, wondering what we can do to improve ourselves. We try proving ourselves to both friends and romantic partners who are not worthy of us, who often put us down and make us feel worse about ourselves. And often, we reach for what we believe will save us: beauty.

Female beauty, especially when you're male-centered, has the approval of men in mind. It encourages us to change our bodies to reflect what we believe men want: large eyes, fluttery eyelashes, full lips, smooth and pore-less skin. While beauty can be a great source of joy, there is *nothing* joyful about believing you need to appeal to men to feel pretty or valuable within.

The beauty industry is very ugly indeed. Under capitalism, beauty is not just sold to us as an aesthetic but as a feeling. Capitalism is built on the idea of selling people product after product; on creating desire and need. It uses insecurity as a weapon and psychology as a tool.

The beauty and cosmetics industries assert control via both physical and psychological means. Their messaging can be shamelessly brutal. Most women are aware of their manipulation and the self-hatred they instil in us, yet we still buy into them, secretly hoping they will make us prettier and, therefore, better and happier people. While the patriarchy is to blame for much of this, so is capitalism and our own part in keeping it alive.

Companies repeatedly sell us products that are meant to make us sexy and beautiful, while simultaneously reminding us of what we can improve on. Really, when you take a step back, you can see how a global, multibillion-dollar industry convincing women of their faults – made up of brands often owned by men – acts as a powerful means of controlling the masses and keeping women in their place.

When you hear validating comments about your beauty, you think to yourself, *That's how I get praised. This is how I get attention and love.* And so, for as long as you allow it, you remain focused on achieving this false sense of accomplishment: what we have come to believe female power to be. Like many women, I truly believed that everything I'd ever wanted would manifest itself, including my inner confidence, should I randomly wake up one day and appear stunning.

When beauty is wielded as a source of power, it provides women with a false, unwarranted sense of accomplishment. Teaching women that the prettier we are the better our lives will become creates an unhealthy form of competition, as well as a sense of unjustified power over other women. When it comes to beauty, there are truly no winners.

Beauty, much like other external practices involving the female body, has become associated with improved inner feelings as much as physical improvements. We live in a perpetual cycle where we're made to feel terrible about ourselves; taught that beauty is the cure for every problem and negative feeling, and so therefore believing that continuously buying products or having surgeries will make us *feel* better. Then, of course, we become confused when our lives, feelings and emotions don't miraculously improve after we use a specific product or undergo surgery that has promised to achieve this for us.

Then, to feel confident within we often end up circling back to the same old oppressive standards that created the problems of low self-worth to begin with.

The system sets us up for failure. A hot woman is 'good', but a hot woman *knowing* she is hot is 'bad'. We're told that being beautiful will empower us, yet if we achieve that, we become more powerful and aware of ourselves, which means men will try to knock us down. Patriarchy has created the system in which beauty helps generate our worth, yet they actively stop us from achieving the empowerment we're subconsciously promised once we achieve it. Therefore, even if a woman is pretty and unaware of it, many men will try to keep her down, making sure she never gets too ahead of herself. To many men there is value in a woman having self-esteem issues.

Many men want a woman who is naturally beautiful, but a woman conscious of her beauty is seen as 'vain'. The image-conscious woman cannot be both beautiful and intelligent. To be vain *must* mean you are selfish, though a woman must retain a certain level of vanity to be beautiful. Being vain means a woman is consciously aware of how her beauty can milk the system. She knows it will get her places. And if she knows she can milk the system or play men at their own game, men know she has become too powerful to manipulate or control.

However, being vain portrays women as shallow, as society says that a woman can't be both a good person and care intrinsically about how her own body looks. This is because beauty is linked to how we impress or satisfy men – not something we can do for ourselves or a means of making ourselves feel better. You're not allowed to see yourself as pretty, for your beauty is supposed to only be judged and measured by men.

In a male-gaze society, women aren't supposed to brag about their achievements or think highly of themselves at all, because we can't, God forbid, be better than men in any way. Once we're put down enough, we revert back to chasing what we're told is what makes us valuable – beauty – and the cycle continues.

The problem with beauty is that it both empowers and disempowers us; makes us both the oppressed and the oppressors. Our current beauty standards force us to conform to unrealistic expectations, keeping our nervous system in a constant state of hyper-vigilance. Beauty thrives in a capitalist culture, where women are encouraged to remain invested in their own self-improvement as a means of reflecting who they are.

But, like many things associated with femininity, beauty is often unreachable. Achieving a form of perfection is one thing; maintaining perfection is another. Beauty profits from our feelings of self-loathing and self-sabotage, forcing us to keep our bodies under constant surveillance, whether that's dieting, having Botox or buying copious skincare products. Beauty is so integrated within the performance of femininity that looking anything other than polished and hair-free is seen as a hygiene problem.

To lie to ourselves that beauty means nothing and that self-love is what counts most ignores how much of a very real impact beauty and the beauty industry have on our lives. Lying to ourselves may help us feel better temporarily, but it doesn't ignore the very real repercussions and pressures that beauty has on women, their self-image and their mental health.

Whether we like to admit it or not, beauty *does* matter and often has consequences on our life and opportunities, including our careers. A study on Italian women from the University of Messina found that attractiveness played a big part in the likelihood of making the second stage of the recruitment process. It found that 'unattractive' women only had a 7 per cent callback rate, while 'attractive' women were called back 54 per cent of the time. Depressingly, the paper concluded that 'searching for a job seems to be just like a beauty contest: it is better for unattractive women to invest in aesthetic surgery, than in education.' When it comes to weight – a supposed classic signifier of beauty – another study shows how there is clear evidence of discrimination against obese women for job openings but *not* against obese men.

Our bodies are treated like objects, which can be disassembled, commodified, retouched, slimmed and then returned to us as a polished, completed version of femininity. This is sold back to us as empowerment: making choices that are supposed to make us feel better, though leave us feeling empty and disassociated from ourselves. Beautifying ourselves on the outside conveniently skips the problems within us that seek help, soothing or care and promises to eradicate those problems quickly.

I have come to understand my own failures in constantly obsessing over the way I look. I know I am doing myself a disservice when I consider changing my body or face. I have felt shame in both hating how I look and not being able to reject my own internalised misogyny to accept the way I look naturally.

I also know that no matter how much I come to accept my body, men will still leer at me, make inappropriate comments or even assault or grope me. No matter how much I love myself or choose to love myself, I can never – will never – be entirely free from their unwarranted comments and actions.

But is it wrong to *want* to feel pretty? Is it unfeminist to like beauty products or use products to make us feel better, or even for male attention? Even on my most depressed days, I admit that plucking my eyebrows, shaving my legs or underarms, or applying some mascara or lipliner does make me feel better. Feeling more *attractive* makes me feel better.

So, can we enjoy beauty, while also being aware of how it disprivileges us and our own lack of social capital? Can beauty ever be empowering and something we enjoy truly for our own sake?

I believe it's not a question about what's right or wrong, necessarily. It's about awareness. When you're aware of how the system works, you will be more informed to make better decisions. By focusing on our inner selves, improving our inner confidence, beauty will become less important and less of a chain around our lives.

A self-aware woman is less likely to be walked over. A self-aware woman who can enjoy beauty, without worrying about how a man may view her, is very powerful indeed.

For over 200 years, many brilliant female writers and thinkers have criticised the way feminine beauty has created impossible standards to which women should aspire. In her 2009 book

Living Dolls, author Natasha Walter shows how for centuries many women have repeatedly brought to light the way beauty has pressurised women and girls, to no avail. From Mary Wollstonecraft's *A Vindication of the Rights of Woman* in 1792, Simone de Beauvoir's *The Second Sex* in 1949, Germaine Greer's *The Female Eunuch* in 1970 to Naomi Wolf's *The Beauty Myth* in 1991, generations of female writers and thinkers have demanded change around impossible female beauty standards and the pressures women face to meet them.

Yet despite their best efforts, the beauty standards expected of women are becoming increasingly stricter and narrow-minded. They now often involve cosmetic procedures to help attain them. Having visible work done, such as overfilled lips or a bigger chest, can be seen as a sign of wealth within some communities, a sign you have the viable means to afford expensive procedures. Conversely, more recently there has been a societal shift for women to choose procedures that are not visible, as though their augmented beauty is completely natural.

Social media, beauty and the rise in misogyny are heavily interconnected. Sites like Instagram and TikTok trap women and girls into self-doubting spirals, where constant scrolling and looking at faces undoubtedly make them question their own self-worth, attractiveness and value from a series of follows or likes. If they don't receive the likes they want, they panic, believing their worth is diminishing. So they find themselves constantly comparing themselves to other women, finding never-ending ways to seek (often sexualised, male) approval over their bodies while reinforcing the same type of cookie-cutter beauty standards.

Acceptable beauty is still heavily Eurocentric and white. In fact, the paler the skin and the closer to Anglo-European features, the higher the social, economic and financial advantages. Studies show that those who look less white tend to have lower incomes and occupational status.

Similarly, women with non-white skin tones are often equated to something edible: described as 'chocolate', 'caramel' or 'mocha', as though they are something to be devoured, their bodies to provide pleasure through consumption. Any non-white woman will have assumptions made about her based on her skin colour. Asian women are submissive and innocent; Latinas are feisty; Black women are hypersexual. Women of colour become objects of gratification, rather than women with minds and emotions, feeding a system that keeps women subordinate.

Culture critic Jia Tolentino states how we're in the age of 'Instagram face', a familiar amalgamation of beauty where women have borrowed features from different ethnicities and cultures: full lips, big eyes, thick eyebrows, long eyelashes, fuller cheeks, a tiny nose and pore-less skin, but where white women, ultimately, retain the most advantage.

For example, big lips, thick eyebrows, curvier behinds and large breasts are celebrated on white bodies yet are often made fun of on women of colour. While big lips on white women may be viewed as 'just' lip fillers, they are often ridiculed or used as racist tropes to mimic Black women.

Many white women take the aesthetics of Black women and Black culture and imitate Black beauty ideals in hairstyles, make-up and surgical enhancements for both cultural and financial benefits. However, white women do not have to face the same challenges and oppression that Black women experience daily simply for not matching what society says beauty is.

Beauty can now be attained in so many ways, given the wealth of treatments and technologies available. With the right amount of investment, time and energy we can, more or less, morph ourselves into the models and filtered women we see online or in magazines. At least, that's what we're promised, anyway. Fillers, Botox, hair extensions, nails, threading, waxing, tanning and surgery can mould us into something better. And if not those, then photo-editing apps and filters will suffice in the meantime, granting us a look at a more beautified version of ourselves, as though we're looking through a crystal ball at the woman we could possibly – hopefully – become.

But in chasing these ideals we're slowly losing our individuality; morphing into nothing more than factory-made dolls, ready for male consumption.

My desire to go on the Pill was less about preventing pregnancy and more about having glowy, ravishing skin. My vanity overpowered the need to stay safe sexually and, besides, I knew that to be wanted sexually, I had to be pretty.

Instead, within a matter of a week, my skin, especially on my face, erupted into huge painful acne cysts. My face was red, painful and sore. There was not one part of my face that didn't have a cystic spot on it. As the weeks progressed, my skin became worse. When I went to my GP he insisted that this change in my skin was probably due to my diet and that the Pill was not to blame, nor should I look to blame it for my problems and to keep taking it. I specifically remember him telling me that other women took it and they were fine. Essentially, it was my problem, and mine only.

Not only was my skin excruciatingly painful to touch – an accidental touch could bring me to tears – but my periods suddenly became horrendously heavy and painful. How can any man, regardless of whether they're a doctor, empathise with the pain many women experience from our cycle? There is no pain to measure it against. Each month I would lie in bed, sometimes for days, writhing in agony. One day, I even fainted from how painful it was. Albeit too late, I decided to go against my GP's advice and stopped the Pill, but the damage had already been done.

I googled this specific brand of Pill – Yasmin – and discovered that certain US states had banned it because some women had died as a result of taking it. There were ongoing lawsuits from the families of these women and websites asking for it to be recalled. Other women spoke on forums about how they'd gained large amounts of weight; how they, too, had excruciating periods and, of course, how many had also experienced terrible acne breakouts. Not too surprisingly, the drug also happened to be very cheap to manufacture, which is probably why the NHS used it as an option to begin with.

The evidence was there. Women were talking about their problems, sharing their experiences and even campaigning for safer medication, but they weren't being listened to. Even family members of the deceased weren't being heard. That's the problem with women's health. We are lumped together as one, treated as though our bodies are all the same. Men's bodies are far less complex than ours, and yet I guarantee that if only *one* man had died from taking a contraceptive pill, let alone if it were discovered that they were being given out to women like sweets, there would not only be outrage but a global intervention.

When I started off modelling, I was fresh meat. Photographers, masking behind their cameras, could smell the desperation of girls wanting to be the next supermodel.

Perhaps one of the scariest moments I've ever encountered happened when I was around twenty-two. I had become somewhat obsessed with a beautiful up-and-coming model called Emily.

Emily was stunning. She was booking all the jobs. On top of that, she had a mother who clearly wanted her to be famous and successful, who reposted all her modelling photos out of pride on Instagram and Facebook.

I viewed Emily's life with a mixture of envy and jealousy. My own mother did not support my modelling dream, thought it was a waste of time and was keen for me to get a regular job after years of trying to 'make it'. Now that I'm older, I get where she was coming from. Despite being signed to an agency at this point, I was making no money from modelling whatsoever, dragging myself from casting to casting only to be told my skin was bad or I wasn't tall enough or I wasn't thin enough or whatever other excuse they had for me that day. It felt personal because it *was* personal.

Emily had recently posted some photos on Facebook of her on a yacht with an older man called John, who I soon discovered after much FBI-level stalking was a Hollywood film producer. Her mum was pictured on the yacht alongside her, toasting each other with glasses of champagne and surrounded by plates of exotic canapés, laughing and joking, her tanned arms around John's shoulders.

One day, Emily reached out to me privately.

'*Hey!*' she wrote. '*I know this is random but my friend John has seen your photos and really wants to meet you. He's really powerful in Hollywood so it would probably be cool for you to get to know him. We're doing brunch on Sunday if you're available? Xxx*'

I couldn't believe it. That Sunday I travelled into Central London to meet Emily and John for a breakfast I knew I couldn't afford. We were meeting at an expensive hotel in Soho. I arrived ten minutes early to make sure I gave a good impression.

I headed into the restaurant and grabbed a table. Emily and John were nowhere to be seen.

'*Hi!*' I texted her. '*I'm here at the restaurant!*'

A few minutes later, she texted me back.

'*OMG! I'm so sorry, I forgot to tell you but I can't make today!*' she wrote. '*But don't worry, John is the BEST. You will love him. Let me know how it goes.*'

I had travelled all this way on a Sunday to come and see them both. It would be silly, wouldn't it, to turn back now? No, I had to be brave. I had to fake confidence. I was going to make my dreams come true, no matter what.

'*Hi John,*' I texted him. '*I'm just downstairs at the restaurant.*'

'*Hey Charli!*' he texted. '*I'm running a few minutes behind, just finishing a call. Why don't you come upstairs and meet me, then we can head down?*'

I knew there was no way that Emily's mum would be hanging around with John, let alone letting Emily hang around with him, if she thought that he was some kind of a problem. *No* mother would put their daughter in danger for a shot at success.

He texted me what room he was in – the penthouse – and I got into the lift. My gut was telling me this was stupid and to just wait downstairs a while longer, but my legs continued to guide me to the elevator and towards John's room.

I knocked on the door.

A short, stumpy, grey-skinned man in a white dressing gown opened the door. He had a huge grin on his face.

'Charli!' he said, reaching out and giving me a hug. 'It's so lovely to meet you! Emily's told me all about you. Come in, come in.'

I remember the feeling of the towelled bathrobe against my body and standing there rigid. He was clearly not on the phone. My body was saying LEAVE. Yet my brain kept telling me that by leaving, I would be making a mountain out of a molehill – or, worse, I'd be accusing him of being a sexual predator, which wasn't necessarily fair.

And so, like many incidents involving strange men in my life,

I decided I'd act cool about the fact a stranger was hugging me in his dressing gown and downplay it all.

'Aww, that's OK!' I said. 'I'll just wait here.'

'There's nothing to worry about with me,' he said. He opened the door wider. 'See? This whole room is like an apartment. Just take a seat in the living area, and I'll get dressed and be right with you.'

'And then we'll go and get breakfast, right?' I said.

'Of course!' he said in his Californian drawl, smiling. 'I'll literally be five minutes.'

As soon as the door shut, I knew I'd made a huge mistake. John put the security latch on the door and my heart sank.

He was right about one thing. His room was exactly like an apartment. There was a dining room for meetings, a kitchenette and a 'living area' – a sofa and TV positioned in front of a bed.

I walked towards the sofa and sat down. Immediately, I began trying to figure out an escape plan. I knew I had to get out.

I pretended to look at my phone.

'Gosh, I'm such an idiot! I completely forgot!' I lied. 'I'm supposed to be meeting my boyfriend in a minute—'

'Your boyfriend?' John said, his eyebrows raising. 'You never said you had a boyfriend.'

'I know, I know,' I said, trying to sound upbeat. 'He's literally waiting for me downstairs, so I should probably go and meet him.'

'Don't be rude,' John replied, his demeanour changing. 'You promised to have breakfast with me.'

John clearly had no desire to get changed into his regular clothes, and never had. I began to sweat from anxiety; the fabric of my top was stuck to me like glue from how much I was sweating. I had to get out of there.

My plan was to make a beeline for the door as soon as John

went to the bathroom. The problem was, he was stood in the way, blocking my route to the door.

'Shouldn't we go downstairs to the restaurant now?' I asked nervously.

'Sssh,' he said. 'Stop worrying.' He handed me an in-room dining menu. 'Order something from here.'

I decided that once the concierge delivered the food, I could then make a run for it.

Waiting for the omelette felt like hours. Eventually, room service knocked on the door and John went to open it. The man strolled in with the wheeled tray, not looking either me or John in the eye.

Why didn't I run? I don't know. I didn't want to cause a scene. I didn't want to get him into trouble. He hadn't actually *done* anything to me, so I didn't want to sound dramatic or blow things out of proportion. I kept telling myself he couldn't do anything bad to me because Emily hung out with him all the time. He invited her to fancy LA parties and flew her around on private jets.

The man left and John relocked the door, then came to sit next to me on the sofa.

'Let me give you a massage,' he said suddenly.

'I'm OK,' I replied. I felt physically sick. 'You know, I really need to get going. My boyfriend will be worried—'

'Take your top off,' he said.

What?

'No.'

'I said, *take your top off.*'

I sat there, frozen. This was it. I was going to be raped, I was sure of it, and I was watching it happen in slow-motion.

I accepted my fate. I did as I was told. I sat there in my bra, my back towards him, staring out of the window and focusing on the velvety texture of the chair. He put his hands on my shoulders and began rubbing my skin sensually, the hardened, dry skin of his fingers digging into me like some sort of serpent.

By now, sweat was dripping down my back in streams of droplets, dotted across my forehead and hairline.

'What's wrong?' he asked. He began kissing the back of my neck. 'You nervous, baby?'

It was apparent that my anxiety appeared to turn him on.

'God, you're *gorgeous*,' he said in what I assume was an attempt at a sexy voice, and he began undoing my bra.

The bra fell to my waist. At this point, I seemed to disassociate. I stared out of the window and into the courtyard below, fixating on a tree with twinkling string lights. I remember thinking what a waste of electricity it was, having string lights on in the day.

He began massaging my arms before moving to my front, his hands rubbing and fondling my breasts. And do you want to know the most bizarre thought I had at that moment? As I continued to sweat, my heart beating profusely through my chest, I remember hoping I didn't smell sweaty. Despite everything he was doing to me, I didn't want him to walk away thinking I was *dirty*.

'Why don't you come and lie down next to me?' he asked quietly, pointing to the bed.

Something inside of me snapped. I had to at least *try* to run. I jumped off the sofa.

'I need to go,' I said forcefully. I left the bra on the couch. I pulled the T-shirt over my head as quickly as I could.

'Oh, come on,' he said. 'Don't be like that.'

I glared at him, thinking how repulsive he looked. I'd never met anyone with such dull, grey skin or dark under eyes.

And then I made a run for it. I ran towards the door.

But John beat me to it, holding his arms either side of the doorframe.

'Move your arms,' I said. I wasn't even aware I'd said it. The voice seemed to come out from the depths of me – a voice far more confident and assertive than I'd ever thought possible.

John stood there, grinning like the Cheshire cat.

'I said – *move*.' I didn't back down. 'If you don't move, I'll scream.'

We stared at each other for what felt like minutes, though it would've only been seconds.

'Jesus, *relax*,' he said. 'Emily said you were cool.'

Reluctantly, he moved out of the way and I unlocked the door. I ran past the elevator and down the corridor, running down the stairs, my heart still pounding. I couldn't believe I'd got out of there unscathed. I ran out of the hotel, my face flustered, all the way to the Tube station and home.

I nearly broke down when I saw my boyfriend. I told him what had happened.

'What the fuck is wrong with you?!' I remember him saying. 'Don't blame him for this. You went to his room. You clearly wanted the attention. You brought this on yourself.'

I was watching TV one evening not too long ago when my doorbell rang. I knew my neighbour had a parcel for me, and it wasn't unusual for her to drop parcels round in the evening after work. I didn't even bother to check the peephole, assuming it would be her.

Standing in front of me was an attractive man, looking as though he'd come from the City, smartly dressed in a grey suit, his hair groomed and well kept.

'Hello,' I said, a little surprised.

'Hi,' he said, appearing nervous. 'I'm here for the house viewing.'

I told him he had the wrong house.

'Oh!' he said, laughing. 'Yes, you're probably right.'

And then he just stood there. He didn't move. He just stared at me, smiling, staring directly into my eyes.

After a few seconds of unease, I broke the silence.

'Anything else?' I asked.

'No.'

He continued to stare. He didn't budge an inch. He just glared at me, the noise from the TV playing in the background.

'Well . . . OK,' I replied, trying to sound unbothered. 'Have a good night.'

As I went to shut the door, he lunged forward.

'*I LOVE YOU!*' he yelled.

I shut the door quickly, slamming it in his face. I stood for a couple of seconds in silence, my heart pounding. Who the hell was this guy?!

'That was Charli! That was Charli!' I heard him saying. My heart stopped. I squinted through the peephole, trying to see who he was speaking to. While he'd appeared alone, I couldn't work out if he had other friends with him.

After a few seconds, the doorbell rang again. The sensible thing to have done would have been to ignore it. But I couldn't. This was my house, my home. I didn't want any man to think he could scare me, and not only that, think he could turn up to my house unannounced.

I opened the door once more, peeking my head out from the side.

'What do you want?' I snapped.

'I'm lost,' he replied.

'Look, go and speak to one of my neighbours,' I said. 'Some of them have lived here a lot longer than I have and will know the address of where you need to go.'

Again, he just stared at me gormlessly.

'Are you high?' I asked.

He looked at me and smiled.

'Yes.'

'What have you taken?'

'Coke.'

As many women will attest, it's moments like these where you are unsure of what to do next. Do you slam the door and tell him to fuck off? Do you yell? Do you swear at him? Do you call the police? For all I knew, he could have a knife or acid. Besides, he clearly knew my name and address, which meant if I angered him enough, he could always come back.

Instead of responding aggressively, I decided – like many women instinctively choose, and as I have numerous other times in my life – to be nice, to downplay the situation. I didn't want to make this man, whoever he was, think he was freaking me out. I also didn't want him to think I was rejecting him. I have turned a man down before and been met with insults and threats. I didn't want to make him angry, because as any woman knows, an angry man can be highly dangerous indeed.

Despite the fact he was standing in the pathway leading to my front door, I decided I'd ask my neighbours for help.

'My neighbours have lived round here since the nineties,' I said while forcing a smile, my heart racing. 'They'll be able to help you find where you need to go. Let's go and ask them.'

I knew he wasn't lost, but thought getting help would be the safest thing to do. I grabbed my keys from the side table, holding them in between my fingers as I've long been taught and pushed past him.

'I'm not in trouble, am I?' he asked as I desperately waited for them to answer.

'*No!*' I said, trying to sound friendly and downplay my nerves. 'No, not at all.'

'Good,' he said. And then, in perhaps the most menacing tone of all, he added, 'I'm not going to hurt you.'

I felt sick. As soon as the words left his mouth, my neighbour, thankfully, answered the front door.

'This guy has turned up out of nowhere and somehow knows my name,' I murmured to her.

She could clearly see how frightened I was.

'What do you want?' she asked, turning to him.

'I'm . . . I'm . . . lost,' the man replied.

'Well, you can't be ringing people's doorbells at eight o'clock at night,' my neighbour said. 'You're obviously scaring her. You need to go.'

'Am I going to get in trouble?' the man asked again.

'You will if you don't leave,' my neighbour's son said.

He stood there for a few moments, then began to walk off. I let out a sigh of relief.

'Thank you,' I said to her gratefully.

And then, just a couple of minutes later, he began to walk back down the street towards us again.

'WILL YOU JUST *LEAVE*!' I yelled.

'Get inside the house and lock the door,' my neighbour instructed. I did as I was told, rushing into my house as fast as I could.

I was left shaken by the experience. I called the police but they couldn't do anything. As he'd only been to visit me once it didn't yet count as stalking, which is bizarre, as he'd somehow got hold of my address. I ordered a rape alarm and set my house alarm at night.

I was suddenly aware of myself in ways I'd never been previously. Even as part of my everyday protocols as a woman, where our safety has to forever be considered, I was worrying about what I was doing all the time. I would glance out of my bedroom windows at night into the park opposite, wondering if he was watching me from the shadows. I took taxis everywhere, which ended up being costly, refusing to take the train as it would mean having to walk five minutes down the street from the station in the dark. I would clutch my keys in between my fingers in my coat pocket whenever I went for a walk, even during the day, expecting him to jump out and grab me at any moment.

Within a few days, I began receiving threatening and sexually aggressive messages on Instagram from anonymous accounts. '*Tell your neighbour if he comes near me again, I'll kill him,*' said one. '*I want to fuck you and blow your back out,*' was another. Almost as soon as I took a screenshot of them the account would be deleted and a new message from another new anonymous account would take its place.

'I suppose you should stop posting photos of yourself online in lingerie, then,' a female friend suggested. 'He's obviously seen them and got the wrong idea.'

Her internalised misogyny was staggering. And yet despite knowing she was essentially slut-shaming me, I began to consider her comment, questioning whether she was right. It made me paranoid thinking of other women and other 'friends' who'd clearly been judging me on what I'd posted in the past. I wondered how many other people may have assumed I'd 'deserved' a random man appearing at my door at night simply for choosing to bare my skin.

Although I was angry, her comment of course made me doubt myself and think about the problem I'd clearly helped create. Later that day, I scrolled back through the photos on my

Instagram account. Bare skin after bare skin after bare skin. I was completely oblivious to how much I'd paraded my body, all under the guise of 'body confidence'.

Truth be told, I could find any way to make something 'sexy' – and by sexy, I mean something that would ultimately appeal to men – while under the guise of 'empowerment'. When my parents got their new puppy, I posed topless with her covering my chest. I would regularly post photos of myself in swimwear. When I posted a photo in a push-up bra and my crush hearted it, I took it as more of a compliment, or having deeper meaning, than I should have.

The more likes I received, the more validated I felt. Really, these were nothing more than pixels on a screen. But the hearts, likes and follows made me feel good. Most of all, they made me feel *validated*. They made me feel I was worth something, even if I didn't feel worthy myself.

When I discovered the body positive movement in my midtwenties, I finally felt like I could reclaim my body and my sexuality and embrace the skin and body I naturally had. I had spent *years* as a model starving, purging and attacking my body, and finally, I saw my relationship with my physical body could be positive. I had found the movement on Instagram, where women proudly flaunted their cellulite, stretch marks and dimples for the world to see. They were sexy. Their photos were met with enthusiasm; their smiles infectious. Their bodies weren't what I'd been sold as female perfection, but they appeared happy and content in who they were. Surely that meant I could feel pretty in my imperfections, too.

As I simultaneously recovered from my eating disorders, gained weight and became more curvaceous, I wanted to change the narrative of what I'd long believed flesh to be. Flesh could be what *I* made it. Fashion and the media had told me that flesh meant sexual. By choosing when, or where, I wore skimpy clothing; choosing when to post suggestive pictures to Instagram; choosing who I could sleep with; I was empowering *myself*. I could make sexy what I wanted it to be.

Despite being petrified of posting a photo of my body looking anything less than perfect, when I first posted a photo of my body with a slight tummy, I was met with positivity. I began sharing stories of my eating disorders and before and after photos of how my body had looked in the past. I quickly gained a following, posting photo after photo of my new, curvier body.

Of course, I loved making other women feel as though their bodies were good enough. I am a huge believer in body diversity, in encouraging women to love the skin they're in. I still very much believe that. But, if I'm being completely honest, I knew that by showing my body, I was also appealing to men. Part of me enjoyed men telling me I was beautiful; telling me my body, which didn't resemble that of a Victoria's Secret model, was beautiful. Another part of me hated it. Somewhat ironically, I couldn't understand why so many men I dated saw me as nothing more than a sex object and how little empowerment I experienced in *feeling* like a sex object.

Really, who could blame me for wanting to bare skin; for viewing my selfies as anything other than a radical act of self-love? I have been sexualised and objectified since I was a child. As a result of my sexualisation, I not only had incredibly low self-esteem but subsequent eating disorders, all based on control over how I was perceived. I desperately wanted to regain control over my own body and my own sense of self.

That's what I told myself, anyway. I couldn't understand why often this so-called act of empowerment didn't make me feel that empowered at all. If anything, I'd feel depressed and hollow, as though something had been taken from me. While I absolutely preferred living a life where I wasn't having to count calories and was modelling at my natural size, I can't pretend I always felt confident in posting these pictures. Posting photos online in lingerie while men slid in my DMs telling me how they wanted to fuck me or stick their dicks down my throat didn't make me feel like some sort of sexual goddess. Having men leer at me on nights out in tight, provocative outfits while not being able to have me sexually didn't make me feel powerful in my sexuality. More than that, it never made me feel beautiful.

But while I continued to promote this message of choice, empowerment and loving the skin I was in, there came a deeper, more male-centered origin to my actions that I was choosing to ignore completely. It would take almost ten years, while I healed from my borderline obsession with men, to question what I had believed to be empowerment all along.

Currently there is a fine line between overly sexualising yourself on sites like OnlyFans, where women charge money to see their naked bodies, and Instagram, where women post provocative content for free. It begs the modern-day feminist questions of whether showing skin can *ever* be an act of sexual empowerment and whether profiting from your undoubtable sexualisation can ever be liberating.

Like me, many women search for scraps of what feels like power in the form of validation and acceptance through sexualising their bodies, without questioning why we feel the need to parade our bodies or skin to begin with. Whose acceptance are we craving? Is showing our skin truly for our sake or are we just trying to make ourselves feel better in a world where beauty and sexuality reign supreme? If we truly loved our bodies or felt content in ourselves, would we be posting this content to begin with?

I told myself that my body positive photos were empowering, that I was doing something positive for fellow women by teaching them to love the skin they're in. But when I think about it, there was still a huge part of me trying to convince *myself* that I was worthy enough – of inner love, outer love and beauty. The more I tried convincing myself I was sexually liberated, the more disempowered I was becoming.

Of course, anyone who has an Instagram account knows the best way to receive likes and validation is by posing with fewer clothes. Sex absolutely sells and if not sex, then bare skin. Posing in a bikini can make a difference between upwards of sixty thousand likes, versus fewer than a thousand for, say, a photo of a cute dog. When social media is tied to paid opportunities – and paid opportunities come off the back of likes – the need to routinely upload photos like these becomes apparent.

For many women, showing their body in a bikini is often regarded as an act of confidence, especially if the woman is not rail-thin or cellulite-free. Yet we don't expect men to prove their inner confidence by posting photos of themselves in Speedos or by showing off their stomach rolls or beer bellies. Why? Because their bodies aren't a reflection of their value. We haven't reduced men down to their body parts, beaten and berated their appearance within an inch of their lives or taught them that their beauty is their only viable trait. Men don't need to 'reclaim' their curves as a means of recovering a sliver of self-acceptance. Their bodies are just . . . well . . . *bodies*. Wouldn't it be wonderful if women could view our own with the same neutrality?

The irony of the body positivity movement is that it still focuses on bodies and appearance. It still tells women that feeling good about our bodies is important: that if you love how you look on the outside, you'll feel great about yourself on the inside. It skips over the most vital part of self-love, which is loving yourself from within first.

One man I dated told me he could never introduce me to his

parents because of the content I posted. While I wouldn't say my photographs were OnlyFans level, it infuriated and hurt me that he couldn't see beyond the photo and the body confidence message I was trying to promote: to love the skin you're in. I don't know why his words stung but of course they did. Because the photos of me in lingerie were clearly what sparked his interest in the beginning, and now that he'd got what he wanted, he no longer viewed me as worthy enough to date. He joined a long list of men who saw me as nothing other than a sex object, who refused to view me as anything more.

The choices we make to show more or less skin aren't necessarily our own. The female body is political, and men from all sides of the political spectrum will convince us that the choices we make about our body are ours to make and ours alone: either through guilt-tripping and slut-shaming, or through pushing a false sense of empowerment. The choices we make about our own bodies often benefit the men in our lives rather than ourselves. The question is: how do we know what is true empowerment versus what we believe will make us feel wanted?

I think society has always separated women into categories of those who show skin and those who don't. Women have judged each other in these categories, too, viewing those who show skin as immoral or slutty and those who cover their skin as prudes dominated by men.

Purity culture views anything vaguely sexual relating to women as dangerous, seeing modesty and modest dressing as signs of a woman respecting herself, but in today's society no amount of clothing will stop her from being objectified or treated as a sex object. The irony of purity culture is that it assumes women have more sexual agency over their bodies and how they're perceived than they do.

While it may not seem like it, deciding to dress modestly is still based on men's thoughts and viewpoints about your body. You're still as male-centered as if you were posing semi-naked. You're still living outside of your body, thinking of how men may judge you or ogle you and additionally how fellow women or elders may view you.

If you believe that dressing modestly will somehow protect you from being objectified or sexualised by men, you are sadly mistaken. Regardless of whether they're dressed in skimpy lingerie, a burka or in an apron and long dress like a 1950s housewife, a woman has no control over how a man will treat or respect her and her body. And a woman, whether she dresses modestly or immodestly, won't stop a man from treating her better or worse. Only he has the option to do that.

It's not the showing of skin which is the problem but the socio-cultural pressures *around* skin that create the issue. After all, in a world of *true* female equality, showing or covering skin would mean absolutely nothing. When we constantly think about our beauty through the eyes of men, it deprives us of our individual freedom to express ourselves in ways we'd truly like, especially when it comes to fashion and cosmetics, which can provide a great deal of self-expression.

When we focus on modesty and dress codes, we keep the focus on women as body parts, not as people. Really, it is these forces that should be fought against, not the women stuck in the middle, attempting to live life as they please. Whether a woman chooses to wear revealing clothing or not shouldn't mean that she's letting feminism down, playing into patriarchal ideals or furthering sexism. But one thing's for certain: we cannot possibly decenter men if we concern ourselves with how other women choose to show their bodies.

Coming to terms with beauty – and the connection it has to

our overall life – is difficult. Beauty is intertwined with sex, politics, gender and power. So how can we redefine our philosophy of beauty in a culture that demands physical perfection at all times?

Aspiring towards outer beauty kept me outside of my body. I was constantly seeing myself through how others potentially viewed me. I became fixated on other people's perceptions of me, assuming if I had a skin breakout or if my make-up wasn't applied right it would somehow make me lesser. Less important. Less worthy of friends, of love, of life.

I did OK in my modelling career and still land the occasional job now. But I am not the most beautiful woman to have ever walked the planet, nor the most photogenic or symmetrical, and as a result, I will never be a millionaire from my looks or my beauty.

To have understood this as a teenager would have likely broken my heart. I would have taken it as a reflection of my worth; seen my future as doomed to fail. How pathetic is that? I now wonder what I may have achieved without modelling at the forefront of my life's ambition; what talents I may have developed had I focused on being emotionally or intellectually fulfilled instead.

Accepting the way I look and coming to terms with the fact that I am not the most beautiful person on earth (let alone attempting to chase it) has strangely been a form of self-acceptance. I still love beauty – dipping my fingers in make-up pots, trying new mascaras, having relaxing facials and my eyebrows threaded. But I now use these products as a form of self-care – *not* as some sort of miracle that will somehow make my life worthwhile or make me more desirable. Instead, I now take myself as I am and work with what I've got.

Since accepting this, I have focused on other talents. I have spent a ton of time writing and creating. I leave the house without worrying whether I have a spot or whether my face is caked full of foundation. Beauty feels like a treat for me, instead of the sole thing that gives me purpose.

Removing body hair has long been a marker of an appropriate or sexy woman in the modern age, as well as a means of gendered social control. A hairy woman has become synonymous with a lazy woman, a failed woman, and in recent transphobic times, even trans-ness. A woman *must* be a lesbian if she refuses to shave her underarms or legs, because there is no possible way she would want to be seen as unattractive – let alone make unattractive choices – in a world where the male gaze ultimately rules supreme.

It is estimated that more than 99 per cent of American women currently voluntarily remove their body hair and more than 85 per cent do so regularly. Although hair removal practices have existed across continents and cultures through time, in the late nineteenth and early twentieth centuries, white men became especially fixated on controlling white women's beauty regimes, especially around the removal of body hair. In the book *Plucked*, Professor Rebecca Herzig notes how regulating a woman's appearance became a strategy to maintain control over women and help define a clear contrast between the sexes and races – with hair removal understood in the mid-1800s to early 1900s as an indicator of 'civilised' women. This became the accepted norm and continues to this day.

The origins of hair removal are heavily rooted in racism. Despite most women having natural body hair, in the nineteenth century, European thinkers saw body hair as an indication that certain people hadn't evolved into 'civilised' (i.e. white, Western) humanity. Hairlessness soon signified racial progress and superiority. Over time, any hair on a white woman's body became symbolically associated with dirtiness because of its cultural association with 'inferior' races and 'animalistic' qualities. Hairy women were put on display in 'freak shows' across the US, reinforcing not only how far white women had progressed from looking primitive, but also how shameful it was for women to have body hair at all.

From the late 1800s, magazines featured white, hairless models in their pages, creating a new beauty standard for women. Jewish, Italian and Eastern European women were targeted with advertisements for electrolysis that would help achieve this white ideal. However, the machines were dangerous and killed hundreds, if not thousands, of women in the process.

While perceptions of female beauty are constantly evolving, body hair is still seen as grotesque. When I think of the *centuries* of women who have gone to great lengths to be deemed pretty by men, at least in a socially acceptable sense, I wonder why we're still allowing ourselves to feel pressured into looking a certain way – into having to pretend we're mythical, naturally hairless creatures. I wonder how much more of ourselves we must eradicate and how much pain we must go through to feel accepted, desirable or 'womanly'; why our natural selves never seem to be good enough.

One of the first moments I knowingly decentered the male gaze was when I questioned how I wanted my *own* vulva to look, which, as a grown woman, sounds rather insane when you think about it. Even before I'd ever actually had sex, I realised I'd spent my life removing my body hair in the event someone else may see it. I've personally never liked the way my vulva looks aesthetically when it's completely hairless, let alone the prickly rash that would develop afterwards as the hair grew back. I realised that even before I became intimate with someone, I was forever imagining how they might view my body hair and rate me because of it – whether they'd assume I was dirty, lazy or unkempt for daring to have my vulva not resemble that of a child. Rarely had I ever sat back and questioned whether *I* wanted my vulva to look that way.

As someone who used to regularly have bikini or Hollywood waxes; smeared horrendously acidic-smelling hair removal creams over my body and vulva; underwent sharp laser hair removal every six weeks; and nicked my skin with razors in the shower all in the attempt to appear feminine, pretty and hygienic, I finally decided I'd no longer spend my time attempting to create a dolphin-like body. I was exchanging society's view of female perfection for my own preference and comfort.

I refused to wax or shave my bikini area completely hairless any more, refused to worry whether someone viewing my naked body may deem me hot or not. Trim and tidy? Sure. Wax it all off? No. In just a small radical act, I was choosing to present my body the way *I* wanted.

This choice of mine came, ironically, from finding old *Playboy* magazines, where beautiful models sported full pubic bushes and somehow looked far hotter to me than the bare, prepubescent-like vulvas I'd seen in later issues or on porn stars. I became confident in my choice. If someone doesn't like my pubic hair, then they don't deserve to see my body naked, sleep with me, or date me in general. This was my first form of body rebellion: reclaiming my body, and my choices, as my own.

As I get older, I notice lines around my eyes when I smile. They have become one of the first tell-tale signs that I am ageing – something which, if I'm being completely honest, is hard to come to terms with. I often mourn my youthful skin and wonder whether I made enough use of my youth while I still had the chance: whether I used it enough to my advantage. I am trying to remind myself that these lines didn't exist a few years ago for a reason. I simply didn't laugh. My life was not joyous, let alone humorous. I was persistently sad. So these lines, which have appeared fairly recently, are a sign that I am living again: proof that there *are* things to smile and laugh about and that I have laughed at them.

As I age, I know I am losing male attention. Many of us will agree that we received the most catcalls when we were younger. While some of this can be attributed to our youthful looks, the uncomfortable truth is that much of this attention comes down to power and making girls feel small. Disguised as compliments and something they should feel grateful for while they still 'have it' ('it' being 'youth'), catcalling young girls sets them up for a lifetime of sexist comments and behaviour; reminding them that they are objects, secondary to men; said at a time when we are usually the most naive, insecure and malleable.

It is both a heartbreaking and empowering reality in knowing that by the time our bodies do sag and youth is no longer on our side, many of us mourn the loss of being desired by men, while simultaneously feeling relieved that we no longer need to push ourselves physically to get their attention.

I know there is power in embracing ageing. I know that to live fully, I must learn to accept the natural changes in my skin. We see ageing as a punishment, not as a privilege. I am trying to view this dwindling attention from men with relief. Like many women, I would never choose to go back in time to my teens, not even my twenties. But embracing these lines is still a learning curve – learning how to push back against everything we've been taught our value to be. We must stop centring our entire lives around beauty standards and pandering to men who are attracted to young women.

Having said that, I would be lying if I said I didn't occasionally look at my reflection and consider what I should tighten, fill, lift or alter through tweakments or surgery. As I age, I do of course worry about growing older. I think most women in this image-driven society feel the same way. Every day, I see perfect faces on social media. I try to tell myself that I am comparing myself to the faces of twenty-year-olds, yet when you see enough of the same type of line-free, pore-less face, you manage to convince yourself this is what beauty is: that this is what you should aim for.

Our bodies have become products with a best before date. We erase older women from the media, shunning them from public view. Women are supposed to be experienced but their skin should not look lived in. We are supposed to smile but not so much that it leaves the remnants of crinkles or lines afterwards. We expect women to look youthful but without the teenage, acne-ridden skin texture. Skin must look smooth, every blemish eradicated. Ageing gracefully requires women to tiptoe on the edge of acceptable treatments: to look polished but not overdone.

Once fertility is no longer apparent, women become invisible. Too often, we hear older women talk about feeling as though they've lost their identity once they begin to age, as though their desirability made them who they were. Mothers express how forgotten they feel once they've given birth, how they no longer feel desired by their husbands or partners after they've had children. In the society we live in, beauty *does* equate to being seen.

I am blown away by some of the modern-day celebrity cosmetic surgery results, which are nothing short of incredible. While I tell myself these celebrities are women too – that they'll have issues and problems of their own – I often fantasise about how much easier life may be, how much happier I may be, should I happen to become more beautiful or youthful than I already am.

Because of social media, I am now aware of the names of certain parts of my skin that I had no idea about previously, not to mention the names of specific cosmetic procedures needed to correct them. In fact, I'm now aware of problems I wasn't even aware *were* problems. I have learnt names of famous doctors that celebrities pay hundreds of thousands of dollars for, and friends share them with me. Wherever there is a flaw, with the right amount of money, it can be fixed.

Users will frequently post photos of themselves to Reddit cosmetic surgery forums, sharing the results of their own surgeries or asking other users what cosmetic procedures they recommend they undertake, as though they are experts. And best believe, these users are willing to dish out this advice. There's also plenty of unsolicited advice and opinions given on different body parts than those the user asked about, undoubtedly fuelling even further insecurities.

One user asks what procedure she should get to 'widen' and 'fill out' her lips. Others ask if they should have rhinoplasty. One woman, who is thirty, posts before and after photos of her facelift and neck-lift which she'd had to try to eradicate the jowls and extra skin after losing weight. Other users, who aren't doctors, give them 'advice' based on their own very selective, narrow-minded versions of beauty.

One Instagram user shared a post about a mid-facelift she had aged just twenty-eight. *Twenty-eight.* While she insists she didn't have a facelift because she hated how she looked, she wrote it was because she was holding herself 'to a new standard' after partying and burning out. Women are being sold the false promise that cosmetic surgery will miraculously make them feel better about themselves. And, like many women, this woman believed surgery would fix it.

Nothing will waste your youth or age you more than fighting for male acceptance. It depletes your energy, your spirit, your confidence. Instead, focus on the things that light you up from the inside. Read books by female authors, go to the theatre, hang out with old friends that make you laugh, make new friends, try new foods, play sports and watch films. But don't waste your one precious life pleasing men in the hope it will make you feel better about yourself.

The beauty industry is designed to make us appear more youthful than we are. The younger we appear, the more fertile we seem; the more fertile, the more worthy we are of love (marriage) and babies (family). Beauty, therefore, is far more complex than just 'looking good'. It defines much of our female life and value. Beauty is a complex accumulation of assumptions, norms and attitudes.

What I've learnt is that we can never win in a society that is set up as ours is. Beauty will exist for as long as there are humans. But beauty can be enjoyed, separate to the male gaze, and become something we can do for ourselves, rather than for men. Beauty, I believe, can be reclaimed solely for female pleasure. Rather than constantly trying to convince ourselves that we are beautiful no matter what, we should instead tell ourselves that beauty does not need to matter as much as we think it does.

How might beauty look under the female gaze? The female gaze, I think, is more of a feeling; a representation of women's true bodies and lived experiences in the world. It is intimate and personal, rather than objective. It is how we view women as people with intelligence, soul and feelings. It's not about what the eyes see necessarily, but about what the *heart* feels.

As of now, there is no female gaze because there is no matriarchy. Men control and dominate the media, leaving little space for women to show life from our own viewpoint. While the concept of the female gaze needs work, we can – and deserve – to see womanhood through our own lens.

I am still trying to figure out my own relationship with beauty, and I don't know if I'll ever be truly satisfied with how I look naturally. The system we're in is complex, and we must allow ourselves grace as we try to untangle ourselves from the false importance of it all. We can enjoy beauty and take pleasure from it, but beauty shouldn't be the thing we focus on at every moment.

Why are we scared of being average? Why are we frightened of being unseen or forgotten? Why are we so obsessed with needing to be beautiful?

Would you rather look good or be happy? Perhaps, like an average man, it's OK for women to feel *good enough*.

stomach.

One of the most emblematic parts of womanliness is the female stomach. Soft to the touch and the eye, the stomach represents everything we assume femininity to be: nurturance, care, motherhood and vulnerability.

In paintings from the Renaissance, a woman's stomach appeared warm, soft and inviting; its rotund appearance comforting in a way unique to the feminine. A few hundred years later, the image of the ideal female stomach changed: flat, tight and taut; muscle protruding; ribs outlined through the skin, as though you could slice your fingers on their bony edges. What was once a timeless signifier of femininity must now be everything it was told it wasn't, couldn't, *shouldn't*, be: tough, rigid and strong.

For both women *and* men, our stomachs and guts are perhaps the most central and unique parts of the human body, yet instead of appreciating how they're instrumental in maintaining our body's health and survival, as women, we have chosen to fixate and obsess over the way they appear aesthetically.

While beauty standards have consistently changed across generations, it is the stomach, the abdomen, the midriff, whose ideals have seemingly stayed consistent in modern times. Even the so-called 'perfect' female body of today, which is the hourglass, cartoonish, curvaceous shapes popularised by the Kardashians, seems to require a flat abdomen. These body shapes very, *very* rarely exist naturally so are achieved with hours of exercise, specific diets or surgical procedures, which, for the most part, take money and/or time. A flat stomach, therefore, has become somewhat of a luxury, awarded to either the youthful or the wealthy.

A 'beautiful' female body has become synonymous with pain, and perhaps even more strangely, with complicity. The waist, especially, is associated with the worst parts of female control and restriction. The flatter the stomach, the higher the willpower; the higher the willpower, the stronger the discipline; the stronger the discipline, the higher the beauty. To reject readily available fatty foods, exercise until your abdominal muscles hurt or even undergo cosmetic procedures like liposuction, requires the utmost discipline.

Historically, the aesthetic ideal of the stomach was hard on men and soft on women. The fat we carry in our lower abdomens is so undeniably feminine, our anatomy differs so far from the bodies of men, and yet for some reason, in our patriarchal society we shame ourselves for appearing differently to them. We are not built the same as men genetically, though we expect our bodies to tone and lose weight in the same way. We hate our softness, we feel ashamed of the way our abdomen protrudes in our clothes, the way it wobbles when we're intimate with someone. After all, to be soft is to be feminine and to be feminine is a form of shame.

It is a strange, yet undeniable truth, that the softest and squidgiest parts of our female bodies – our tummies, our buttocks, our thighs – are not only often the parts of ourselves women tend to hate the most but are the hardest for us to physically change. They're the parts we anger ourselves over when they don't resemble the thin, toned bodies of famous and beautiful women; the parts that seem to rebel against our gym sessions and dieting; the parts we become frustrated and disappointed about for not shrinking in the ways we'd like. We refer to our stomachs as 'muffin tops' or 'spare tyres' when our skin overflows in jeans, placing the importance of how our bodies look in clothing over the way clothing should accommodate us. When our waists don't co-operate in the ways we'd like, whether that's through calorie deficit, surgery or from doing numerous sit-ups, we somehow view our entire selves as failures.

On some days, our protruding abdomens dictate what outfits we wear. On particularly bad self-image days, the way it looks in clothing can dictate our mood entirely. It's crazy that a body part has this much of an influence on our feelings and self-worth, yet when we're consistently taught that our bodies should appear lithe and lean to be desirable and that any form of 'fat' makes us disgusting and grotesque, it's not that surprising at all.

The female body is biologically designed to store fat and to burn it slower than that of a male. And while washboard abs are certainly attainable for some women, the truth is, most women simply aren't built for it. Biologically, a woman's body is supposed to have more fat cells in the abdominal area to help protect her reproductive organs and a foetus if she becomes pregnant. During adolescence and childbearing years, females typically produce additional body fat cells in the abdominal area for pregnancy, which results in the softly rounded lower tummy most women possess, even if they are fairly fit and lean.

If females ever happen to have flat stomachs in their lifetimes, it's usually when they're children or teenagers. We've come to see a flat stomach as not only beautiful and youthful but as something incredibly hard to achieve. The women with the flattest stomachs are the women most revered. On popular apps like TikTok, teenage girls in low-cut jeans and crop tops dance innocently with their midriffs on show, with adult women comparing their bodies to them and adult men lusting over them. Expecting adult women to resemble body types like these is not only unfair but nigh on impossible. Lusting over their youthfulness is another matter entirely.

Thinness plays a huge role in our perceived sexual value. Along with youthful skin, a flat stomach and tiny waist can also be viewed as a representation of female virginity. Like the hymen, many men still value the unstretched, unsaggy stomachs of younger women whose bodies don't appear to have been 'lived' in or 'ruined' by pregnancy.

But if a rounder, lower abdomen is a natural part of our female DNA, why do we fight against it so much? Why does society view this part of our femininity with such revulsion and disgust? What is so wrong with embracing the bits of ourselves that define us as women?

Having struggled with an eating disorder for most of my teens and twenties, it's clear to see the correlation between the area we try our best to make smaller and the unsettling, often confusing emotions that lie within it.

While we associate the heart with our feelings and emotions, it is the gut, really, that stores, absorbs and digests our feelings. Our guts not only act as a storage facility for food but also thoughts and emotions our brains can't quite make sense of. It's the part of our body we grab while crying hysterically from laughter; that convulses while crying hysterically from sadness. It's where we feel jitters of excitement; where sadness gathers and pools; where butterflies flutter when crushing on someone; where we feel a sudden punch of grief or an abrupt drop of fear; where anxiety leads to nausea; where jealousy swirls in its bitterness.

More often than not, our gut stores feelings and emotions we try our best to ignore, feelings that are bigger than our entire selves, too complex for our brain to dissect. Too often, we ignore our inherent gut feelings for our brain's logic, focusing on what we choose to believe, or what we hope for, over our instincts.

Perhaps this is why we take so much anger out on our 'unruly' tummies. It isn't necessarily the fat we dislike, per se, but the unease and anxiety churning in our guts that we can't make sense of. Our emotions scare us, unsettle us, infuriate us. As a result, we focus on this fat, going from diet to diet and picking apart our bodies, believing that starving ourselves will somehow shrink our anxieties and negative self-image.

And so when we wake up with a flatter stomach, when we see the outline of a new bone beneath the skin, when people tell us we look 'great' because we've lost a few pounds, what many of us really believe is: *I am one step closer to my dream life. I am one step closer to perfection, and if I am perfect, then I will finally be happy. I am on my way to feeling OK. I am one step closer to all my problems disappearing. I am that bit nearer to feeling beautiful, and if I am beautiful, then the feelings of loathing, hatred and disgust I feel about myself will finally end.*

Many women have an intense fear of fat, in a way that can only be described as pathological. Fatness is very often viewed in Western society as a failure in women: a failure to meet societal expectations around beauty and marriageability and a representation of a lack of self-control.

Anti-fatness is big business. Barclays say that the global obesity therapeutic market could be worth $100 billion by around 2030, all from convincing women that there is nothing worse than being fat and nothing better than being thin. But rather than the majority of these diet products or programmes providing long-term results, studies show that only 20 per cent of all dieters successfully maintain weight loss.

Despite this, the diet industry thrives on keeping women in never-ending cycles of betterment. After all, why would it not?

Without keeping women in a constant loop of insecurity enticed by a false promise of internal fulfilment, it wouldn't be worth what it is today.

Most of us will have been on some form of a diet at some point in our lives. I, personally, have tried many. Diet culture sells women the ultimate fantasy: a dream life, full of love, adoration, success and beauty, that can all be yours if, and when, you're thin. Rather than living in the present, we build a fantasy around the potential achievement of a 'dream' body, telling ourselves that once we slim down, we'll finally wear a bikini on holiday; that we'll treat ourselves to a new outfit; that by reaching a certain number on the scale, we will suddenly become irresistible to men or worthy of love.

Being thin is associated with being attractive, being attractive means more attention from men and more attention from men means an easier, 'happier' life. Instead of focusing on the way we feel internally or aiming to better ourselves mentally or emotionally, we imagine how we'll feel in the future fitting into smaller clothes and how men may view us in those clothes. As a result, we will often undertake extreme regimens to help us achieve what we believe happiness to be, beating our bodies up physically and mentally in the process.

At the crux of society's obsession with thinness lies the importance of desirability. Whether we choose to accept it or not, the thinner you are, the more sexually desirable you become. When our sexuality dictates our worth as women, it's no wonder we choose to go on a diet. More often than not, dieting is less about becoming healthy for yourself and more about being deemed beautiful by others. As per most of the female experience, diet culture affirms how much of a woman's value lies in how attractive she is to men, forcing her into a constant cycle of self-objectification and self-loathing.

We are told that thinness will cure us. It will make us desirable. It will make us healthier. It will make us worthy. Most of all, it will make us *good*. Starvation becomes something to be proud of, masked as discipline. The more we starve ourselves, the *purer* we become. We will not only starve away fat but also the feelings that come with fat: unworthiness and disgust. Thinness will grant us acceptance, safety and love in a world that made us beg for them to begin with. In a world where we are never enough, we are starving for love and attention.

But thinness was and is never about looking good. Not really. It is deeper than that. It's about a feeling of unworthiness that we hope the number on a scale will fix. Thinness is about women being manageable. It is about being palatable. After all, a woman who is full, fed, rested and strong is harder to control and manipulate.

A hungry woman, as many of us can attest, is anxious, weak, fearful and distracted. Her mind is foggy, her thoughts incoherent, her brain obsessive. Nothing matters except for her appearance. As her body shrinks, so does her voice. Within her shame, she becomes frightened to speak up, stand up, rise up and take up space. Hungry, she becomes too tired to fight back, not only physically, but mentally; not only for herself but against the system that forced her to be this way to begin with. Being thin benefits men more than it does the women chasing it.

Sexual harassment and abuse can also be a trigger for self-surveillance and dieting. Thinness can become a strange combination of wanting to be youthful and attractive enough to be desired by men but also a means of hiding from them; disappearing so as not to attract attention. We know how many women experience unwanted sexual touch and sexist comments, so it's not hard to understand why we try to shrink ourselves to disappear and escape this.

Diet culture is marketed to us as empowerment, as wellness, while not providing much positivity at all. Still, it works. From childhood, thinness is sold to us through magazines and books, films and TV shows, supermodels and runways, and even our own mothers, who know little better – want little better – for themselves.

Of course, the promised fantasy dream life of thinness never materialises, because even when you *do* reach your 'goal weight', you often feel as insecure as you did before. But diet culture continually teases you behind further bright lights and false promises: through the lure of the latest fad diets, weight-loss drugs, skinny teas and smoothies or fat-burning exercise classes, encouraging you not to give up.

And so develops a long-standing relationship with self-hatred, where we become angry and disappointed at our body for not behaving in the way we think it should, when our body doesn't fulfil its promise of thinness, beauty and contentment, even after meticulously following the rules. We can't understand it. If other women on Instagram and TikTok appear happy and content in their thin bodies and expensive gym gear, then we must be doing something wrong.

As a result of feeling unworthy, we tend to 'punish' ourselves through food – or, rather, a lack of it. We become angry at our stomachs crying out in hunger, disappointed when we give into temptation, when our hunger gets the better of us. But we're told that our dream life is on the other side of that ravenousness. *Keep going.* Diet culture successfully gaslights us into thinking that by ignoring our hunger or fullness cues, we can override our body's natural needs and wants and finally own the body that promises us a lifetime of happiness.

So, what does the toll of constantly monitoring our waists do to us psychologically? The Mental Health Foundation reports that one in eight British adults aged eighteen and over have been so distressed about their body image, they had experienced suicidal thoughts or feelings because of it. The *Guardian* also reported that 10 per cent of women in the UK have deliberately hurt themselves because of their body image, compared to 4 per cent of men.

It's not just our stomachs that feel the physical effects of constant dieting. Our entire bodies become consumed and affected by it. Our brains become starved of essential nutrients, our moods spiking from sugar highs and dives. We're unable to concentrate or focus properly, our thoughts obsessive around food. In extreme weight loss, tremendous strain is placed on our heart, which in the most severe cases can lead to actual heart attacks, even in young people. Our hormones become disrupted, which leads to our skin breaking out. Our periods become irregular, even heavier.

The likelihood of maintaining a life-long diet, let alone life-long results, is vanishingly small. This doesn't deter us from trying new ways of achieving thinness, though. Treating our bodies like objects, we routinely reach for anything that promises us a svelte figure.

But if the chances of long-term weight loss are as slim as the bodies we try to emulate, why do we keep putting this much pressure on ourselves to achieve it? Instead of choosing to accept the bodies they're in, a lot of women spend most of their lives attempting new diet after new diet, hoping that finally, *eventually*, the weight will stay off and that the happiness, confidence and self-acceptance promised to them will prevail.

Most importantly, who are women doing all of this for? In most cases it's not for their own gratification. Not really. Not if you truly think about it. If the option of freeing themselves from a lifetime of needless, painful and, quite frankly, boring dieting is within reach, not to mention letting go of the incessant need to focus on their looks, why do women keep themselves shackled to the numbers they weigh on a scale?

Experience has taught me that whenever a woman says she feels fat, what she *actually* means is that she feels bad within herself. She's experiencing feelings and emotions she can't quite describe or find the words for and, as a result, her brain reaches for the worst description a person – or, at least, a woman – can be: *fat*. Feeling fat has become less of an accurate, physical description of bodies, and instead, a way of describing our internalised negative inner feelings and shame. Fatness has become associated with ugliness, laziness, weakness and failure. To be fat means you are 'other', an outsider. Most of us yearn for societal and cultural acceptance, which makes fatness, or becoming fat, a scary prospect indeed.

So deep is our fear of fatness that according to the *Wiley Handbook of Eating Disorders*, 80 per cent of teenage girls in the US say they are scared of becoming fat. A shocking study by researchers at Arizona State University revealed that 14.5 per cent of women would rather be *blind* than overweight, or would rather have one of twelve socially stigmatised conditions, including herpes, depression or alcoholism. An estimated 45 million people go on a diet each year, and people who go on diets are eight times more likely to develop an eating disorder. Thirty-five per cent of dieting becomes obsessive, with 20 to 25 per cent of those diets turning into full-blown eating disorders.

Studies show that by the age of three, children already have preconceived ideas that fat people are slow and gluttonous. By primary school, children believe fat people have no friends; by secondary school, they believe fatter people are undesirable and unintelligent. These childhood prejudices often linger in the back of our minds, following us into adulthood, and we not only use them as a fear tactic but as a means of segregation.

It doesn't take a lot to be considered fat. Any body part that isn't slimmed or toned within an inch of its life has the possibility of being ridiculed, which is probably why so many of us fear our bodies being seen naked or in a bikini.

Many of us will imagine how others view our stomachs and try to suck our stomachs in to appear thinner. Excessively sucking in your stomach can lead to a condition called 'hourglass syndrome', which includes breathing difficulties, incontinence, back pain and muscular imbalances.

Even as a nine-year-old in the playground, I distinctly remember the boys didn't want to be seen with the bigger girls; how being seen with a bigger girl would reflect badly on the boy and his choices. 'Fat' was used as an insult, a means to hurt or belittle girls, even if the boys weren't slim themselves. I also remember the distinct feeling of being 'picked' as somebody's girlfriend in the playground: an honour not bestowed on the girls who were chubbier.

It was cruel. It was sexist. Even then, girls like me were learning that our bodies were only important if a boy found you attractive.

Oppression is often intersectional. A fat woman's experience, especially, is often aggravated by other forms of discrimination, such as racism, classism, ageism and ableism. These patriarchal expectations around female bodies, beauty and femininity lead to women being punished for not conforming to thinness. Women of all ages, ethnicities and sizes are expected not to take up space; to remain quiet. Fatness defies all of that. Accepted archetypes of femininity do not grant space for fat or unattractive female bodies, excluding them from their humanity. There is no room for fatness – or so-called 'unruly' bodies – in the current patriarchal, image-driven society we find ourselves in.

Maybe that's what scares us about 'fat'. Many women can't

comprehend how another woman wouldn't want to be thin to be considered attractive or desirable to men. While it may not seem like jealousy, deep down, she wishes that she, too, could be free to live her life as she pleases, to eat what she wants and be free from male sexualisation.

This is not to say that bigger women are not sexual beings or worthy of sexual attention. Far from it. Men will sexualise women of all sizes. But a man who fancies a fat woman is often seen to have a kink or a fetish. Fat women aren't treated as fellow humans but as freak shows. Thinness, however, tricks women into believing that by being thinner, they will, indeed, be worthy of respect from men.

Throughout much of history, a small waist – through dieting, exercise, corsetry or waist training – has been an indicator of feminine desirability, beauty and self-control. Corsets became common from the late Middle Ages onwards, especially among wealthier women, and by the mid-nineteenth century, factory-made corsets became readily available for women of all classes, making them a beauty standard.

Wearing corsets as tight as possible could lead to numerous female health problems, including organ deformity, muscle weakness, respiratory issues and fainting, leaving women vulnerable. It was common to leave a window open whenever a woman was sitting indoors, just so she had fresh air and wouldn't faint.

The vulnerability, daintiness, demureness and innocence associated with a small waist started to provide men with an unwarranted feeling of masculinity and physical strength. Women would have legitimately required and depended on men for a variety of reasons, especially financially, and a small, thin body – especially when next to a man's – would have provided men with a sense of physical 'manliness'. In other words, much of the appeal of thinness is how it's designed to make men feel more important and macho.

Even now, a woman's waist is a symbol of control, both physically – waist trainers, corsets and dieting – and metaphorically – conformity, obedience and self-discipline. Smallness is a signifier of femininity, and it has existed for centuries.

Women will spend untold billions in achieving the appearance of a thinner body or waist. In more recent times, shapewear brands like Spanx (created by Sara Blakely, whose net worth Forbes estimates to be $1.3 billion) and Skims (owned by Kim Kardashian, which, too, helped her to become a billionaire), have become billion-dollar companies from helping women achieve a svelte, lump-free, 'snatched' figure, without needing to hit the gym.

Despite this, cultural ideals around ideal female body shapes tend to be difficult to achieve in reality. In the Renaissance period, women were depicted as having a fuller figure, which, essentially, showed you could readily eat and were therefore wealthy. Even nowadays, in countries with pervasive famine, a rotund female body is often perceived as the most attractive body type, an ideal echoed by the women of my grandparents' generation, who, after Second World War rationing, preferred curvaceous body shapes, like those of Hollywood starlets.

I have been aware of my stomach and fatness since I was a child. Aged around nine or ten, a friend of mine lined me and my friends up in the playground in order of fatness, biggest to thinnest. I came second from the thinnest. I recall feeling jealous over not having made first place. If, say, we were competing in a sport, this jealousy or competitiveness could be somewhat understandable, even healthy. But we weren't. Our *bodies* were the competition. I couldn't help but question my body and internalise my worth. My friend's ranking of my body clearly represented what other people saw, especially boys, and I wasn't sure I liked being second-best.

It didn't help that the girl who was number one was the girl that all the boys supposedly fancied; the girl who the mums at the school gate would repeatedly claim to be beautiful; who everyone deemed to be sweet and kind. She was seen – and treated – in ways I was not.

I had never compared myself to my friends before and suddenly I felt as though I should. After all, no one complimented me. No one was saying how pretty I was. I felt completely average.

Then, when I was twelve, I went to an all-girls boarding school, a result of my parents' constant travelling (I'd lost count by how many houses we'd lived in by then), my naughty behaviour and, apparently, in the hope I'd focus on schooling over boys. In hindsight, my unruly behaviour was likely due to the feelings of angst around sex and previous behaviour from men that had made me feel incredibly out of control and lost. Nothing felt stable. Boarding school was supposed to provide that stability. We weren't wealthy or well-off by any means, but my dad's job helped subsidise some of the school fees. In wanting to offer me opportunities they hadn't had, my parents stretched themselves to give me a better life.

I know I should've been grateful for a so-called great education, but I wasn't. The British class system means that unless you come from wealth or old money, you will never truly be accepted in upper-class circles. This is just fact. It's one thing going to a private school. It's another being able to maintain the lifestyle and culture that comes with it, from being able to afford the latest clothes, to understanding cultural traditions like fox hunting. Despite coming from the same country, it was a total clash of cultures and I didn't know where I fitted. It was incredibly disjointing going to visit my family on council estates at the weekend, where poverty was rampant, to sitting in class with a girl whose family had a private jet or with another whose family raced horses for the Queen.

Suddenly, I felt as though I was having to fend for myself. There was an emptiness in my body, a yearning for something that I couldn't find the words for. I was constantly surrounded by people but felt entirely alone, in ways I couldn't quite make sense of.

My grandmother was the nearest relative I had living nearby. Every weekend, she would pick me up from school to stay with her. During those days I'd finally be able to relax; would finally feel cared for.

As someone who'd grown up with rationing in the war, my grandmother's love language was food. Food meant care. To care was to love. There was no shortage of food in her house. I was constantly offered it. We'd have takeaways, often twice a weekend, ate our lunch out and then had numerous desserts to eat in front of the TV in the evening. My grandmother, I think, could sense my sadness and helped fill my void with food, hoping it would show me I was loved. It wasn't healthy, exactly, but having experienced food shortages in her life, I could understand why she wouldn't ever turn it down.

There was no better comfort for my loneliness, anxiousness and homesickness than food. *Food, glorious food*. I had no idea that something so readily available and accessible could provide such comfort. I hated feeling empty. I especially hated having to make sense of my insecurities, anxieties and other feelings of sadness. Food filled that space, leaving me temporarily satisfied and whole; my hunger, which wasn't always related to food, temporarily replenished.

I had always been thin. But as I began developing from a

child into a teenager, so did my flesh. Almost overnight, my body expanded, in height, cup size and, especially, around my waist. I went from wanting to be pretty to not wanting to be noticed at all.

There was something about being curvy that went beyond the worry of looking fat. Everything about femininity and womanhood filled me with disgust and, even more than that, a sense of fear. To be womanly meant being feminine and to be feminine meant having flesh on your bones. I was worried that the more I started to look like a woman, the more men would sexualise or take advantage of me.

The more meat I had on my body, the more flesh there was to grab. 'Flesh', I'd learnt, was another term for 'sexual'. 'Sexual' meant 'shame'. And looking sexual meant you were more likely to be treated as a sex object, more so than you already were. The thought of my body being touched and squeezed in ways I wasn't comfortable with made me feel physically ill, transporting me back to moments where I felt completely out of control.

The other issue was that I was one of the first girls in my class to start my period. My body and its maturity preceded me. I couldn't control it, nor could I control the ways other people saw me. My body became bigger than who I was ready to be, who I was able to be. I wanted to remain small, unseen, and yet I was forever feeding a monster within me that was never satisfied with how much I tried to punish it into submission.

Everything about womanhood made me anxious. The flesh, the curves, the breasts, the bleeding, were all intrinsically tied to sex. I would repeatedly think about the times I'd been sexualised, especially by Sean, as well as other moments with men, feeling as though my body was 'other' to me.

And so I became fat. I don't mean in a slightly chubby way. I mean in a genuinely obese way. It was strange. While I actively detested curves, I ate and subsequently become curvier, in order to become less attractive and therefore less noticeable.

At just thirteen, I weighed around 14 stone. I was disgusted by myself, my lack of control around food and how I looked, yet I couldn't stop eating. I would binge on packets upon packets of crisps, bars of chocolate, fizzy drinks, slices of cake. I would eat two, three portions of dinner at school, before going to the school's tuck shop and ordering more food from there. I knew girls were judging me, laughing at my body and yet I couldn't stop.

I decided not to pay much attention to my body at all. As the months rolled on, especially in that first year, I hid my body underneath baggy sweatshirts in ugly colours. I didn't feel deserving of fashion or pretty things. Pretty clothes did not belong on bodies like mine. The only time I'd look in a mirror was when I was having a shower and even then it was a brief glance. I could barely catch my own eye.

Without technology like FaceTime to keep us connected, months would go by where I wouldn't see my parents. When they saw me in person for the first time after going to school, I remember the shocked looks on their faces at my new body.

I knew I was gross. I knew I was unattractive. With no boys around, it didn't bother me *too* much. But girls could be equally judgemental and cruel. I was fat and so I was picked on because of it. My body became a mockery – my weight, my puberty, my clothes. And not just that, but all of me – my accent, my class. My body fitted in nowhere. One day, a friend's mother came to pick her up and announced I had put on a 'tremendous' amount of weight. I could physically feel the disgust in her voice, my cheeks burning in shame.

Sport especially became an anxiety-inducing nightmare at school. I dreaded getting changed, girls seeing my fat, fleshy stomach. I hated running across a sports pitch and feeling my tummy wobble. The thought of going swimming, being in a tight swimsuit, would leave my stomach in knots. I repeatedly used the excuse of 'forgetting' my swimsuit or being on my period as means of getting out of it, though of course there's only so many weeks you can have a period without your teacher taking notice.

One Sunday, I overheard my great-grandmother telling my grandmother that I had put on a ton of weight and that other members of the family had noticed it, too. I heard my grandmother hiss at her, telling her to keep her voice down. I pretended I hadn't heard the conversation, though her words stung.

That evening, I stood in front of my grandmother's bathroom mirror and took my clothes off, dropping them to my feet in a pile. For the first time in a long time, I analysed my body properly.

I couldn't believe how fat I was and, not only that, how I hadn't ever noticed much of it. I looked nothing like the girls in my class, whose bodies were tiny, small and cute. My stomach was flabby and hung over my trousers, layers of flesh around my ribs. My arms shook when I held them up. My thighs rubbed together. How could I have missed this? When did I become so *grotesque*?

Perhaps, subconsciously, I thought the more I ignored my body, the more my problems would go away. But that's the issue with anxiety and trauma. The more we ignore them, the bigger they get. They swirl within us, anxiety churning in our guts.

I sunk my fingers into the skin around my ribcage until I felt bone. My body was squishy, fleshy, chubby. I decided from then on that something needed to change. I couldn't look like this any more. I had to lose weight – and fast.

It started off with chocolate bars. Cadbury's, to be precise. The following day, the Monday morning, as my grandmother handed me a bag of confectionery and snacks to take to school to last me the week, I decided to hand the chocolate bars out to other grateful girls.

I started noticing numbers on packets of food. 250. 300. 80. These, I learnt, were calories. I'd never considered them before, but I knew that the higher the calories, the fatter you'd become.

The next time I went home to my grandmother's and weighed myself, the number on the scale had gone down. I couldn't believe it. Weight loss was simple. Instead of eating my daily two, three, four chocolate bars, I would simply have one. It wasn't difficult at all.

But then, I cut chocolate out entirely and not just chocolate but anything 'fatty'. Over the next couple of months, the weight dropped off. The more I lost weight, the more girls began to notice me, while others, used to me being somewhat mediocre, became visibly jealous of the new-found attention I was getting. While I wasn't 'thin', I had lost a couple of dress sizes, and people began treating me better. The same friend's mother who told me I'd put on a tremendous amount of weight one day pulled me into a hug, claiming she was worried about me becoming so skinny. The more dress sizes I lost, the more accepted I felt.

Food had become less about comfort and more about restriction. I became acutely aware that if I dared to begin to eat as much as I had before, I'd lose the nicer treatment. People wouldn't care any more. I didn't want to be fat again, let alone be treated as a fat person, which meant, on the whole, subhuman. And so I continued to monitor my body intently.

Weight loss didn't eradicate the feelings of self-loathing and unease within my gut. No matter how much I restricted my food, they were still there, fighting their way to the surface. I had to go further. I had to *punish* myself further. And one day, I found the cure.

I can't remember when I discovered the art of making myself sick. I can only assume that one day I felt as though I'd overeaten like the pig I thought myself to be and therefore had to rid myself and my stomach of its contents.

What I *do* remember is that bulimia became a regular act of 'self-care'; a ritual to make myself feel 'clean' and 'pure'. It became a routine: stuffing and stuffing my mouth full of food, so much so that my stomach could barely move or until I needed to physically throw up to make space. I would take myself away into a bathroom to do it. Food became a sin. Emptiness felt like virtue. Anxiety, stress, shame and embarrassment could all be eradicated, simply by shoving my fingers down my throat.

For a brief moment I would feel calm. My throat would burn from the acid, my eyes would be bloodshot and water from the stress. But it didn't matter. My stomach was empty once again.

Every time I was sick, I rid my body of my pain and emotions. For a second, my body would reset; my head empty and clear, my thoughts coherent, my anxieties dissipated. My heart would thump as though I'd done a rigorous workout, my forehead dotted with beads of sweat. I was empty. And in that emptiness, I felt finally pure.

At least, for a moment.

If I was lucky, this peace could last overnight. I'd go to bed promising myself that tomorrow would be a chance to wipe the slate clean, to no longer give in to temptation and feed into my greedy desires.

Life had become a strange combination of both wanting to be 'seen' and cared for, while also remaining small enough to go unnoticed and unbothersome. I became consciously aware of my body taking up space. I was starving away my body's soft parts to make myself smaller, all in the hope of feeling bigger. By slimming myself, I was hoping I could disappear from male view, all while being viewed as worthy by women, worthy of friendship, of love, of care.

While, initially, I'd wanted to lose weight for women, the weight loss brought with it the attention I was trying to avoid. The more weight I lost, the more male attention I seemed to attract. Men, clearly knowing I was underage, would catcall me out of vans or approach me in the street and ask for my number. I learnt that it didn't matter if I was thin, fat or any size in between. Men would repeatedly find a way to leer over me, to objectify me, to make me feel like all I had to offer was my body.

At least I could decide how my body looked. At least I could have some control over it. I may not have been able to stop the sexualisation, but I could control how I felt about myself.

In modern Western society, with a never-ending supply of food, entertainment and other forms of excessive capitalistic consumption, thinness has become a sign of beauty, wealth and even class. A flat, *toned* stomach, however, became particularly popular in the 1980s, made famous by beautiful women like Jane Fonda. Female fitness suddenly became associated with glamour and sex appeal. Aerobics videos featured presenters barely breaking a sweat in their high-waisted Lycra, their hair remaining perfectly coiffed and make-up in place. While these videos were aimed at women wanting to improve their health, unsurprisingly, men, too, enjoyed watching women thrust their hips.

Perhaps not uncoincidentally, this new body ideal was likely a push-back to the obesity epidemic and rise of fast food, as well as a more sedentary work lifestyle, where women were now sat at desks and contributing to an income, rather than on their feet doing housework. A tight, lean, fat-free body signalled a woman's willpower to reject and avoid the abundance of fast food, but also the fact she had the money, freedom and dedication to achieve one.

Since the eighties, this flat-stomach body ideal has rarely changed, plateauing throughout much of the nineties (as seen on supermodels), before women were encouraged to diet further and achieve size zero physiques: a size made famous from the US.

Size zero culture was proof that a woman's body is nothing more than an object; something she may live in but will never entirely be her own. As a teenager, there was no escaping this 'trend'.

It's hard to explain the level of pressure placed on women to be excessively thin throughout the early 2000s. Without social media, our only sources of entertainment, fashion advice and celebrity news were via TV shows or cheap gossip magazines (of which, there were many), magazines that seemed to compete for the most shocking celebrity photos to make regular women feel worse about themselves.

Each new cover would feature celebrity women's bodies, zooming in on their so-called flaws. I still have no idea how these magazines thought this was OK, considering that the journalists writing these pieces probably wouldn't have been rail-thin themselves.

Most of these female celebrities had no idea that they were being photographed, out and about, usually on a beach in their bikinis, where they were simply living and having fun. Shots of them from deliberately unflattering angles or with bad lighting highlighted the 'issues' that so many of us have: untoned, squishy stomachs, cellulite, flabby arms, stretch marks. You couldn't help but feel unworthy too. If a woman lost a ton of weight, they would then feature articles claiming how friends were worried about them; how she'd taken dieting 'too far'.

Vanity sizing was also popular, where brands made their dress sizes smaller to make women feel better about themselves. In the early 2000s, aged around fifteen, I recall feeling absolutely ecstatic when I fitted into a pair of size 2 Abercrombie & Fitch jeans, which were actually designed for a size 8.

My eating disorders mirrored the incessant images of 'wrong' female bodies. *Weight, weight, weight.* It was all these magazines spoke about. If it wasn't about who'd gained weight, it was diet plans explaining how to lose it. It made you feel as though your dress size, your body, was genuinely all that mattered. Studying other women's bodies, let alone my own, became a full-blown obsession.

I recall cutting out a magazine article which included the supposed diet plan that helped Nicole Richie achieve her size zero physique. I followed it religiously, eating fewer than eight hundred calories a day. I even went so far as to order diet pills off the internet using a friend's credit card, pink tablets that were meant for obese people – which I was now not – and which would swell in your stomach to make you less hungry. I would spend hours of my day – and I mean, *hours* – scrolling through pro-anorexia websites, where anonymous users would encourage you to lose weight and starve yourself. I even had a notebook where I would glue and stick 'thinspirational' images of thin women, alongside the items of clothing I'd buy once I deemed myself thin enough – and worthy enough – to wear them.

As someone who had previously ignored mirrors altogether, suddenly, they were all I looked for. I would find any way to judge, objectify and insult my body, looking for 'problems' that I could starve away. Looking in the bathroom mirror, I'd lift up my school shirt to analyse whether my waist was any thinner; whether I'd gained weight; whether there was any more skin around my midriff to squeeze. I'd grab rolls of flesh with my hands, pinching myself until it hurt, praying it would shrink. I dreaded to think other people viewed me with the same levels of disgust and shame as the women I saw on magazine covers.

When my periods stopped, I viewed this as success. When I began growing down hair on my face and body – a soft, white layer of hair your body creates in starvation to keep warm – I knew it was because I was successfully eating fewer calories.

By the mid-noughties, size zero disappeared from mainstream view. Numerous studies showed the damaging effects it had on many women's and girls' self-esteem and how it led to eating disorder issues. But the damage had already been done. Disappointingly, however, twenty years on, excessive thinness has reared its ugly head again thanks to the internet.

Misogyny is intrinsic to fatphobia and the objectification of women, but fatphobia is also heavily rooted in racism, and in particular, anti-Blackness. In her book *Fearing the Black Body: The Racial Origins of Fat Phobia*, sociologist Sabrina Strings examines the historical ways slimness became the ideal body within society and how fatphobia emerged as a response to slavery.

Strings explains how it wasn't until the mid-eighteenth century that fatphobia really made its mark on society, a reaction to the burgeoning transatlantic slave trade. In Europe specifically, the period before this was littered with portraiture of voluptuous white women, women whose shapely curves and rounder stomachs came to be known as the epitome of beauty. The pale, plumper bodies of white women who stayed leisurely at home and out of the sun, being waited on hand and foot by servants, and who were lucky enough to eat rich and delicious foods for pleasure on the daily, became an ultimate signifier of wealth and class, a total contrast to thinner, poor women yielding crops, who would not only tan while working in the sun but who would have little access to nutritional food and would naturally burn it off from working on their feet all day anyway.

By the late seventeenth century, fatness became a way of

categorising race. Colonists believed that Black people loved food and were obese due to lack of self-control. Early 'race scientists' – white men who sought to biologise and systemise a racial hierarchy – began regarding gluttony, curvaceous bodies, fatness and unintelligence as characteristic of Africans. This is quite the turnaround from previous racist depictions, considering that before the transatlantic slave trade Black women were portrayed in Renaissance paintings as sickly thin servants, a way of demonstrating their lowly and inferior positions. Scientifically, studies show that Black women actually have more bone and muscle mass but *less* fat as a percentage of body weight than white women, meaning this 'fear' of appearing fat was completely unfounded.

By the eighteenth century – and following these supposed 'intellectual' findings of the anthropologists, scholars and race scientists – white women (in particular, British women) began to shun fleshy and voluptuous figures in exchange for thinness, sticking to diets that would keep them lithe and svelte. Now considered a 'Black trait', fat became the enemy. A thin physique was no longer seen as 'sickly'. This, Strings explains, was a means of white women differentiating themselves from the Black slaves they were treating so abhorrently, as well as creating an ideal that would make them appear superior to the naturally curvier bodies of Central and West African women. Of course, this is not to say that anti-fatness did not exist prior to the slave trade, but fatness did come to be despised in a highly rampant and systemic way once slavery became as prevalent and normalised as it did.

With the rise of the American Empire in the nineteenth century, ladies' magazines, like *Harper's Bazaar* and *Godey's Lady's Book*, began publishing articles that linked fatness to 'African savagery', crime and even deformity. As new immigrants arrived on American soil, anxieties began to form among settled Americans around sustaining the image of north-western Europeans

– white, blonde and blue-eyed. As a means of maintaining white supremacy, as well as this new ideal of American beauty, thinness became a further marker of racial distinction, wealth and class.

Fatphobia could also have been developing from a concern of remaining attractive to men. Interestingly, while media did not exist in the ways it does now – nor, obviously, phones, the internet, or mass fashion – women were, even then, self-objectifying, aware of their bodies in ways that did them a huge disservice and caused needless anxieties.

While it is easy to assume our obsession with weight is a female issue, men have repeatedly played a bigger role in fatphobia and body image problems than I think we like to believe. Although modern media certainly has a role to play in the ways women view themselves objectively, self-objectification and sexualisation came long before it. Self-objectification stems from the male gaze and the patriarchy, a system designed to make women feel unworthy and second-class, as though we have nothing else to offer other than our bodies.

After all, who were these Renaissance, rotund, Rubenesque bodies painted by? Who developed these racist, racial biases based on body type? Throughout history, what we've come to know, discover and understand of female beauty is through the male lens and not via women themselves.

During times of political unrest, and certainly within the rise of right-wing parties and conservatism, thinness tends to rear its ugly head. This is not a coincidence. Thinness is not only a trend, but a misogynistic political strategy, used to remind women of their place and that their bodies are, ultimately, for the sexual gratification of men. More often than not, it is women themselves leading these ideals, defining clear standards of what constitutes a 'correct' woman, and keeping themselves and fellow women bound by misogynistic ideals under the guise of 'traditionalism'.

The return of ultra-thinness – whether that's promoted through the guise of #SkinnyTok, weight-loss injections or fashion designed for smaller figures – is usually a reflection that women are becoming too confident within themselves. As a result, the system begins to panic. To regain control, it convinces women that their worth and value lie in their smallness, not just physically, but in their mannerisms and behaviours as a whole. Staying thin distracts women from creating real collective change and the issues in life that are genuinely important.

Enter the 'trad-wife'. Trad-wife subculture is becoming more and more mainstream, encouraging young women to give up work and become picture-perfect versions of what they believe women should be; where gender roles are hardwired. The topic has over 300 million views on TikTok alone and is continually growing.

While not a popular opinion, women can be red-pilled too. Topics like extreme fitness, clean or obsessive eating, extreme weight focus, anti-vaccination and medication, conspiracy theories and religion are all sides to trad-wifery, masked by Instagram photos of home-cooked pies, aprons and tight little bodies.

In some ways, it's understandable why so many women want to stay at home as housewives. Right-wing ideology and framework provide order in times of disorder, structure in times of chaos and meaning in times of existential struggle. If looking good for your husband is an exchange for feeling protected, what's the problem?

To conservatives, ideal femininity resembles docility, infantilisation, the rejection of feminism (read: opinions or a backbone) and a strict adherence to heteronormative binaries. Women should be thin, white, young, traditionally feminine in the way they dress, non-disabled, straight and middle to upper class. They need to act and dress modestly but also look sexy, not have kids outside of marriage and within it be willing to populate the world with as many children as possible.

Conservatism rejects everyone who doesn't fit these norms. To be chosen by these men requires you to embrace traditional roles, to be demure, quietly intelligent (as by no means can you appear more intelligent than him) and well behaved. Your existence is for nothing other than servitude.

Among many conservative women, there is no such thing as 'body positivity' or 'body neutrality'. There are 'correct' bodies and 'incorrect' bodies. Thinness becomes a representation of a female's restraint and a willingness to submit. It is as symbolic as it is pathological warfare.

Far-right patriarchy promises women safety from a world of abuse, poverty and isolation. Succumbing to its ideologies provides protection, love, money, salvation and meaning for women, tied together within a neat family structure. Far-right men have an ideological commitment to the idea of traditional families and women's subordinate places within them, all while selling women the idea that they're 'winning'.

Trad-wifery is marketed as domestic bliss, where a woman does nothing but bake, care for children, animals and the home, all while looking beautiful doing it. What's not to like? In such an image-driven society, the trad-wife lifestyle appears calm, safe and cosy. Besides, isn't this what feminism is about – allowing women to make their own choices? Her right to take on traditional gender roles should be respected.

However, like many false promises of choice, in submitting to this lifestyle I believe a woman exchanges one form of oppression for another. A trad-wife will give up her freedom, her intellectuality and bodily autonomy in exchange for protection. Really, she doesn't have much choice at all. The right accurately articulates the threat of violence and poverty many women face, despite hiding behind oppressions of their own. Although the solution right-wing men offer may not be trustworthy, right-wing women prefer the ideology that they feel puts their (justified) fears to rest.

Naturally, the promise of protection for these women comes at a cost. These right-wing men still want hot, sexual women. The trad-wife is very much a pornified version of what a woman is supposed to be. Unintentionally, she merely reinforces patriarchal norms and contributes to devaluation of women who don't fit the mould.

When you take a step back, there isn't much of a difference between sex workers and trad-wives. Both are used for their bodies and labour. Both are expected to be picture-perfect images of femininity. Pimps promise women physical protection, care and, in some cases, drugs, all while exploiting women for their own monetary gain. Husbands will trap their wives with babies, telling them this is all for their own good. Unfortunately, this false sense of protection is a callous means of keeping women in a constant state of need.

How ironic, and cruel, that the men we often look to for protection, know they can take it away on a whim if we don't comply with their rules. Perhaps we should explore why many women feel so unsafe and are therefore willing to settle for less-than-human behaviour for what they believe is the safer option.

Andrea Dworkin wrote of the disgust and fear she elicited from other women as a lesbian in the 1970s. Conservative women of that time feared lesbians would sexually assault them (not too dissimilar to the conservative women you see online today who fear trans women). Dworkin wrote how many right-wing women transfer their fear of assault from men on to another group, an 'acceptable' target. It is more acceptable in right-wing spheres to be angry at trans women, lesbians, immigrants and people of colour than it is to be openly angry or upset at men. After all, why would you bite the hand that feeds you?

Today, men like Donald Trump, Andrew Tate and Elon Musk explicitly sell misogyny, barely hiding their contempt for women, and yet many women continually buy into their beliefs. Over half of Republican voters in the US 2024 general election were women. Yet despite its promise of traditional familial values, many conservatives want to slash public services and welfare, making many women's and children's lives harder. Therefore, when they advocate for traditional families, what they mean are families that resemble the white, suburban, picture-perfect portrait of 1950s America.

As we know, many politicians are opportunists, strategically hiding behind religion as a means of winning elections. Abortion rights are a prime example. Donald Trump, who was once vocally pro-choice, shifted his position to pro-life in order to appeal to right-wing voters as he stood for president, all while marketing a new version of the traditional American family, claiming he wants the best for women and using trans women as scapegoats.

It's important to remember that misogyny and patriarchal systems benefit each and every man on all sides of the political spectrum. Femininity is still defined by both correct and incorrect ways of being, where a woman is seen as only of value if she is visually pleasing to men or her body can benefit them.

Even left-leaning, so-called liberal men still benefit from women's bodies, usually at the expense of their health, under the guise of female sexual liberation. Of course they advocate for abortion rights and sexual autonomy. Why wouldn't they? These choices benefit men, too. It's why, as I've got older, I view casual sex less as sexually liberating for women and instead as a means of men furthering their own narrative and sexual agenda.

Hugh Hefner, for example, frequently advocated for pro-abortion rights within *Playboy* and was a huge donor to Planned Parenthood. But while *Playboy* rode the wave of new-age sixties feminism and the newly invented Pill and marketed itself as a forward-thinking, sex positive magazine, really, its messaging and the lifestyle it promoted was all for the benefit of its male readers: where men could finally engage in non-committal, casual sex without the fear, responsibility or consequence of marriage and children. While women had always been treated as objects, this form of liberalism provided women with a false sense of bodily ownership.

On many trad-wife forums, women ask for advice on how to look the best for their husbands. It's as though the 1950s have suddenly discovered the internet. I discovered a thread where a 23-year-old woman asked for advice on keeping her husband attracted to her. Many other women congratulate her on her willingness. One man replies: *'Good for you for recognising that you need to become the best version of yourself in order to have better odds at getting the man you want!'*. I can practically feel the patronisation through the screen.

Like overly sexual women, these women are continuously attempting to keep their men by any means possible, believing – as many of us do – that becoming a mother, housewife or picture-perfect woman will stop your man from straying, treating you badly or looking elsewhere.

Once again, the allure of thinness and beauty keeps us trapped within a false sense of empowerment, making us believe we're in control of our bodies while disempowering women.

In the past, I viewed my weight as a representation of the love I deserved. The fatter I was, the more space I took up; the more grotesque I looked, was and subsequently felt. I knew that the thinner I was, the more desirable I'd not only be to men but to fellow women, and, therefore, the worthier I'd believe myself to be.

True self-worth and true love could only come if I reduced my body, reduced myself, not just by becoming thin but from shrinking anything about myself that would be deemed too loud, too unladylike or too visible. Being small wasn't just a body shape. It was an entire sense of being.

Sometimes I look at my squishy tummy in the mirror and barely give it attention. Other times, I am wholly conscious of it. Usually, I become aware of my stomach during anxious or stressful times. My eyes revert to the pieces of myself that don't sit quite right in clothes, the parts of myself I assume, know, other people judge me on. I focus on my stomach and the way it hangs over my underwear; the way it wobbles when I move and folds together when I sit down; the slight outline of cellulite underneath my belly button, which seems to have slowly moved its way up from my thighs and across my abdomen. I wonder how I may feel if it were flatter, smaller, more toned; whether I should give it more focus and more attention instead of focusing on the worries in my brain. And then I must work hard to remind myself that no amount of starvation or dieting will rid me of my anxiety.

I don't know whether the lifelong messaging I've learnt about 'fat' and curvy bodies is so ingrained within me that I'll never be able to feel completely satisfied or comfortable with how it looks. But still, I must try my best to unlearn what I've been told, to teach my brain new, positive messaging and separate the feelings of low self-worth from the promises of an easier and better life. Moving forward, how I think about myself and what I choose to focus my attention and energy on are choices about my body that *I* get to make.

But whether my stomach shrinks or swells, lays flat or protrudes, whether I am thin, fat or any size in between, I now know my weight will never be an indicator of how worthy I am of love or a representation of who I am as a total person. And if a man can only love me if I mould myself into a woman I'm not, then he is certainly not deserving of me or my body. And a body, no matter how toned or trimmed, will never be satisfied or complete without feeling good within. It will never miraculously attract love or a partner or a better career, and if it does, then perhaps you need to consider whether this is the sort of love, partner or career you truly want.

thighs.

'Are you sure you want to do this?'

I was sitting with my friend in an upmarket beauty clinic in West London, a place where the couch in the reception likely cost more than my entire year's rent and where I was conscious of ruining the glossy tiles with my shoes. She had roped me into giving her moral support while watching her get 'ass shots', designed to make her 'hip dips' disappear and help achieve a smoother, curvier silhouette around her thighs and bum.

'Well, it's either this, or a BBL [Brazilian butt lift],' she replied, as though choosing not to undertake such procedures at all wasn't also an option.

It seemed easy enough. Like in other parts of your body, filler would be injected into the hips, thighs and bottom to make them appear fuller and curvier. It was expensive – over £5,000 for the injections alone – but the results she'd shown me in photos did appear impressive, with no downtime required unlike major (and permanent) surgery. If it was going to make her happy, who was I to judge?

When the nurse called my friend into the little consulting room, I sat on a nearby chair in the corner and watched. It appeared my presence was not welcomed by the nurse and it took some persuasion from my friend to allow me to accompany her.

'Is it going to hurt?' my friend asked the nurse anxiously.

'Only a bit,' the nurse replied. 'We use hospital-grade numbing treatment, so it shouldn't be too bad.'

As my friend stripped down to her knickers and I saw her barely clothed body, I couldn't help but feel this was totally unnecessary. Were those little inward dips *truly* that much of an issue to live with? Worth spending £5,000 on?

The nurse rubbed a numbing treatment all over my friend's bum and thighs. A couple of minutes later, my friend lay down on her side.

'I'm so excited!' she squealed, a huge grin on her face.

I knew that grin. It was a smile that said, *I will be better now*; a smile that said, *Once I have this procedure, I will finally feel beautiful, and I will never, ever complain about myself or how I look again – I promise.*

When I saw the size of the needle, I felt physically sick. It resembled something from a Victorian operating theatre, around half a centimetre thick and half an arm in length.

'Perhaps don't look,' I suggested, trying not to throw up.

What I witnessed next was terrifying. The nurse injected my friend's so-called 'hip dips' with the thick needle. My friend squeezed the bed and began screaming in agony, her knuckles turning white from how hard she was gripping. It was like witnessing an exorcism.

'Good girl,' the nurse told her, which felt somewhat patronising. 'You're doing so well.'

Once the needle was removed, the assistant immediately began trying to soak up the blood with tissues.

'Wait. It definitely needs more there,' the nurse said, then proceeded to inject her some more.

My friend then had to turn to the other side, holding herself up in a sort of side plank so as not to undo the injected area.

'That was the most painful experience of my life,' my friend said, glaring at me through tears.

'Are you sure you put enough numbing cream on?!' I asked the nurse in concern as she began prepping for round two.

'Of course I have,' she replied, irritably.

And so the screaming continued. I watched my friend yelling as she planked in this position, her body shaking as she held herself up and endured the injection, all to fill and round out a couple of centimetres of flesh.

For the grand finale, my friend lay on her front, bandaged on either side, while the nurse injected her buttocks with *more* filler from that giant, scary needle.

'It looks amazing,' the assistant said, though I can't say it made a profound visible difference. She handed my friend some tissues to wipe her eyes with.

'Oh, I forgot to mention,' the nurse added nonchalantly as she dumped the needle in the bin, 'as I've had to use more filler, I'll have to charge you an additional £250.'

My friend insisted she wanted to go home and be alone that night. I helped her into a taxi as she winced from the pain. She was given a few painkillers to take for a couple of days, as well as some clean bandages.

The following morning, I woke up to photos and videos of her bloodied, bandaged lower body. The bandages were soaked in brown, reddish blood, her thighs and bottom bruised all over from the needle.

'I haven't slept at all,' she wrote. *'It was too painful to lie down so I spent most of the night having to stand up. Spent most of it crying.'*

But despite all of that, my friend only had one question.

'Does it look good?'

*

To be a female thigh in this day and age is confusing. While on the one hand, the overly curvaceous, cartoonishly rounded, Jessica Rabbit silhouette is widely considered the pinnacle of beauty, many women and girls are still attempting to achieve a thigh gap as a means of appearing dainty, delicate and thin. While one requires excessive squats, exercise or surgery, the other often requires starvation. Either way, our thighs and bottoms are noticeable: parts of us that feel metaphorically larger than we are.

Throughout history, wider hips have been used as indicators of female sexuality and fertility, despite there not being any scientific evidence to suggest wider hips make childbirth (or carrying babies) easier. Even women with so-called 'childbearing hips' have had difficult and traumatic deliveries, while women with narrower pelvic shapes have had easier births. Prehistoric figures, like the Venus of Willendorf which has exaggerated hips and breasts, demonstrate the association (if not obsession) many people – specifically, men – have with hips and female fertility.

Like other curvier parts of the female body, a lot of the distaste we feel towards our thighs and buttocks predominantly comes from a place of sexual shame, a shame that follows us from childhood. If our bodies aren't being eyed up for future motherhood, they are sexualised as placeholders in the meantime, with wider hips especially used as a measure of a woman's sexual appeal. The types of female bodies seen in music videos, advertising and pornography contribute to the idea a woman can only be sexy if she is curvy.

And yet despite this sexual shame, as I have shown throughout this book, often women choose to battle this sexualisation with *self*-sexualisation. You can now buy padded shorts to give the illusion of a bigger bum. Shapewear helps you achieve a 'smoother' profile, meaning no 'hip dips' – a perfectly natural yet new female 'problem' that women and girls are trying to eradicate. TikTok and YouTube tutorials show squat exercises to achieve a perkier, tighter bum. Denim companies send emails promising to give you the 'best butt of your life!'.

While I try to embrace my thighs – and this new standard, which is far easier to achieve than starvation – the comments I've received about them (and my bum) have probably been the hardest to shake off and forget. It's hard trying to undo years of social messaging around bigger thighs, where women constantly spent their time trying to lose weight around their thighs and bum and whose bodies were mocked ruthlessly via celebrities in the press. No matter how much I diet or exercise, my thighs are the parts of my body where fat doesn't drop off, the parts of my body embedded with cellulite, the parts that rub together and drip in sweat when it's hot outside. They feel sexual in ways that make me nervous.

Men have groped my bum in bars and in the street. One evening, when I was walking home, two older men grabbed me. One held my arms so I couldn't run and the other squeezed and groped my bum. As I yelled for them to get off, they called me a 'slag' and laughed while walking away. As a result, I've felt like the curvier I am around my thighs and bum, the more 'grabbable' I am. I am terribly conscious of wearing anything tight, as though I'm actively encouraging stares or hands.

For years, I fixated on and hated my thighs and bum. I couldn't understand how, unlike my friends, they were dimpled in cellulite, cellulite that stretched from my knees upwards and across my buttocks, dimpled across and underneath my skin like orange peel. I convinced myself that there must've been something terribly wrong with me, because only ugly women had cellulite. You merely needed to pick up a gossip magazine to see photo after photo of female celebrities on beaches, their cellulite zoomed in on in unflattering lighting, alongside captions expressing pure disgust.

As a result, since I was a teenager I have spent hundreds on cellulite reduction creams. I have brushed my thighs and bum with hard brushes, which I was told would help break down the fat and toxins. I have downed tons of water. I have avoided dressing rooms and their dreaded lighting while trying on clothing. I have avoided mirrors altogether. I have avoided beaches and wearing bikinis. I have turned the lights off when being intimate with a partner. I have spent hours exercising and squatting.

And nothing has fixed it. The cellulite has remained stagnant.

There are some parts of us that may not be societally perfect but which we have no other option than to accept. It's only been recently in my life that I've accepted my cellulite for what it is: a part of me. I do not love my cellulite. If there was an option to remove it entirely, I would choose to. But instead of fretting over it or wasting my energy on something I just can't change, I am focusing on the parts of myself I do like.

Whenever I post a photo online of me in a bikini, I guarantee that at least one man will comment on how 'sexy' and 'real' it is: that 'real' men like a 'real' female body such as mine.

When size zero was at its peak, one of the repeated key reassurances from women and men alike was that thin bodies weren't something men found attractive. Real men liked curves apparently, which I knew wasn't true, as I'd repeatedly been made fun of in my teens for being 'fat'. What they *actually* meant is that there are correct and incorrect ways of having curves and storing fat. There's fat which can appear sexy and grabbable and fat that appears unhealthy, dimply and 'gross'.

I've lost count of the times people have said that men like women with meat on their bones; that a thin body isn't something men find attractive. A lot of these comments come from women. While I'm sure many women say this with good intentions and to encourage a healthier approach to food, comments like these prove just how ingrained their internalised misogyny has become. At the time, I could never understand why these comments made me feel uncomfortable. They never made me feel good, and years after the hell of size zero and overcoming eating disorders I still don't like my body being given 'approval' by men. It makes me aware of how much men are staring and eyeing up my body; that unless they consider my shape beautiful or just right – carefully making sure I don't lose or gain too much weight – I will ultimately be unattractive.

But isn't that femininity in a nutshell? Femininity is essentially defined by how a man perceives it, not how a woman *herself* may define it. Our bodies are narrowed down to a specific ideal; our individualism slowly lost among the expectations of beauty.

Transgender women are also expected to perform a certain type of femininity to be fully accepted. Trans women cannot exist how they want to or dress how they want to without being compared to cis women. The 'accepted' transgender women are usually those that dress up in the most feminine (or sexy) outfits; whose facial features appear as petite and dainty as possible; whose breasts, thighs and bottoms are curvaceous and 'sexy' – all of which involve a host of cosmetic surgeries to achieve.

When Caitlyn Jenner announced her transition on the cover of *Vanity Fair*, she was commended on how 'lovely' and 'womanly' she looked. Although cosmetic surgery has advanced in ways that are incredible, I think about those transitioning without Caitlyn Jenner's budget; those who can't afford the procedures. How must they feel? Does the inability to afford gender-affirming surgery make them feel less womanly, less seen and less accepted?

I spoke with Maxine Heron, a 31-year-old trans woman and

advocate, public speaker and writer, about her relationship with femininity. I was curious as to how someone not born a cis woman may view femininity, womanhood and beauty pressures.

Maxine is an undeniably stunning woman: glossy hair, glowing skin and high cheekbones. She began taking puberty blockers at the age of twelve, which meant she managed to bypass much of her body's masculinisation. This early intervention has meant she appears outwardly feminine, as well as being gendered correctly; something she describes as 'passing privilege'. This, alongside her parents' support, is something she feels immensely grateful for.

'My access to puberty blockers – now banned in the UK for trans people under the age of eighteen both privately and via the NHS, despite being prescribed for other reasons to patients who aren't trans – played a key role in allowing me to slip under the radar with ease and be gendered correctly through my teens and into my adulthood,' she explained. 'At times, slipping under the radar effortlessly, I often feel unremarkable, and I hate that it is a privilege to feel unremarkable instead of unsafe as a trans person. I hate that a lot of the time it's the safety standard, given the transphobia I experience is online and not from strangers in person. While I feel incredibly grateful to have had access to this care, and to have been prescribed oestrogen since the age of thirteen, I do wonder sometimes if my privilege of being able to assimilate with mainstream society is upholding a pressure on trans people to become normative in presentation in order to be accepted or even in order to stay safe.'

I asked whether she thinks trans women who transition later in life or who don't have the support or financial means to have access to oestrogen, puberty blockers or surgery at an earlier stage (if perhaps ever) may feel less accepted by society or secure within themselves.

'Given I've only ever had one procedure and was privileged

enough to have my parents cover my medical transition, I can't speak on the experience of trans women who endure multiple procedures through their gender affirming care. But I know from speaking to my friends that it can be tricky to determine which physical features you naturally feel disdain towards due to your own discomfort within your body and which need to be amended in order to feel "normal" and safe within an increasingly transphobic society,' she said. 'My sex worker friends in particular feel pressure to exceed patriarchal beauty norms, both for their long-term stability and for their survival. The patriarchy is truly something none of us are free from.'

I asked whether she, herself, has ever felt the need to have more surgery; whether she feels the pressure so many women do to look beautiful.

'I'm fortunate to only ever have had one surgical procedure in my life, the one we refer to as *the* surgery many trans women get, so that procedure is not relevant to how strangers perceive me in public,' she said. 'The need to have surgery came from the dysphoria I felt alone and not from people pressuring me [to look womanly]. This procedure felt enough for me [to feel feminine].

'That said,' she added, 'looking like a conventional woman hasn't made me feel any safer from men, only from transphobes. A man did accost me in the street recently accusing me of being trans, simply because I didn't flirt back with him. Given many other women are being accused of being trans recently, and it's the first time this has happened to me fifteen years after my transition, I wonder what the worth in my "passing privilege" is if we're at a point where so many women in the street are being transvestigated, regardless of whether they're trans or not.'

Being accepted as a woman, it seems, cannot come from a place of simply 'being'. Trans women must appear *more* womanly, *more* beautiful than their cis counterparts to feel accepted or safe.

In Maxine's case, beauty can actually be a form of protection.

I asked Maxine how she feels within herself now – whether she is happy and confident in the woman she is today or whether she feels pressured to maintain never-ending beauty standards.

'During the times I didn't disclose my transness, I felt pressure to make the most of my youth and thinness, and I definitely put too much emphasis on these as defining traits about myself. Now I'm a few sizes bigger than I was and obviously older, yet somehow, I feel freer than I did a decade ago. I'm at a stage of looking into anti-ageing procedures and covering up my first greys, and at times I wonder how empowered I truly feel in these choices, but neither feels like punishment in the way dieting and my never-ending pursuit for hotness once did.'

And then she said something which resonated with me and my own journey completely.

'I feel decentering men in my understanding of beauty and of my worth has been one of my greatest gifts to myself. I haven't weighed myself in months, and I don't plan to. When people comment on my appearance online, I remember that their beauty standards are harmful to all of us – trans or not.'

Maxine's feminine traits have also previously been used to humiliate, dismiss and devalue her.

'Before I'd transitioned, at school, I'd often be bullied for having feminine traits, with comments such as, "*You're such a girl, go and get the sex change you've always wanted*", and then when I *did* transition – during a time of minimal trans representation and discourse and particularly after I came out online nine years after transitioning – the comments rolled in, saying, "*You still look masculine – you'll never be a woman.*" While strangers used to weaponise my femininity against me and now opt to hold my transness against me instead, I've made peace with the fact that it's impossible to win.'

Isn't that the case with all women? If we play into our feminine traits too much we're told we're annoying, girly and unserious. If we don't make any effort with our appearance, grow out our body hair or act angrily or aggressively, we're condemned for that as well. 'It's not attractive,' people will say when you don't appear, speak or act feminine enough, because beauty is not just a standard, but an expectation of our gender.

In the modern-day debate of women's-only spaces, we watch how men have the final say over who gets to define themselves as 'women'. The system makes it so anyone who doesn't appear as feminine as possible is rejected – even cis women. Because of these unfair requirements, there are even cases of tomboyish-looking cis women being thrown out of locker rooms simply for not appearing womanly enough.

Being rejected for not appearing feminine enough is something that cis women face: a rejection for being undesirable and unfuckable. If a cis woman appears too flat-chested, refuses to wear make-up, wears baggy clothes or refuses to conform to any other standards of acceptable female beauty, she can be accused of being trans or 'manly'. I, too, have received comments from trolls online asking if I'm 'secretly a man', all for having bushier eyebrows.

As masculinity is considered the default, it is possible to 'emasculate' a man. But there's no such equivalent for women, because femininity is already defined as something embarrassing and weak.

There are even correct and incorrect *emotions* to have as a woman, and life becomes a balancing act in knowing how to react correctly. Femininity does not grant a woman 'masculine' emotions like anger. For Black women, especially, anger is often used as a stereotypical racist trope. There is a particular portrayal of Black women in the media as unnecessarily aggressive, obnoxious and frightening. In films, Black women are depicted as angry, the nagging housewife or quick to start a fight. Black women are portrayed as animalistic in a way that white women can't *possibly* be.

Hips and thighs are considered as sexual as they are motherly. Hips indicate either undeveloped youthfulness, which many men will be attracted to, or motherhood and fertility, which many men will also value. Often, they represent an impossible standard, where virginal girls are seen as flawed for not yet being mothers, and mothers for not being virgins. Either way, a woman's hips and thighs often represent what a woman can offer *him*.

I think about the time a man told me I had perfect 'child-bearing' hips and how uncomfortable that made me feel. While it was presumably said as a compliment, I felt reduced to somewhat of a broodmare – my body ready in waiting to be impregnated by someone; it's ultimate purpose to become a mother.

I can't say I have felt an intense, burning desire to be a mother and this has been a problem within some of my relationships. As soon as I meet a friend's cute baby and feel the flicker of broodiness, a news story about the way women are treated will bring me back to reality and remind me of the world we are currently living in; the ways mothers are frequently undervalued and how raising children is often a thankless task. I am not alone. Across much of the Western world, and particularly since the pandemic when mothers were more likely than fathers to take care of children at home, women are feeling undervalued. While in the past it was seen as unfeminine to discuss the ways motherhood wasn't fulfilling, more recently women are choosing to stay childless, with mothers speaking openly about their grievances, mental load and pain.

Motherhood has been fetishised since the dawn of time, creating unrealistic pressures and expectations on women and making those who *aren't* fulfilled or happy feel ashamed and unfeminine. Often, society focuses on the idealised image and experiences of motherhood, while minimising the challenges, complexities and realities of what actual mothering entails. Discrimination against mothers is still highly prevalent in the workplace. There is still an expectation to snap back to our pre-pregnant bodies, to appear as though we never had babies to begin with. Women frequently take on the majority of housework. And many feel a total loss of identity once they give birth, as though their role as a mother has stolen the identity of who they once were.

The birth rate 'crisis' the West is currently experiencing isn't really to do with the birth rate. It's about control. Because if society truly cared about women not having children, they'd focus on *why* it's happening, not just the figures. They'd care about the women they're so desperate to get to reproduce. They'd help build systems that support mothers, systems which supply affordable childcare, flexible work schedules, paid parental leave, a healthcare system that values women and their reproductive rights. They would encourage shared domestic responsibilities. They would encourage a culture which doesn't punish women for being nurturing while also ambitious and career-orientated.

Perhaps the issue isn't that more women are choosing themselves over having children, but instead the fact that society hasn't done enough to make motherhood safe, sustainable, empowering or rewarding. It's not about women rejecting motherhood, necessarily; it's about women knowing they deserve better. It's about women refusing to lose themselves for a role that maybe doesn't fulfil or complete them.

And really – is that so bad?

*

In the early 2000s, when I was probably no older than fifteen, a family member commented on my 'J.Lo bum' as I walked ahead of them in jeans. This, I knew, was not a compliment, and when I turned to look at the person's face it confirmed it. I am not being sensitive when I say this. It was a secret dig at the fact I had gained weight. Referring to my bigger bum was a form of shame, a means of letting me know that I had let myself go.

Although Jennifer Lopez is a goddess and will be until the end of time, that family member might as well have come out and said point blank to my face that I was ugly. They might as well have said I was classless or even that I was a slut, because no self-respecting, high-end white woman would *ever* let herself get to a size like this or have thighs and a bum that stretched jeans. At most, I would've been a UK size 10–12.

Now that I'm older and have read and engaged with the works of Black theorists, I know there was likely a racist element behind the dig, too. White women in the early 2000s were not supposed to have curvy bodies. Back then, every white woman you saw in photos in the media looked nigh on skeletal; their bums flat, their hip bones protruding from their skin. To have an ounce of fat or a body part that jiggled meant you'd let yourself go.

Before social media, curvaceous thighs and buttocks were a characteristic limited to women of colour, women whose bodies we rarely saw in the media unless in hypersexualised music videos. For many Black women, having curvier thighs or bums meant they have been repeatedly sexualised and/or tormented for them for centuries.

Before the Brazilian butt lift (BBL) trend, Black women were frequently shamed for having bigger bums, their butts used as a means to racially depict or stereotype them. With white bodies seen as the standard to measure beauty by, curvier butts were seen as undesirable. In her book *Black Looks: Race and Representation*, bell hooks describes Black women's traits and how they have been portrayed sexually by society. In the chapter 'Selling Hot Pussy', she associates the racial stereotypes of Black female sexuality with sexual deviance and primitiveness.

Before the Kardashians made bigger butts an 'acceptable' – and even glamorous – beauty standard, women would frequently look in the mirror and ask whether their bums looked too big and endlessly tried to slim themselves into smaller jeans sizes. Big bums were associated with being 'fat', i.e. ugliness, i.e. the worst thing a woman could be. But there were also deep-rooted links to racism, with Black women's bodies seen as the 'other'.

Under capitalism, beauty can be plucked and picked from different cultures, creating a globalised ideal which many women can buy into and which white women especially can use as currency. While white women can choose to opt out of BBL surgeries or fat injections when the 'trend' of curves dissipates – which, knowing the ways women's body types and shapes frequently go in and out of fashion, is highly likely – Black women cannot opt out of their natural body shapes. The objectification of Black female bodies dates far back in history. In fact, during the slave trade, Black women's thighs and bums were considered 'exotic' and fascinating enough to be showcased, with women taken around the world in 'human zoos'. Saartjie Baartman, an enslaved woman from South Africa, was brought to Europe and paraded in 'freak shows' in London and Paris, where crowds would come to look at her naturally large buttocks. Baartman had what was called 'steatopygia', resulting in extremely protuberant buttocks due to a build-up of fat. Author Rachel Holmes, who wrote *The Hottentot Venus: The Life and Death of Saartjie Baartman*, explained how in the 1800s it was fashionable and desirable for white women to have large bottoms. Many women envied Baartman's natural body and the fact she didn't have to accentuate her figure. In fact, it is thought that the Victorian fashion of tight corsets and large, billowy dresses to accentuate the derrière was based on Baartman's body.

After her death age twenty-six in 1815, her brain, skeleton and sexual organs remained in a Parisian museum to be ogled over until 1974. It took until 2002 for her remains to be repatriated and buried in South Africa – a situation that was nothing short of grotesque. Baartman was treated like a freak show throughout her short life – and even in death.

In 2014, Kim Kardashian posed for a now infamous front cover of *Paper* magazine, balancing a champagne glass on her overexaggerated, protruding bottom. Some critics argued that the image was reminiscent of contemporary drawings of Baartman. The image actually referenced a 1976 photo of Black model Carolina Beaumont, taken by the same photographer, naked and in a similar pose.

The obsession with curvier bums and thighs is increasing. BBLs, where fat is transferred from parts of the body to the buttocks or thighs, are the most dangerous and deadly plastic surgery procedures a person can undertake, yet because of the pressures to have a curvier figure, led heavily by pornography and the need to be sexually desirable at all times, women are travelling worldwide to have them done. The International Society of Aesthetic Plastic Surgery's 2022 Global Survey reported over 800,000 buttock augmentation procedures worldwide (which includes both the buttock lift and buttock augmentation), with a 56.8 per cent increase from the previous year. And, despite the dangers, the British Association of Aesthetic Plastic Surgeons says BBL procedures are the fastest-growing type of cosmetic surgery, with its popularity increasing by 20 per cent year-on-year.

I watch videos of women in excruciating pain, their bodies leaking yellowish fluids and blood; flights from countries like

Mexico and Brazil where women are lying in aisles of planes, unable to sit down from the pain. And yet despite the physical agony, these women all have one thing in common. They believe it will make them more attractive.

The first time I realised bigger bums were in fashion was on a modelling job for a denim brand sometime around 2018, where I was made to wear butt-padding shorts beneath jeans. Considering I was the only model asked to wear them, I assume my bum wasn't considered juicy enough to sell the product – slightly ironic, considering much of my modelling career had been spent trying to slim my thighs and bum into nothingness. It was strange that while, in hindsight, my bum could never have been considered large, once bigger butts became culturally acceptable and sexy among white people, suddenly, it couldn't have been bigger.

As a white woman who had to tolerate cruel, degrading and objectifying comments about the size of my bum for much of my life, including from fellow women and soul-destroying model agents, I must admit that seeing bigger bums and thighs become acceptable has made me feel less conscious about my lower body. But acceptance shouldn't mean further sexual objectification. It is also important to acknowledge and reflect on where these beauty standards developed from and how we may be contributing to the further objectification and sexualisation of women of colour by allowing this sexualisation of butts to continue.

One Black woman I spoke to, now in her thirties, recalls tying her school jumper around her waist in school to stop boys from commenting on it. 'My bum felt bigger than me, somehow,' she said. 'Boys would constantly comment on it or grope me. I was the only Black girl in my class, and so I felt it fed the stereotype of Black female bodies. It is frustrating seeing white girls celebrated for having bigger bums now, when it used to be something used to mock women like me.'

*

To me, surgeries like BBLs are indicative of how violent beauty culture is: how these systems turn us into objects at our own expense. While we can literally see how recoveries from surgeries such as BBLs impact our *physical* health, no one seems to discuss the damage of these systems and expectations to our *psychology*.

In society's idea of physical perfection, there is no room for joy. Beauty is sold to us in both glossy and alluring ways but also in menacing and threatening ways: *use this, or else*. 'Or else' can mean 'you will be ugly'. It can mean 'nobody will want you'. Ultimately, it means you will lack male admirers and therefore have no societal or internal value.

'Beauty is pain,' people say, as a means of justifying the physical pain women have endured throughout centuries to maintain beauty standards. And this is true. Beauty can be cruel and unforgiving; something you must prove yourself to. A body that is punished or starving has become synonymous with the feminine body: a *beautiful* body at that. To be beautiful requires a huge amount of self-mutilation and self-surveillance. Beauty cannot mean anything unless it's painful.

'If suffering is beauty and beauty is love, she cannot be sure she will be loved if she does not suffer,' wrote Naomi Wolf in *The Beauty Myth*. We must repent for our aesthetic failures to have any worth or value.

Under capitalism, we have become marketable objects. There is always something we must change to prove ourselves worthy of love; a product or treatment that will *eventually* make us feel worthy. There is no part of the female body too small to be augmented, controlled or eradicated. During difficult times, such as a break-up, we often use beauty as a form of self-soothing, believing a glow-up or new haircut will make us feel better or make our exes see what they're missing out on.

Women have lasered and plucked their hairlines; waxed and threaded their body hair; worn corsets that led to fainting; bleached their skin until it caused irreversible damage; starved themselves to fit into tiny jeans; bound their feet to make them more dainty and delicate; undergone dangerous surgeries with long recovery times – all to feel worthy. Trends like weight-loss injections are fuelled by the same pressures and inadequacies women felt during the nineties and noughties era of heroin chic. These pressures are ultimately rooted in a place of shame.

Capitalism sold humans the idea that we must suffer at work to achieve success and enjoy our lives to the fullest. The same is true for beauty. Being beautiful is the ultimate prize for a life of dedication. The more we suffer for our looks, the more committed we are to them, the more we believe we will deserve them. Beauty will cure us. For example, if we wear a waist trainer for long periods throughout the day until we feel sick, we will achieve a tiny waist as a reward. The harder a skincare ingredient stings our face, the more it must work and the smoother our complexion will become. When did self-care become another word for self-harm?

Will I ever truly love my thighs with all my being? Will I ever truly feel comfortable with the dimples embedded within my upper thighs and bum? Be satisfied with the copious cellulite that litters across my skin? Have confidence to wear tiny shorts or skirts that shows it off in public? The truth is . . . no. Probably not. Not 100 per cent. I can *accept* the way my thighs look and I can learn to tolerate them as parts of my body. I can even learn to turn a blind eye to them while wearing a swimsuit on a beach for a few hours. But if there was an option to eradicate cellulite entirely and replace it with smooth skin, I would probably take it.

Having said that, I also know how various cellulite creams,

special massages and lasers do not eradicate this so-called 'problem' in the long run. Trust me, I've tried them. I spent years trying to reduce a problem that actually isn't much of a problem at all, but a man-made, capitalistic-driven issue pushed to sell beauty products.

Although it is estimated that 80–90 per cent of women have cellulite, including most women I know, I must somehow still convince myself that what I see on my skin is 'normal'. It is more uncommon to see a woman without it, and yet my brain, whose knowledge of female bodies (and female beauty) has long been formed from seeing countless retouched photographs, knows not of cellulite-ridden skin. Despite the similar bodies I see in daily life, I must still convince myself that I am not a freak: that having dimpled thighs like this is normal.

The vast majority of us do not have cellulite-free skin on our thighs. The majority of us do not have thigh gaps, or hips that appear perfectly round and smooth, or bums that are completely pert or round. But every one of us has a heart. Instead of focusing on the parts of ourselves that we think should be bigger or smaller, perhaps we should focus on that: the thing that has remained consistent, and loyal, and loving, overall.

Nowadays, the relationship I have with my hips and thighs is one of acceptance. It falls into a place of neutrality, where I neither detest them, nor celebrate how I look. The only way we can embrace self-love is to reject the idea that beauty will cure us. It means rejecting the misogynistic and patriarchal beliefs that teach us our value lies in our appearance and to embrace a love that extends past our external selves.

brain.

Killing yourself comes with a great deal of pressure.

There would be nothing more embarrassing than failing my own suicide. I could picture it now: the pitying glances from people at parties once I'd returned from hospital; the murmurs and whispers as I walked into a room; people gossiping over what could possibly have made me want to kill myself to begin with, and intrigue over whether I'd potentially attempt it again. Some people would view me sympathetically; others – *most* – as selfish.

Deciding on a method wasn't exactly straightforward. I knew I wanted to die but with so many options available, it became rather difficult to choose.

The first – and perhaps easiest – option I considered was an overdose. It seemed simple enough: if I mixed enough painkillers together with alcohol, I'd pass away in my sleep. The problem was, I don't drink very much. I'm a total lightweight. Most of the time, I'm sick from just a couple of glasses of wine and spend the entire night throwing up. If this plan didn't work – which could very well be the case as I've never been great at maths or measurements – the likelihood, Google told me, would mean dealing with a series of intense and debilitating stomach pains. That is, unless I managed to get to a hospital in time to get my stomach pumped, which would not only feel like a waste of my own time but also a terrible strain on the already struggling NHS.

There was also drowning. Drowning was meant to be relatively painless – peaceful, even, like a warm hug, according to those who'd survived it. Plus, I'd always been a bit of a water baby. My dad always enjoys telling the story of how he'd take me swimming as a toddler and how people would watch in amazement as this little girl, with her blow-up swimming bands, frilly Ariel swimsuit and fat tummy, would go up on to the highest diving boards, waving to her spectators below like she was performing some sort of show, before taking the plunge. Perhaps the water element could be somewhat of a poetic acknowledgement of my earlier life, a nod to when times were easier. It is a time I don't remember, though from what I've been told, I was *good* then; relatively well behaved and cute. But I didn't like the thought of my body being wrinkly and ghostly-white when I was found. My skin is pale enough as it is. Let's be honest: corpses aren't the prettiest things to look at. I wanted my body to appear relatively attractive, at least.

Jumping in front of a train was another option, but an ex-boyfriend's uncle killed himself that way and it genuinely sounded too gruesome for my liking – not to mention *permanent*. Once you took that jump, there was absolutely no going back. There were times I'd stand as close to the edge of a train track as possible, past the yellow lines, and close my eyes, feeling the hair blow off my face as a train screeched past. I often wonder how his uncle did it, the sheer guts it must've taken to have gone through with something like that. But in a lot of ways, I know *exactly* how he could've done it. When you feel absolutely nothing, it's easy to do anything.

No, this was something that needed to be done privately. Something ritualistic, almost, somewhere quiet and peaceful that wouldn't interrupt the lives of too many people. I was once stuck on a train that'd hit a person and overheard a couple in front of me tut at how selfish the victim had been; how these delays were going to make them late for their meeting. I didn't want to be *that* person – my life's ending associated with annoyance.

The paradox of being suicidal is the desperate urge to feel something while simultaneously not wanting to feel anything at all. For someone who didn't seem to care much about life, I longed desperately to feel something – *anything* – again. I think that's why my brain created the darkest, most vivid images it could: a way of acknowledging I still had senses, that I was still alive. I'd imagine the sensation of a razor blade against my wrists, dragging the metal through my skin until it hit a vein or artery; would the blood splurt across the room like a horror movie or dribble slowly down my arm towards my elbow? When I stayed in hotels, as I often did, I pictured jumping from the window of my room, the way my bones and skull would crack against the concrete, my body collapsed and broken in various angles on the pavement below.

After much consideration, I concluded that I'd hang myself from the banister of my new house, which I'd just finished painting a nice shade of dark, glossy green. If I jumped from the right stair, there'd be just enough of a gap for me to swing and break my neck.

Compared to most ways to go, hanging had a pretty high success rate. Seventy per cent, according to the internet. I decided I could put a Spotify playlist of all my favourite songs on as I did it. Make an event of it. Have a toast to my life beforehand; maybe a few snacks from M&S.

Like a lot of terraced houses, the house I'd recently bought became *boiling* in the summer – so hot you had to leave all the windows and doors open. I'd spent days painting the walls wearing nothing but my underwear, dripping in sweat. All this hard work seemed an utter waste now. I began to wonder how long it would take for someone to find me. Days? Weeks? As a single woman that was the element about my life that depressed me the most. Who would raise the alarm? By the time I was found, my body would probably be rotting, and the summer heat would mean the smell was horrific.

I knew buying a house in London as a single woman was something to be proud of, something millions of young women, let alone men, aspire to. I had achieved all of this from the way I look. My career was going from strength to strength. I was at fabulous parties with fabulous people and wearing fabulous clothes. I'd started cultivating a dream life for myself, becoming the type of woman I used to draw as a child in my notepads. I was a single, jet-setting, party-going, financially independent woman! What could be better than that?!

On paper, there was absolutely nothing worth killing myself over and that's what made me feel even worse. I can't tell you how ashamed I felt. I was achieving everything I wanted, achieving things that *so* many people want, yet I felt nothing about anything, anyone or life. I was merely existing and playing the game, knowing the right times to smile or drop a humorous comment, disassociated from reality while floating within the realms of human consciousness.

My brain became my prison, a constant whirl of feelings and emotions I couldn't process properly; a dark, misty fog engulfing me whole. I was beyond fatigued, often waking up at two o'clock in the afternoon and then back in bed by eight. I could no longer run from my thoughts. My memories were catching up with me.

I know there'll be people reading this rolling their eyes, tutting at a woman who doesn't know the meaning of struggle. And that's what made me feel even more terrified to speak up about how I was feeling. I am incredibly privileged for many, many reasons.

One of my best friends had passed away from cancer during lockdown and all he'd prayed for was for some extra time on earth. I'd seen how desperately he'd wanted to live; how devastated he was for not getting to achieve or experience all the 'normal' things in life, like marriage and children. And yet here I was, wanting to throw all those possibilities away. I felt utterly, utterly guilty and ungrateful for feeling the way I did, yet remarkably at peace in the thought of joining him.

I wasn't going to be swayed from my plan.

I felt awful for the person who was going to find me. I knew it wouldn't be pleasant. But life goes on, doesn't it? There'd be an initial shock, obviously, but people would move on. Time heals everything. That's what people tell you during difficult times: that the more time passes, the longer you sit with things, the easier everything gets.

Everyone is forgotten eventually. That's life. Soon, I would be nothing more than a body on a slab; a statistic; a pile of ashes. And before long, a distant memory, just as I'd hoped.

I have never felt truly deserving of love, yet I *so* want to be, and somehow, even when people try showing me love it barely fills the void. There is a hollowness in my body, a gaping hole that has been scraped or carved out. Something is missing, and I have spent a lifetime figuring out what to fill it with.

I've sought that missing piece externally: by being desired by the latest fling; from people-pleasing; from buying things; from hitting milestones in my career. I have starved, eaten, purged, drunk, numbed, partied, bought, bled my way through life in an attempt at discovering what that missing part of myself needs.

Love, I think, is what will fix me. It is easier to search for love within things or other people than it is within me. External validation feeds the vacuum in my soul, if only for a minute, proving I am, indeed, worthy.

At this stage of my journey, aged thirty-two, I do not know that attention doesn't mean love, that attachment doesn't mean connection and that the bare minimum from someone isn't effort. I don't understand that caring about someone won't automatically mean they'll care about me or that intense chemistry doesn't necessarily mean we're right for each other. All I know is that if I love someone hard enough or morph into the woman they want me to be, that one day my efforts will pay off; that *eventually* someone will notice how great I am and that they will love me and then all the pain or invalidation I feel about myself will suddenly disappear.

I want – no, *need* – someone to find my heart and take care of it. The media has taught me that a man will protect me – which, ironically, is a far cry from my actual experiences with them. Like in Disney movies, I grew up believing that someday my prince will come along and save me; that you can, of course, be a strong and independent woman but that your life will ultimately lack meaning unless you're wanted, or chosen, by a man.

Men are supposed to be our saviours; our protectors. They are supposed to rescue us and keep us from harm. Despite being taught to be vigilant and to keep our wits about us at any given time, there is still hope that the *right* man will protect us from other men out there.

Perhaps I put so much emphasis and urgency on being in a relationship because without a partner I don't know what else there is to live for; what my purpose in the world is. Every time a friend gets engaged or becomes pregnant, I fall further and further into solitude, as though I am failing. Family and friends are forever asking me who I'm dating; if there's been any luck on dating apps; if I ever want to get married and have children. While people tell me it's OK to be single, society affirms it is not. I try to pretend that I am OK with being single, but truthfully it leaves me feeling sad, as though I am doing womanhood wrong.

Isn't the purpose of life to love? To share the best and worst of times with someone; to explore the world together; to take care of each other? Being in a relationship not only feels like a goal, but also my last hope; the very thing that will give my life meaning.

I have felt lonely for an incredibly long time, lonely in a way I find hard to directly pinpoint or describe. I feel alone even when I am not. It's hard to explain loneliness when you are constantly surrounded by people, whether that's at dinner with friends, at loud and vivacious parties, among a city crowd, in a WhatsApp group chat or at a family gathering. No matter what I'm doing or who I'm around, nothing makes me feel complete. I don't know what 'feeling complete' *means*, exactly, only that I long for it.

In the past, I have felt so physically lonely that an accidental brush of a hand on a Tube carriage has sent sparks flying throughout my body. A massage has the ability to bring me to tears, the traces of their fingers lingering on my skin for hours. I have booked a hair wash at a salon just to feel another human being's touch; wrapped my thighs around a pillow in bed just to pretend it's a partner; listened to podcasts as though I am having a one-on-one conversation; deliberately ordered a takeaway in the hope the driver will speak to me or ask me how my day has gone. I feel disconnected from everyone and everything, as though I am watching every interaction, every event, every conversation, from above.

But this current version of loneliness – this cavernous, empty sensation I feel within the depths of my body – is like no other. I am surrounded by people daily yet feel zero connection to them.

My romantic relationships – the very thing I believe will fix me – haven't fixed me at all, instead leaving me with more questions. I cling to these people in the hope that they can give me whatever it is I need, yet they happen to be people so emotionally unavailable, so choosy in the ways they give their affection, that they only add to my problems. I can never understand how I'm never enough.

I feel almost robotic in my behaviour: knowing the correct time to smile; how to sound legitimately OK when I tell people, 'I'm fine!' I know how to play the game, even though I feel like an outsider peering in on my conversations and relationships. After any interaction, no matter how fleeting they may be, I somehow find myself feeling more isolated than I did before, sinking further and further into a pit of nothingness.

There was a family intervention.

For a long time, part of me hoped that someone, or something, would miraculously appear from somewhere and bless me with whatever it is my soul yearned for. But this godlike figure never arrives. Not in a mystical sense, anyway. Hope instead appeared via the people closest to me: my family.

It turned out I wasn't very good at hiding my depression. My thoughts were etched across my face, impossible to hide. I had tried dealing with it for as long as I could. I'd tried absorbing ways of 'thinking yourself better'; bought into the idea that a bit of positive thinking and words of affirmation would be the miracle cure to my depression. 'Stay positive!' may act as an occasional comfort blanket but eventually left me feeling cold. In a world of preachy self-love messaging, it's hard to admit that, sometimes, the only thing your brain needs is chemicals.

After much persuasion, I tried calling my local GP surgery to ask to see an emergency doctor.

'There's about a three-week wait to see a doctor at the moment,' said the receptionist on the phone. 'Would you like me to pencil you in?'

Three weeks?! Just to speak to someone? I genuinely couldn't see myself lasting that long. Besides, even if I *did* wait that long, there wasn't necessarily a guarantee I'd be given the antidepressants anyway.

Images of my pale, limp body swinging from the banister kept replaying in my head.

'Can I please just get some antidepressants?' I asked anxiously. I am embarrassed by my vulnerability, embarrassed to be begging. But I'm also scared. Scared that they're not taking me seriously enough; scared that I don't sound ill enough; scared that I'll be stuck in this cycle for ever. Scared that my demons will take over, and I will actually do the unthinkable.

'Only a doctor can prescribe you those,' she replied, matter-of-factly.

I knew, in my heart, that unless I sought help elsewhere, I would do it. I would kill myself. I'd already planned it. I knew the day, the time; the notes I would send to people thanking them for their friendship during my time on earth; the songs I would ask to be played at my funeral.

I needed to do something – and fast.

Dr Patil's office is small and uninspiring, hidden at the back of what would've been a townhouse once upon a time in Victorian London. It is clinical-looking and dull. The room is a lacklustre shade of white, with bits of cheap paint peeling off around the windowsill. Aside from his desk and chair it has nothing in it except for a single leather armchair, a rubber potted plant and a box of tissues.

Dr Patil is an expert in the brain and trauma. For the amount

I'm paying him for this 45-minute psychiatric assessment I should certainly hope he is. Money talks, and it has allowed me to see him within a couple of days.

I am grateful to have the funds to see a psychiatrist on Harley Street. Money is one more thing my body has provided me with. I am fortunate to be able to see him at such short notice. I think about the people who can't, the people who feel they have no choice but to end their lives because of the lack of funding, the long waiting times and limited availability of the NHS's mental health service. Even amid my depression, I know I am one of the lucky ones.

I am fifteen minutes late to our meeting and out of breath; my hairline beaded in sweat. The reason I am late is, ironically, because of a suicide on the train tracks.

'I'm so sorry I'm late,' I say breathlessly. 'I'm never late. I never am. Someone killed themselves on the train track.'

Dr Patil doesn't seem bothered at all. Then again, why would he? He's making £750 from me alone this afternoon. He's already taken out his notepad and clicked his pen, peering at me above his glasses.

'No need to apologise,' he says, and he seems like he genuinely means it. 'That's a horrible thing to have to deal with. A suicide is always a traumatising thing.'

'Hardly,' I reply. I don't even feel bad about saying it. In the selfishness of my depression, nothing except my own pain matters. Why would I care about a stranger's suicide when I have been busy planning my own?

Dr Patil is a tiny man with a kind face, dressed smartly in a shirt and tie. He is smiling at me sympathetically. He appears welcoming, but I can't fully relax. I know, from the second I start speaking, that he will be analysing every move, every quip, every comment I make, and I feel uneasy at being this exposed.

'Well, all these little dark or traumatic things we deal with or see day-to-day can slowly add up into one *big* thing.'

I've decided I'm not sure I like being analysed, and I'm not sure I agree that some random stranger's suicide has the ability to impact me to such great depths. Am I supposed to care? I don't mean that sarcastically, I mean it genuinely. If I don't care about a stranger's suicide, am I a sociopath of some sort? Or am I just inherently selfish? As human beings living today, our brains are constantly bombarded with bad news after bad news, scary image after scary image. What makes today's incident any different?

'You see, these traumatic little things we experience or unconsciously absorb might not *seem* like a big deal at the time, but eventually all these negative experiences add up, and then you find yourself somewhere like . . . *this*.' He gestures around the room.

Dr Patil is being kind and understanding and I do not like it. I do not feel worthy of it. *I will not cry*. I physically detest being vulnerable and talking about my feelings. I always have. I tell myself that I will be composed throughout this session.

'So, on a scale from one to ten, how happy are you right now?'

'A one.' I pause. 'Maybe a two, on a good day.'

'When was the last time you felt like a ten?'

'I don't think I've ever been a ten.'

Dr Patil scribbles in his notepad.

'What do you think would make you happy?' he asks.

I don't have to think too hard about this. I have thought about this for a long time.

'A relationship,' I respond, which although an honest response, I already sense is the wrong answer.

'Why is that so important to you?'

'I don't know.'

I do know.

'Well, you must have a reason.'

I'm embarrassed to admit the reason.

'Because then I won't be lonely.'

Dr Patil continues to scribble in his A4 notepad, licking his fingers while intermittently flipping the pages. I don't *want* to keep talking, yet I feel as though I must fill this silence with commentary. I'm not even sure if what I'm saying is meaningful.

I continue to talk.

'Because I don't want to be alone. I'd like someone to share my day with. I'd like to talk about my problems with someone. I want to go out for dinners with them or go on trips with them.'

Dr Patil jots all this down on his notepad, then looks up.

'But a relationship isn't a necessity,' he says. 'It's not going to solve your problems.'

I stare at him as though he is talking nonsense. To me, it *is* nonsense. I feel as though I am being judged for wanting, *needing*, the most basic thing in life: *love*.

'A relationship would be *nice*,' he adds. 'Yes, it would be nice to do all those things and to have someone to spend time with. But you don't *need* a partner. Being in a relationship will not fix how you feel about yourself.'

So people keep telling me.

'There is a difference between having a partner that adds value to your life, versus having a partner just because you don't want to be alone.'

I spot the wedding ring on his left hand. I am genuinely sick and tired of married people telling me that it's OK to be single. It's easy for them. They do not understand the difficulties of modern dating; how impossible it is to find genuine love nowadays, in a world where you constantly need to perform.

'I know you don't think I'm right,' he says. 'But believe me, you *can* be happy on your own. And being happy on your own is where we need to get you to.'

But I'm not sure I *want* to be on my own. I truly do not believe that I can ever be happy as a single woman, because since my late teens I've rarely been by myself. When I am alone, my thoughts and memories consume me, swallowing me into a deeper pit of anxiety and despair. I do not trust myself to be alone with my thoughts. I seek romantic relationships and attention from men as a means of keeping myself occupied; so as not to explore the pain within myself.

It feels dangerous and unsafe to sit in silence. And so a man – *any* man – acts as a distraction. Getting them to love me gives my life meaning, even if I don't particularly *want* to be with them. Without the constant need to perform for a man, to be wanted by one, I don't know who I am, and I don't think I care to figure it out.

Anyway, is it so wrong and unfeminist to want to be desired by a man? To want nothing more than to become the center of someone's attention and affections? Because it is all I want. I want a man to crave me, to need me, to devour me whole. I *want* a man to objectify me, to sexualise me, to have his hands over my body in public. I want people to know I am his and his alone. I am willing to go to whatever lengths to become whoever he wants me to be, just so he will stay.

'How do you feel physically?' Dr Patil asks.

I explain how I feel as though I'm constantly supporting an invisible weight; a thick, heavy pressure that's weighing down my heart. When I walk upstairs, I wheeze. *Everything* is tiring. I am exhausted in a way no amount of sleep manages to fix.

He asks me if I've lost weight. I have. People are commenting on my weight loss regularly, though instead of seeing it as a concern, the majority are complimenting me on it, saying how great I look. As a 'curvy' model, I am now losing jobs because of it. I have no appetite whatsoever. Even lifting a fork feels difficult. I am crying out to be noticed, and nobody seems to see me at all.

Scribble, scribble, scribble.

'And how do you feel mentally?' he asks.

I tell him the truth. I want to die.

'Are you planning on hurting yourself?' he says.

This is a trick question. If I say yes, the likelihood is that I will be sent to a hospital or psychiatric unit. The first rule of suicide is not letting people know you want to commit suicide, otherwise you will be swayed from your plan altogether. I am still unsure whether or not I want to cancel my plans. Admitting your feelings is a balancing act between being truthful, versus being hospitalised.

'No,' I reply, honestly.

Well. Not today, anyway.

'Why do you think you're so depressed?' he asks.

I truly don't know what *the* defining moment is that led me here. If I were to sit back and think about it, there could be many. This is why I try not to think about them. This is why I distract myself with anything other than my feelings.

I suppose, if someone were to view my recent history, one might assume my depression is due to my most recent break-up. I broke off my engagement to a man who had been cheating on me since the very beginning; with exes, married women and so-called female 'friends'. Even now, it feels exhausting going into detail about him. Our relationship could be an entire book in itself.

As a result, I have been left to deal with the aftermath of it all: calling up the registry office to cancel the reception; cancelling the cake order; cancelling the dress fittings; trying to sell my engagement ring for cash, because he owes me a ton of money. One of the most annoying things about this situation is that I discovered his cheating a mere six weeks after getting engaged. People are still congratulating me on my engagement at events, then questioning why I am no longer wearing my engagement ring.

I feel like a failure. As much as he was in the wrong and as much as this is not my doing, I assume people will think this whole drama is, somehow, my fault. I *must* have done something wrong, something to turn him off, otherwise he wouldn't have done this. His cheating is an admission that I am unlovable, undesirable, unmarriable. It is humiliating. Shameful.

Still, he isn't the worst man I've ever dated.

This is my second broken engagement. The first was to a man in his thirties a few years prior who, upon reflection, had most definitely groomed me as a teenager, albeit over eighteen. I see this after entering my thirties myself and feeling repulsed at the idea of dating someone in their teens, let alone sleeping with them.

I idolised him. I clung on to him as though he was the most intelligent, wonderful person on earth. But I'd rushed into that relationship after my first, 'proper' relationship at eighteen with a heavily tattooed gang member – a man I would later discover to be a paedophile. I found a photo album containing photos of him and a pretty, twelve-year-old girl in bed together. He would describe and romanticise their relationship almost as a Romeo and Juliet love story; one where her mother found out about them sleeping together and cruelly kept them apart. In my naivety, immaturity and, admittedly, jealousy, I believed him. I was too scared not to. He would lock me in his bedroom, refuse to let me have contact with my friends or family, cut me off from the world. He would make me wear babyish underwear, I'm sure as a means of fulfilling his twisted sexual fantasies. One of the most frightening experiences with him was when he made me get on to my knees, hold out my hands and choose which finger he should break. He did a multitude of things that I find difficult to speak about, even now.

Dr Patil then asks me to picture myself as a child. He asks me where I am, what I am wearing, what is happening around me. Answering this comes easily to me. For some reason, I have pictured this scene many times in the past. I am about seven, dressed in my school uniform and dancing in front of our hallway mirror to the Spice Girls. We are late for school. My mother is stressed. My sister is crying.

He then asks me what major incident happened to me at that time.

'There was one thing . . .' I say but immediately feel embarrassed to go further. Still, he encourages me to.

I mention how, aged seven, I was touched, inappropriately, by a neighbour.

'It wasn't rape, though,' I am quick to add.

'So you were molested?' he says. 'You were molested by a paedophile?'

I have never allowed myself to admit this story before. Before I know it, I am telling him story after story after story, the memories rolling off my tongue, the memories as painful as the experiences were when they happened. This is the first time I've truly acknowledged my pain. I don't think my brain can handle it.

Once the tears come, they don't stop. I am talking so fast, going into such depths, that I notice Dr Patil struggling to keep up with the note-taking. Between the blubbering, I'm not even sure he fully understands what I'm saying.

When I finally come up for air, dabbing my eyes with a tissue, he looks at me sympathetically.

'The things you mention are traumatic,' he says. 'You have experienced a *lot* of trauma.'

I've never considered my experiences traumatic. They're sad. Unfortunate. But *traumatic*? It feels too serious, too *real*, to claim 'trauma' as a word of my own. I find myself questioning my memories, wondering whether I am blowing my experiences out of proportion, even though, in my heart, I know I am simply recounting exactly what happened to me. Though what I am saying is entirely truthful – parts of my history which, compared to other women, may simply come down to being unlucky – claiming these incidents as trauma feels like an insult to the people who have experienced more traumatic things, and I feel a monstrous sense of guilt because of it.

'Have you noticed that all of the stories you mention involve men?' he asks.

I leave Dr Patil's office with a prescription for antidepressants and sleeping tablets. I am told that sleep is one of the first steps towards feeling better. Despite sleeping all of the time, Dr Patil tells me it is the *quality* of sleep that will help in the beginning.

'Just sleep,' he says. 'Allow yourself twelve hours, if needs be.'

I have no sooner left the pharmacy, armed with bags of medication boxes, than He texts.

'Are you free for a FaceTime tonight?'

I can't quite believe it. My heart soars. I can practically feel the neurons in my brain ignite with sparks. I feel excited again. His attention has given me something to live for.

See? I didn't need antidepressants! This is a case of me being overdramatic. I can relax again now. All I needed was Him.

'Hey, baby.'

It has been over two weeks since I last heard from David, the man I have managed to convince myself will be my future husband. Despite being clinically ill, I could be forgiven for thinking this to be true. After all, this is the man who, after one week, told me he wants us to move to Los Angeles together; wants me to meet his teenage son; tells me he's never felt this way about a woman before; tells me he'd like to father my children someday; tells me about the trips we're going to go on this summer; has spent time engraving my name into a silver Zippo lighter – a handmade, bespoke gift, he tells me, reserved for the people he loves most.

I'm still not entirely sure what love is. I don't know what it's supposed to look like; how it's supposed to feel; how it's supposed to *make* me feel. All I know is that it's the cure to my problems. The cure to my loneliness. It will provide me with a sense of belonging. That the more I show someone what a great person I am, the more they will love me.

In the last two weeks since David's sudden disappearance, my mood has become lower and lower. I can barely eat. I feel rejected, confused and alone. Part of the reason I put off seeing a doctor for my mental health was because I genuinely believed that once David reappeared, he would save me.

As soon as we were back together again, I would be fine. I was sure of it.

David and I met on a dating app a couple of months before my doctor's appointment. It has been a whirlwind romance, far quicker than I can keep up with. From the second we met, we were inseparable. We spent every day together, every night together. He showered me with the attention I wanted – the attention I *thought* I wanted. I've repeatedly ignored my gut about the intensity of his actions because this is what love is, isn't it? No man would say the things he says and do the things he does unless he really likes you. Besides, if a man bombards you with as much attention as this, why should I think to challenge it? If anything, his attention is an honour.

He showered me with gifts; he introduced me to some of his family over lunch; he told me how we're going to make this relationship work in the long run. My mind, heart, flesh, body are for him and him only. I even bear the remnants of bruising from his fingers and teeth marks on my skin; physical memories from our passionate – albeit too rough, for my liking – lovemaking.

This is what a relationship should feel like, right? It should feel all-encompassing. You should crave them like nothing else in the world matters. They should feel like a drug you can't get enough of. It cannot possibly be love unless they play on your mind all hours of the day; that unless you feel an ache or anxiousness in the pit of your stomach when you don't hear from them, let alone at the thought of them, your feelings can't possibly be real.

Towards the end of our romantic week, he tells me he has to go away for work for a couple of months. *No need to worry*, he assures me, presumably seeing the anxiety on my face and the fear in my eyeballs. We will make sure to see each other every couple of weeks and to call and FaceTime in between then. After this work trip, we will be together once and for all.

Once we separate, it's as though everything he said, everything he promised, had been a total fantasy. He went from being so over the top with his affections and attention to suddenly withdrawing them with a jolt. He is pulling away, his calls becoming less frequent, and I don't understand why. We are supposed to meet again in person soon, yet despite his promises of the future, we're slowly losing touch.

I meticulously follow the advice of online relationship experts and self-proclaimed 'femininity experts' and YouTube tutorials in the hope of keeping him interested. I always wait for him to contact me first, and when we do speak, I tell him how proud I am of all his hard work and how wonderful he is. Getting a man to be obsessed with you, I am told, is about making sure he feels like a man. It's about giving him space.

But here he is, after two weeks of no contact, calling me on FaceTime as promised. *Finally.*

As soon as our phones connect, I can tell something has changed. Even through the screen, I sense an energy shift in the way he's talking. It's cocky almost, and I'm not just talking about his dick that has, for some unbeknown reason, suddenly appeared in full view on my phone screen.

'Oh – wow,' I say, out of shock. 'I wasn't expecting that.'

'I thought you'd like that,' he says in his best seductive voice, which is strange, because I'm not sure I do like it.

He is in a hotel bathroom, his voice echoing off the tiles. The bathwater is running. He climbs into the bathtub, positions the phone on the edge of it, then crouches into the bath water and turns the tap off. As I'm talking – I'm not sure what about, exactly – he stares at his reflection on the screen, using it as a mirror, and begins picking his teeth with his fingernails.

Picking. His. Teeth. I have spent the previous hour finding a cute but still sexy dress to wear for our FaceTime date, applied enough concealer to cover the dark circles under my eyes, a thick layer of foundation to mask the dullness of my skin and lip liner to remind him of how kissable my lips are. I have put effort into seeing him, though he hasn't seemed to notice or told me I look nice. And rather than appearing excited to speak to me, he has simply fitted me into the convenience of his bath-time routine.

But my feelings don't matter. It doesn't matter that he's making me feel disrespected, unheard, pathetic or, quite frankly, disgusted. What matters is that I *finally* have his attention, no matter how short or fleeting that may be.

David is not listening to me whatsoever. The more I talk, the dumber I feel. I find myself stumbling over words out of nervousness, trying to think of something interesting to say, something funny or endearing or shocking that will keep him entertained so he'll remain on the phone. But I may as well be talking to a brick wall. I am certainly not speaking to a human being. He is certainly not treating *me* as one. I can practically feel my body shrinking, my brain telling me I need to cut this man off; my heart not having the confidence to do so.

I tell myself he is acting this way because he feels comfortable around me. I make him so comfortable that he feels he can be fully naked around me. Being naked around someone is an intimate act. I certainly wouldn't want to come across as difficult or hurt his feelings by calling him out on his rudeness, let alone have him hang up on me. Most of all, I don't want him to dislike me or to see me as a prude. I want to be one of those women who is totally cool with however a man chooses to behave, because to be tarnished alongside uptight girls would be one more character trait to be ashamed of. I don't care to think that the women who set boundaries with men are actually the women with self-respect.

I begin losing concentration on whatever it is I'm telling him about because I realise I have waited two weeks to speak to a naked man picking his teeth in a bathtub, who murmurs 'yeah' or 'mmm' in the moments his brain deems it correct to do so. He does not care for what I have to say. Just fifteen minutes into our 'conversation', he proceeds to stand up in the tub, his (admittedly) large, wet, soapy dick in full view in the FaceTime frame, and runs his hands across his six pack, admiring his body from different angles in the bathroom mirror. Still focusing on his own reflection, he wraps a towel around his waist, slides his fingers through his damp hair and picks up the phone so I'm now focused on his face.

'OK, darlin',' he says. 'I'm running late for dinner with some friends. I've got to go now. But I can't wait to see you. I'll talk to you soon, yeah?'

He blows a kiss to the camera. And before I can say anything back, he is gone.

I would like to say I finally saw David for what he was: a huge, narcissistic love-bomber. I would like to say I never spoke to him again. But in the depths of my utter desperation, we know this not to be true.

The conversation I'd had with him on FaceTime had left me feeling even more depressed and anxious. Why was he acting so cold towards me? It didn't make sense. My interest in him hadn't waned. My appearance hadn't changed. Why wasn't he interested any more?

To make matters worse, David is back in London at this point. I have seen it on his Instagram stories. He has been here for a couple of days and hasn't contacted me at all, despite promising me he would. Since our last conversation in the bathtub, I can't help but feel my presence annoys him. I am nervous to reach out to him in case I irritate him and am fearful that he may reject or ghost me. *I need to be cool.*

The antidepressants remain unopened in their paper bag. After the amount of effort I put into getting them, I have somehow managed to convince myself that taking these pills may not be so good for me after all. For someone who was hell-bent on killing herself, I am now, ironically, concerned these tablets could kill me: that because they provide synthetic, chemically induced happiness, they can't possibly be good for my well-being. And ultimately, I remain convinced that eventually, as they have done previously, these dark feelings will pass.

'*Hey. I'm here. Wanna meet up?*'

I stare at the text.

My brain says NO. You should absolutely NOT meet with him. But my heart says otherwise. I still have hope that by seeing me, he will realise what he's missing and our fairytale will resume.

I barely leave it for a couple of minutes before texting back.

'*Sure!*' I reply, trying to act as nonchalantly as possible.

Why have I done this to myself?

I am sat in a restaurant the following day, waiting for David to show up. He is over fifteen minutes late. When we'd spent our romantic week together, he'd always been early. Now I'm unsure whether he'll turn up at all.

When he *does* eventually show up, he's even more distant. Cold, even. I can tell that simply being here with me feels like a great deal of effort.

We order food, trying to make small talk. He repeatedly checks his phone, the waitress's bum, the girls at a nearby table.

'You look skinny,' he says.

His phone rings, and he answers it. It's a male friend. *Thank God it's not a girl,* I think to myself. *I have nothing to worry about.* The volume is so loud that I can hear the conversation, though I'm pretending I can't.

'Yo dude!' the person yells down the line. 'You wanna go out tonight with some girls I met?!'

David looks at me and quickly tries to press the volume button down on the side of his phone.

'Er . . . er . . . yeah! Sounds great, man,' he says. 'I'm just out with a friend at the moment. Call you later.'

He hangs up.

'That was a friend,' he says.

I sit there, numb. I want to cry. Maybe he can sense how bad I'm feeling, as he reaches for my hand across the table.

'I've missed you,' he says. He stretches across the table and kisses me, though I notice his eyes scanning the restaurant as though he's trying not to get caught. 'God, I've been so horny.'

'Really?' I reply. This gives me hope. Maybe he does fancy me after all? I feel honoured at the thought.

'Yeah,' he replies. 'It's been like . . . so long since I last had sex.'

I notice what he means. That I am not the last person he'd slept with.

And then, from the corner of my eye, I notice him checking out a dating app. He isn't even attempting to hide it. He switches to WhatsApp, a list of ongoing conversations with girls, one after the other after the other.

Even I, the person who Dr Patil described as having 'chronically low self-esteem', can see I am doing myself a disservice by being here.

I leave. I don't even say bye. My legs feel shaky from embarrassment and hurt. I feel like the rug has been pulled from under me.

For the first time I can remember, I choose me. As soon as I get home, I take my first antidepressant and sleeping tablets – and sleep and sleep and sleep and sleep and sleep.

A week or so after I last saw him, I am back for a check-up with Dr Patil. Antidepressants need constant monitoring. If I take too high a dosage they can lead to mania – a manic syndrome often seen in people with bipolar, with extreme highs and over-active and erratic behaviour.

It is humbling, if you think about it, that such a small white rectangle holds the power of rewiring my entire brain; the ability to stabilise my emotions and feelings. Within a week, I have noticed my brain changing. I wouldn't describe myself as happy, per se, but I am better. My mood can be best described as flatline, like that of a hospital heart monitor. I experience no lows. No highs. My mood is simply . . . *stable*.

I do, however, suddenly have zero libido. For someone whose identity more or less revolved around men wanting her, it was strange to have no desire to act, think or behave sexually whatsoever. I had no desire to flirt, to dress sexily, to masturbate.

For the first time in my adult life, I genuinely didn't give a fuck whether I was seen as desirable or not. There was no internal questioning – *does he fancy me?* No need for male validation. I literally felt nothing. And it felt like a complete and utter *relief*.

I was suddenly aware of sex in a way I hadn't been before. I noticed the way sex impacts everyday scenarios. It was fascinating to watch male and female dynamics play out from afar – not just the sexual interactions but via subtle power differences between the sexes. I noticed how women both seek male attention and are fearful of it.

On the Tube, I watched one woman find a seat further down the carriage, trying to get away from a burly group of obnoxious football fans sitting near her, their chests puffed out arrogantly like pigeons. Later, on another Tube carriage, I watched a woman reapply her lipstick in a hand mirror and puff up her hair, glancing over at a couple of good-looking men opposite in the hope they noticed her. I spotted the nervousness on a woman's face as an attractive woman walked past her and her boyfriend, trying to spot whether he was checking her out and if so, figuring out how she should react. I could see her measuring herself against the other woman, wondering whether she is prettier, what the other woman has that perhaps her partner desires. At lunch, I noticed a single woman dining with her male co-workers, trying to be taken seriously by them, hoping to be treated as 'one of the guys' or perhaps more importantly, as one of the team. At a bus stop, a pretty girl locked eyes with me for reassurance as a drunk man stumbled around us asking for money; we were checking with one another to see if we were safe or not or whether we should move. I noticed the women who clothe themselves head to toe so as to be invisible to the male gaze; the women who show their cleavage for male attention; a group of girls trying to pretend that a group of boys aren't looking at them.

This sudden loss of sexuality impacted the way I interacted physically with men. Men became as much of an 'object' to me as I'd been to them. I realised I could suddenly look them directly in the eye. In the past, I'd shied away from looking at men; glanced down at the floor as though they were somehow superior to me.

I had often sensed some men's enjoyment in knowing they have power over me, whether physically or sexually. Suddenly, I could address them firmly and with conviction, for there was no sexual power issue in the way. As a result of whatever this new-found false confidence was, I even found some men acting nervously around *me*.

That in itself was worth its weight in gold.

'Did you read my clinical notes I sent over after our last session?' Dr Patil asks.

I have not. I look away, working out whether I should lie or not.

'Umm . . .'

'It's fine if you didn't.'

'No.'

'Well, I think you should.'

I don't know why I feel so uncomfortable reading his findings about my brain. I'm worried that he will have discovered something that confirms I am a monster, a freak, or worse, perhaps deserving of everything I've been through.

'My findings show that you have complex PTSD.'

I sit there, confused. He sits there, his expression as flat as my mood.

'PTSD? As in . . .'

'Post-traumatic stress disorder. Yes.'

He must have made a mistake. PTSD is something that happens to soldiers. I am from a military family, full of war veterans, and I know, first hand, the debilitating impact war can have on someone's mental health and well-being. Even though he is an expert in PTSD and trauma, I tell Dr Patil, firmly, that he is wrong. I do not have it. This is, quite frankly, an offence to people whose bodies are blown up in wars, whose entire lives are destroyed by conflict, the innocent bodies so needlessly butchered, raped and mutilated.

Dr Patil explains that psychologists and psychiatrists no longer view PTSD as they once did. While PTSD can be caused by one defining moment – and, of course, affects soldiers and war veterans, complex PTSD, or C-PTSD, can develop from a series of 'little' ongoing incidents over time; incidents which, over a prolonged period, have a detrimental effect on the brain.

C-PTSD has all the symptoms of traditional PTSD – intrusive thoughts and memories, flashbacks, nightmares, being easily startled, problems sleeping and negative changes in mood and thinking – but also additional problems, such as difficulties in emotional regulation, problems in relationships, a distorted sense of self, drug and alcohol abuse, risky sexual behaviour, suicidal ideations, lapses in memory, self-blame and many more. What starts off as trauma in the brain can lead to other issues in the body, including stomach and gastrointestinal problems and headaches and migraines.

'But not *all* of my issues are down to sexual assault,' I insist on pointing out.

'They don't always have to be down to physical or sexual assault,' he replies. 'Remember when we first met, and I told you that all these little incidents can develop over time?'

I nod.

'Well, if you're constantly under threat for being a woman, then ongoing misogyny can be a source of significant trauma, too.'

Complex PTSD. From men. Can you imagine? In some ways, you have to laugh. My friends have previously joked about men and modern-day dating giving them brain damage, and here I was, proof that it could happen.

Men.

I was tired of men. Exasperated by men. Sick and tired of speaking about them, of worrying about them, of what they could do to me, of what they thought of me, of what I thought of them. Most of all, I was angry at them. I was angry at being treated as less important simply for being female. I was sick of being objectified by them and of objectifying myself, for competing with other women for their attention, for *giving* them all my attention. I was angry at myself for allowing them to consume so much space in my brain – trying to entertain them, be beautiful enough for them, be loved by them, to recover from them and the things they'd done.

I am not the only woman who has felt the pressures of the patriarchy. I know many smart, successful, beautiful women who have craved love so desperately that they, too, end up sacrificing the greatest parts of themselves for the most mediocre of men, for a chance of being happy.

Many of us are not happy, and why would we be? The patriarchy tells us we should look better, age slower, be slimmer, be curvier, be sexual, not too sexual, be independent, not too independent, be fun, not too fun, be feminine, not *too* girly (it's annoying), be one of the boys, don't act masculine, be a pushover, look like you've stepped off a surgical table, don't *actually* go on the surgical table, be cool, don't nag, be friendly, don't set boundaries, be confident, don't be bossy. We are living in a man's world as added extras, morphing ourselves to fit into and be accepted by the patriarchal systems and structures in place, unable to be ourselves because we don't know what it means to truly be ourselves. When your existence means so little, what is there to be happy about?

Despite having other exciting things to focus on, men were often at the forefront of many of my and my friends' conversations. Most of our get-togethers in previous years revolved around the men we were dating or the ones who had hurt us, hoping to analyse and dissect their behaviour. One guy had done this, another guy had done that. One guy secretly had a girlfriend, one didn't have the courtesy to text back, one had ghosted, one led me on.

Amid the retelling and heartaches of our silly romance stories lay a deeper desire; a shared desperation for a romantic relationship, because having a boyfriend – and later a husband if you were 'lucky' – ultimately meant you'd 'won'. You'd accomplished life: accomplished the most valuable thing that a woman can, which is being *chosen*.

With a relationship at the core of our soul's purpose, we needed to market ourselves: appearing pretty and attractive for men at all times; posting cute and sexy selfies to remind them of your presence; being available, should he bother to call or want to see you; being accessible enough, but never desperate.

But our lives also revolved around the men we needed to avoid: the catcallers, the abusers, the scary men lurking in the dark at night. Paying extra for cabs home after a night out and then having to remain cautious when alone in the taxi; having to share your whereabouts with your loved ones whenever you went out, instead of being able to simply 'live'. We'd speak about our scary experiences, the ways in which men had hurt us, the ways to *avoid* them hurting us; discussing the horrific, violent stories in the news. I spend my life either avoiding predatory men or trying not to say the wrong thing to upset them, not to offend them; working out ways to politely turn them down without getting murdered for it.

Men, men, men, men, men. Bizarrely, I hadn't thought much about their impact on women at all; nor the idea that forever being treated as objects, and as second-class citizens, was physically altering our brains and the relationship we had with our bodies. When we think of the microaggressions we are constantly subjected to as women and add them up over a lifetime, it is no wonder this has a profound impact on our mental health. It is no wonder that when we are frequently reduced to nothing, we start to view ourselves as nothing. And yet we routinely accept sexism as our fate – not just individually, but as a collective. We consider sexism to be a mere by-product of being female so much so that we rarely challenge it.

According to the World Health Organization, there is a link between growing up in a patriarchal society and a higher risk of mental health issues among women. The mental health charity Mind says women are more likely to have suicidal thoughts and make suicide attempts than men. Young women aged sixteen to twenty-four are more likely to experience mental health problems than any other group in the UK.

Physiologically, the patriarchy takes a profound toll on women: our social circles, our romantic partners, our familial structures as well as our careers, healthcare, culture and wider society. In other words, it's not just toxic relationships or even abusive men that can damage our mental health. It is the patriarchy as a whole.

This is not to say the patriarchy affects everybody in the same way. My experiences of the patriarchy as a white woman will be different to that of a non-binary person or a woman of colour. My experiences with men are my own; unique to me, different from yours. But sexism binds me to women from different cultures, different ethnicities, different religions.

I am not an oddity in what I've experienced. I know this because my friends and I share our experiences with men as though they are unfortunate, yet normal. In fact, most women will attest that we never just experience one bad incident with men. Sometimes there are a couple. Sometimes there are several. More often than not, there are a huge number of incidents over a lifetime.

I'd never truly sat with, or explored, the ways men have influenced my life. Perhaps a lot of my reactions to men, especially the need to oversexualise myself, are acts of survival. I think about the incidents I barely care to consider abnormal: the catcalling in the street that makes me feel nervous and on guard; the men that follow me in the street a little too closely; the copious anonymous dick pics sent to me and my friends, which we've learnt to laugh off. Every woman I know is continually assessing the safety risks of everyday situations, situations that men simply wouldn't think twice about, from taking public transport to walking home at night to giving someone their phone number. For being born our sex, we are rewarded with always having to look over our shoulder.

Could we really consider a dick pic traumatic? Not really, I suppose. Not in the grand scheme of things. But once you're sent enough of them, as well as absorbing all the other misogynistic and patriarchal beliefs and expectations, you start to feel like an object. It is no wonder that this trauma forces many women to objectify themselves; to treat themselves as nothing more than a sex object, believing that to be their only worth.

What damage has the ongoing harm of the patriarchy done

to other women individually? What impact has this had on the development of our gender? How many other women struggle to define the cause of their anxiety or depression, not knowing that they're existing in a world that benefits from keeping them this way?

As I leave Dr Patil's office, I notice the walls are now painted a pretty shade of baby blue. The paint is still chipped in some places but it's certainly an improvement from last time.

'Did you paint the walls a new colour?' I ask, trying to make conversation about anything other than death. 'It looks nice.'

Dr Patil isn't paying much attention, shuffling the paperwork into piles ready for his next patient.

'No,' he replies, closing his laptop. 'But they should. They haven't been painted in years.'

I feel confused. They were white when I was last here, I am sure of it: bland, drab and colourless.

Though as I leave his office, I notice how much more vivid the world appears. It isn't the sunniest of days but the sky is bluer. People appear to be smilier. My pale skin appears a bit rosier. My eyes are a little whiter.

Things may not be perfect but they do seem a bit brighter now.

heart.

In the previous chapter, where I talk about the beginnings of my healing journey, I described a loneliness within me that I couldn't quite pinpoint or understand. But as I began to decenter men and turn my attention away from romantic relationships and on to myself, I started to see how this 'loneliness' was, instead, an inability to communicate the ways I'd been feeling. My emotions were important, deep and heavy and I'd often tossed them aside for somebody else.

Loneliness, I've learnt, isn't necessarily about feeling alone in crowded spaces or not having someone next to you. It's about carrying feelings, words and emotions that you cannot say out loud or express. It's about carrying the burden of truths you don't feel safe enough to share.

Healing is learning how to speak about what matters most to you so that you are no longer alone with your pain. Healing is the work of letting yourself be seen and heard; in being known for who you really are. It's about letting yourself be vulnerable with people so that they understand what lies beneath your flesh; it's about allowing people to see and understand you; it's about the love you have to offer.

Intimacy doesn't have to be about sex. It is possible to fulfil your wants and needs for intimacy and validation with people in your life where the relationships aren't romantic. Once you have enough of these relationships the need to center men will become less apparent. Once you connect with people who truly care about you – and not what your body can offer them – you will you realise that you weren't as lonely as you perhaps thought. You were simply redirecting your energy on to the things that didn't matter, on to the *people* that didn't matter. Once you open up your heart, start accepting your body and your flaws and *allow* yourself to be loved, you will realise that life doesn't have to be lonely at all.

As someone who at one point no longer wanted to live, I remind myself how incredible it is that the heart – a small organ – keeps me alive. Despite all the heartache, pain, strain or abuse we put our bodies through, it continues beating, reminding us that despite everything, we're here. We're alive. We're human.

The heart does not demand perfection. It does not require you to come fully polished. The heart doesn't value you for your accomplishments, does not care how many men find you physically attractive, how big your thigh gap is, how clear your skin is, or how beautiful you appear in a photo. It loves you regardless and unconditionally. Small but mighty, it continuously pumps blood around your body, a constant yet silent reminder that you are alive.

The heart comes from a place of tolerance, of kindness, a place of acceptance, compassion and empathy. The heart knows that you are already whole, that you have an inherent value simply for being you.

You will never regret protecting your heart. You will never regret protecting yourself. You will never regret standing up for yourself or for what you believe in. But you *will* regret – whether it is in five, ten or twenty years' time – treating yourself as though you are unworthy of love, care or kindness. You will regret giving your heart, your energy and your body to someone who treats you as an object. You will regret morphing your body into what you believe is societally acceptable, all in the hope of being loved or chosen. Because while the way people treat you is a reflection on them, the way you tolerate their behaviour is a reflection on you.

The very fact we have a heart that loves and breaks; the very fact we have a body that moves and breathes; the very fact we have a soul that reacts to feelings and emotions is a scientific oddity in itself. The chances of us being alive and existing is a magical fluke. It took the miracle of our parents meeting and *their* parents meeting and all of our ancestors meeting across various continents over thousands upon thousands of years, each with stories and hearts of their own, for our lives to align themselves in blood and in bone, a combination of rhythms that existed long before us; billions of years after atoms and stars and galaxies collided in space.

Our lives are beautiful in ways that are nothing to do with being pretty. So why choose to waste that one precious blip – that minuscule chance of our existence – on focusing on how our body appears to others? Why choose to waste our energy on people that hurt us? Why sacrifice our bodies for those who don't care about our well-being? Why view our bodies with disdain and disgust instead of appreciating the magical, cosmic beings that we are?

It is now 2026, and around the world, many women are finally paying attention. They are realising that there is more to life than this, that they can dismantle and undo the generational conditioning of the patriarchy, live a life of their own and decenter men for good. Is it any wonder women are choosing a different future for themselves?

We're watching incel culture become more and more prevalent, stories of young boys attacking female students and teachers, believing women and girls are inferior to them. A quick search on social media reveals anonymous accounts celebrating rape, paedophilia and other violence. We are still paid unequally for our efforts, time and labour. We have watched a president accused of rape and sexual assault be elected for a second time in the US. We watch young women and girls sexualising themselves repeatedly online in exchange for likes and hearts. We watch the erosion of women's reproductive rights in the US, leaving millions of women at risk of death and children being brought into a world that doesn't provide the funds or resources to help support them. We watch trad-wifery being masked as an aesthetic, where, much like the generations before us, our value as women is diminished to appearance, submission and domesticity, but repackaged as empowerment.

When it is clear that we will not be protected by men or male systems of power, we can't help but ask ourselves: why do men deserve our attention? Men are not helping us, so we must take charge ourselves. We must create a society where we value women for their hearts, minds and spirits and not just their physical attributes; where girls and young women aspire to more than attracting a boyfriend or being lusted over as means of feeling beautiful within.

Many women are choosing to say no; to put themselves first. This goes against generations of conditioning, against the image of what we have long believed womanhood and femininity to be. This new-found 'selfishness' we're supposedly demonstrating is a man's daily right. Women are choosing to pick partners based on attraction, kindness, compatibility, intelligence and shared values; not from a place of desperation, submission or fear, as they may have done previously. They realise that they are allowed to set boundaries. They're realising that they don't owe men sex for simply going out for a meal with them or for receiving bare-minimum treatment. They understand that their bodies and mental health are just as important, too.

Studies show that Gen Z women, especially, are becoming noticeably more progressive in their views, as opposed to their male counterparts, who seem to be on a conservative, right-leaning trend. By 2030, Morgan Stanley economists estimate that 45 per cent of American women aged twenty-five to forty-four will be single. Should this projection be accurate, it would make this the fastest-growing cohort of single women in the US. Several factors are contributing to this. Women are more focused on advancing their careers and financial independence is becoming more desirable. The average age of marriage is increasing. Relationship standards for women are higher and personal fulfilment is a priority. This projected trend could help significantly close the gender gap, creating pressure on labour forces to increase women's wages, promotions and more in the coming years.

In South Korea, women are taking it even further. The 4B movement is a radical feminist movement encouraging women to abstain from sex and relationships with men completely: no dating, no sex, no marriage and no childbirth.

To many men, especially incels, these feminist movements are seen as 'male oppression'. Women having standards is seen as greed or entitlement, while men rejecting women based on their choices is seen as acceptable or 'traditional'. If a man says he only wants to date a woman in her early twenties, that's 'biology'. If a woman says she wants to date a man with a personality and a job, that's 'unrealistic'.

A woman having boundaries goes against everything men have been told they deserve. The manosphere, especially, recruits boys and men in its masses, teaching them that women saying no is simply unacceptable. They complain that women only want 'high-value' men, while mocking average-looking, everyday women, furiously posting online about how they refuse to date older women, single mothers, women on OnlyFans or women who don't resemble Victoria's Secret supermodels, while claiming there is a 'male loneliness epidemic'.

Men aren't furious about women having standards, necessarily, but about being held accountable for their actions. They have never been told no – not by thousands of women at the same time, anyway. They have never had the inclination to improve or better themselves, because why would they? Life has taught them that as a male the world is theirs, that they are simply entitled to opportunities and relationships. Oh, how wonderful that must be.

While it's easy to mock these men and laugh at the hypocrisy of it all, what we should *really* take from this pushback is that women are progressing at a significant rate – a rate which men are noticing. Women are waking up and realising that there is more to life than the bare minimum; that they deserve – shock horror – partners who actually value them. And the more women realise what they deserve from life, the more men will have no choice but to progress themselves to keep up.

What does your heart desire? I don't mean sexually or romantically. I mean the things that make your heart sing, feel warm, feel seen; the things that make your eyes sparkle. Sometimes, when you've centered men for so long, you lose sight of the things that make you *you*; distract yourself from your own passions as a means to appease them. We ignore our heart's desires in favour of someone else's.

Imagine men didn't exist. How might your life look? What conversations would you have with your girlfriends? What would you be investing your time and energy into? What do your goals and dreams look like? What are you prioritising? Who is the person that exists beyond what you believe you 'need' from a man?

The reality, of course, is that men *do* exist, and we can't simply do or say whatever it is we want because our literal safety depends on it. But we *can* try to decenter them as much as possible. We must try to do our best to live a peaceful and successful life of our own, where our hearts, our thoughts, our opinions, matter just as much.

When I first heard about the concept of 'decentering men' it instinctively made sense. I knew, that after everything I'd been through, everything I'd experienced at the hands of men, I wanted to live the rest of my life without them at the forefront of my brain. I no longer wanted to organise my life around a man's comfort, opinions or potential. I wanted healthy relationships with them where I would be treated as an equal instead of a conquest. Moreover, I no longer wanted to sacrifice myself for a system that was designed to consume me whole; a system that profited from my submission and low self-worth.

Decentering men isn't radical. It's rational. It means refusing to make male authority, male experience, male validation the default or the standard. It's about taking back your power from the patriarchy in a liberating act of self-respect. When men no longer occupy a central place in your life, you will fully own your thoughts, feelings, actions and decisions. You don't feel bad for saying no and for having boundaries. You don't question your decisions at all. You break free from craving attention as a means of validating your own worth and existence.

Decentering men requires you to come back to yourself. It requires you to sit with yourself and remember the person you were before someone made you feel like your life's only purpose was to look good aesthetically; before believing your body was there to be used as a glorified servant; before you believed being a wife and mother was your life's sole goal; before you were expected to readily make your husband's or boyfriend's wishes and dreams come true, while ignoring your own.

Decentering men requires decentering that voice that tells you your worth lies in your beauty, your body and your sexuality, and remembering who you are beneath it all. It means freeing yourself from the male gaze and external validation. It is a liberation, a movement towards wholeness – not necessarily away from intimacy. In fact, centering ourselves will only better our relationships going forward. Once we learn to value our entire selves and hold our whole hearts with love, care, support and reverence, we can truly hold space for someone else.

Decentering men requires us to question what we've long been taught culturally, societally and through family. While for some women marriage and motherhood come from an innate biological desire, it might be worth asking yourself whether for you this desire comes from an authentic place, or whether you've *learnt* to chase what you believe fulfilment to be because of societal expectations and conditioning. Once you start to enjoy single life, centering friends instead of boyfriends, you may realise that marriage and having children isn't necessarily a true desire or want at all.

Aren't you exhausted from thinking about relationships? Aren't you tired of thinking how men might perceive you at any given moment; whether a guy likes you or not; how feminine you do or don't appear in their eyes; how many likes you've received on a dating app? Are you tired of questioning whether a man is love-bombing you; whether he's leading you on; whether the relationship is going anywhere; whether he could be your boyfriend, your husband, whether this relationship will last?

Is this it? Is this really what we spend our life's energy focusing on?

When you make men the focus of your life, you are abandoning yourself and your needs. Every time you continue to date someone who treats you like an option, or you stay in a relationship that's just OK instead of truly happy because you fear being alone or 'falling behind' your peers, you are doing yourself a huge disservice. Stop viewing yourself as an object that can be made up or morphed into a doll, or as a few pixels on a screen that can be liked or disliked.

YOU DESERVE MORE THAN THIS. You deserve a partner who sees you for you; who loves you beyond your appearance. The question is: will you allow it? Would you rather settle for something mediocre and so-so because you're afraid of being alone, or stay single until you meet someone who makes you feel like the wonderful person you truly are, who truly *sees* you, instead of uses you? Do not set yourself up for failure or regret just because you're afraid of being alone. Do not waste your one precious life on people who treat you, your body and your heart like an afterthought.

Decentering men isn't about rejecting love or saying no to romantic or sexual relationships with men entirely. It's about rejecting the idea that we must suffer for love for it to mean anything; that we must abandon ourselves, our true wants and desires, to be loved by someone. There is nothing wrong with wanting to share your life with someone; nothing wrong with wanting to be loved or having someone take care of your heart. But above all, center and love the most important person in your life: yourself.

'I think I'm ready to date again.'

A year after going on antidepressants, I am back, once again, in Dr Patil's office. My depression, while still lingering, was steadily declining. My sex drive was slowly returning. As the medication began to settle within my system, my natural biological urges began to come back – not as strong but growing in intensity. I noticed myself finding men attractive again, experiencing feelings of wanting to become intimate again, of wanting to be *seen* as sexual again. While for most people this may be a welcome feeling, I was unsure whether I was ready. Having a sex drive had led me into difficult and uncomfortable positions before.

'Oh, right,' he replies, peering over his glasses. And then, like all therapists: 'And how does that make you feel?'

I sit in silence for a couple of seconds.

'I'm scared that I'll repeat the same patterns with men as I have before.'

'What makes you think you'll repeat the same mistakes?' he asks.

Over the past year, I had abstained from men, sex and dating. This was mostly because the antidepressants had caused me to have zero sex drive, which meant I had zero desire to interact, flirt, date or sleep with a man. The medication had, essentially, made the decision to avoid men for me. It was a relief.

But these pills could only help me so far. You cannot heal what you don't allow yourself to feel. For the first time in my life, especially in my adult life, I was forced to sit with myself and my feelings. Without the desire for sex or the need to focus my attention on someone, I had no other option than to focus on myself.

And so, I opened up. I spoke fully about my traumas in therapy. I learnt how my trauma had not only impacted the relationships I had with men but the relationship I had with myself and my body. I saw the link between my objectified self and the ongoing, daily comments which had led to me treating myself as a sex object. I learnt how repeatedly being sexualised contributed to the ill-treatment of my body, especially my relationship with food. I read about attachment styles and various reasons as to why you might be drawn to romantic partners who push you out. I learnt how being an object erodes your mind, body and soul.

But I had also learnt that I was deserving of more. I was no longer going to feel bad for wanting more for my life, for rejecting the bare minimum. I'd long believed that focusing on myself was a selfish act. Women are not supposed to be selfish. We are often encouraged – and guilt-tripped – into putting the needs of other people before our own. Society and culture teach us to be there for everyone but ourselves: for our boyfriends, then our husbands, our children and our parents. By doing this we lose sight of who we are and remain out of touch with our bodies and our needs.

Learning to believe I could think solely about myself felt uncomfortable. But I've learnt that it is truly possible to hold space for yourself while also holding a healthy amount of love for someone else.

I began redirecting the love I'd reserved for a romantic partner towards my friends, family and – more importantly – towards myself. I chose to romanticise myself and my life. I took myself out on dates. I took myself to restaurants I'd been wanting to try, ordered delicious food while people-watching and soaking up the atmosphere. I took myself to the cinema and watched films from genres I wouldn't have necessarily watched before. I made a conscious effort to see friends and to make new ones, even when I was shy.

Looking after myself felt good. I was becoming a better person – someone who knew herself inside and out. I could feel it. I was becoming content enough in myself not to chase anyone else, and I don't just mean romantically but in every way: in unrequited friendships, in situations where I wasn't welcomed. I just hadn't had a chance to present the newer version of myself yet.

For many of us, decentering men means addressing our deepest fears. It means unlearning the need to please a man to feel worthy. I was concerned about what would happen once I started dating, whether I would find myself drawn to the same types of toxic men or whether I'd repeat the same needy, desperate behaviour. I witnessed many friends in healthy relationships and deep down I knew what I wanted a relationship to be – what a relationship *could* be – but I was worried about making the same mistakes as I had before.

I didn't think I could withstand another heartbreak, another ghosting, another letdown. I felt exhausted at the thought of having to perform again, at trying to morph myself into being someone I wasn't, all in the hope of being chosen. I couldn't bear the thought of being abused again, physically flinching because of a man again, feeling unsafe while being with someone I desperately wanted to trust.

Dating again didn't automatically mean I was healed from all my previous experiences and behaviours. It didn't mean that I was suddenly the world's most confident human being. But the work I'd done to heal myself *did* mean that I was responding to men very differently.

This isn't to say I didn't occasionally make the same mistakes and choose ill-suited partners. I spent three months dating one guy – who was forty years old, I might add – who I genuinely believed wanted to be my boyfriend.

I knew it was getting serious when he gave me the pink head of his electric toothbrush for when I stayed over – pink, because he knew that was my favourite colour. He would repeatedly tell me I was 'wifey material'; how he couldn't believe nobody had 'wifed me up' yet. He told me he loved how things were going, that he hadn't felt this way in a really long time. He would see me three times a week and text me all the time. We would have sleepovers at each other's houses and sometimes go to cafes together to work in the day. We would cook together, laugh at stupid jokes until we cried, watch films curled up on the sofa, go to the pub and play quiz games. It was a relationship without a relationship status.

But . . . he could also be unreliable. He would suggest plans that he didn't follow through on, like going away somewhere romantic for the weekend or checking out a new restaurant. Sometimes he would disappear in the evenings and not text me back until late the next day. But I ignored this, choosing to focus on the things he said – the things I wanted to hear.

Three months in, we were out for dinner one evening when I noticed him checking out other women in the restaurant. I had been bucking up the courage to ask him what we were – that dreaded question which, in today's hellhole of dating, apparently needs to be asked, because spending all your free time with someone and meeting their friends and texting non-stop and sleeping with them still, somehow, doesn't make you official. For all I knew, he could still be on dating apps (the thought of which made me want to throw up).

'What is it you're looking for in a relationship?' I asked. I felt nervous and vulnerable asking him, which is bizarre, considering he'd seen me naked numerous times. 'Like . . . what are we?'

He sat there, picking at his plate while staring at it.

'Don't know,' he replied. 'Haven't really thought about it.'

I felt a drop in my stomach, as though my heart was falling into my abdomen, a feeling I'd experienced many times around men previously.

'But . . . we've been spending so much time together,' I replied. 'We see each other all the time.'

'I just want to see how things go,' he replied. 'No pressure. No rush.'

'What about the future, though?' I asked. 'Are marriage or children something you'd ever want? Not with me, necessarily. I just mean in general.'

It was the first time I'd ever had the courage to ask a guy I was seeing this. I could feel myself tensing up, feeling embarrassed as though I was begging.

'Woah, steady on!' he said, which made me feel stupid, like I was desperate to marry him then and there. 'Like I said, it's just not something I've ever thought about.'

Really? *Really?!* At forty years old, he'd never *once* considered his future or whether he wanted children?

'I know I don't want to be an old dad, though,' he added. 'Anyway, shall we go soon?'

I felt deflated, not to mention confused. How could I have got it all wrong?

Later, when we got back to my house, he asked if I could give him a neck massage. Despite feeling hurt, I did.

'You really are my dream girl,' he said.

I snapped out of whatever fantasy I was living in and listened to what he said. I knew, there and then, that this guy was stringing me along. He had no real desire to become my boyfriend yet he was getting all the benefits of acting as though he was.

I cut him off. I had to, for the sake of my heart. If he didn't think I was worthy of exclusivity at this stage and after all the nice things we'd done, why was it my job to convince him?

Did it hurt? Yes, of course! But I did have to give myself some leniency. I hadn't made up the things he'd said to me, imagined all the nights we'd spent together. I hadn't faked these feelings – not from my side, anyway. I was genuine in my affections and actions.

In the past, I would have ruminated on this man for months. I would've seen this rejection as a challenge to prove myself as a girlfriend even more and in doing so, lost myself in the process. While it felt like a waste of three months, this time, I allowed myself to feel the hurt. I didn't jump back on to dating apps or into the arms of someone else. I removed myself from the situation and moved on.

Your flesh is not a map for lost men to try and find themselves. Your life is not a treasure map, where you spend it trying to find the gold. You *are* the gold. You are the treasure. The treasure has been within you all along. You just have to believe it.

'Write a list of all the things you want out of a relationship, and stick to that list,' Dr Patil suggests to me. 'No one is perfect, and you can't expect them to be everything you ever want. But if you don't share the same fundamental goals for the future, or if you notice red flags, it will help you walk away easier.'

And so I did. I thought about what it was I wanted and desired out of a relationship and wrote them down, including the things I'd previously downplayed as a means not to appear 'intense' or 'needy'.

For example, I knew that at some point in my life, I want to get married. This doesn't seem like a crazy ask, but it's remarkable how modern dating leads you to believe you are out of your mind for suggesting marriage as a future goal. Simply scrolling through Hinge or Bumble will show you how many men are open to short relationships (whatever that means) or still figuring out their dating goals even in their thirties or forties.

I knew that I was no longer going to feel bad for wanting romance. If a man asked me what I wanted from a relationship in the future, I was not going to pretend that I was fine with simply 'seeing how things go', as I had many times previously. I wanted to date with intention. That didn't mean that I expected to marry the first man that came along or that I expected someone to be my husband from the second we met. It meant that I would no longer waste my time dating someone who knew that marriage wasn't *ever* for them.

And so I stuck to my word. I would ask, early on in dating, what somebody's goals were for the future. Some would say that they, too, would like to get married eventually. Some would say that they never planned on getting married. I kindly, but firmly, told these men that a romantic relationship wouldn't work out because we weren't on the same page.

I also learnt to cut out the men who weren't sure; those who wanted to see how things went or who said they'd 'never thought about marriage before'. I knew it was not my job to change someone. They were entitled to their wishes, and I was entitled to mine.

Unfortunately, I did meet a couple of men who told me in the early stages of dating that they wanted marriage, only to completely backtrack on this idea six to eight weeks later and say they weren't ready for a relationship at all. These were usually the men who came on incredibly strong in the beginning, the love-bombers, the men that bombard you with compliments, gifts and attention. Then as soon as I began to trust them they would pull their affections away.

Again, I was surprised at my reaction to this. In the past, their sudden withdrawals would have eaten me up for weeks. While it hurt, I allowed myself to feel the pain. Instead of rushing in to dating somebody else or jumping back on to dating apps, I would let myself feel the pain, have a cry and wait until I felt good enough to date again.

Dating had changed drastically for me. In the past, I would sack off friends if a man's schedule immediately became available. Now, I put my own schedule first. If our plans aligned, that was great. If they didn't, I wasn't going to change my plans or lose sleep over it. My time was valuable too!

You must stand strong in your convictions and beliefs while dating, otherwise you will be taken advantage of. Unfortunately, there are many men who will say what you want to hear to get what they want. Instead, I started believing actions over words. If a guy said he'd arrange a date, I would give him a couple of weeks to sort something. If he didn't follow through, I would cut him off and stop talking to him. I knew I was worthy of more than false promises or being put on the back bench. Lose interest when someone mistreats you. Lose interest when someone doesn't respond to your texts. Lose interest when someone pulls away and shuts you out, when they don't ask questions about you, when they express zero interest in your day, when they don't spend time with you, when they don't express desire for you.

I used to take a man's sexual comments as a measure of my worth or even beauty, but I'd learnt to cut out men who were overtly sexual with me. I now actively avoided this type of man, the type of man who clearly viewed me and my body as things to conquer. I wanted someone to actively show an interest in who I was, in what my goals were. This shouldn't be a huge ask and I was no longer willing to settle for the bare minimum.

I am not the only woman who has dealt with overtly sexual comments from men on dates. Whenever I speak to friends it is clear that many men use dating apps as hook-up apps, seeing women as things to fuck, rather than human beings with feelings.

Since decentering men, my attitude towards this kind of behaviour changed drastically.

I was introduced to an older man by a friend, who told me what a wonderful man he was. He was an incredibly successful billionaire businessman with two children from a previous relationship, a very hands-on father, I was told. He sounded great, a dream, if anything. He booked a table at an expensive restaurant, and he bought me a beautiful vintage Chanel dress as a gift. It was clear he was pulling out all the stops. It wasn't the money I was impressed with, but the effort he was going to to make me smile. It was like something out of a romcom. I'd noticed that despite his success and wealth he was somewhat self-conscious. He asked me a handful of times whether he looked OK, whether his shirt was OK, whether the restaurant was fine.

We hadn't been at the restaurant long when he began showing me a side I didn't like. He asked me if I had ever slept with women. He asked me if I'd ever had a threesome. I couldn't work out if this was a weird sense of humour or if he was genuinely getting aroused at the thought. But my friend had vouched for him, so he must be OK. He *must* be one of the good guys, because good guys are people you know. She wouldn't have set me up with an idiot, I was sure of it. Although I felt uncomfortable, I told him I didn't want to answer those questions and tried to laugh it off.

We were given a menu and he glanced down and proceeded to order almost all of it. While I am not a wine connoisseur, he had clearly ordered the most expensive bottle as the staff were now clambering to serve him. I felt his eyes looking at me, waiting for me to be impressed, waiting for me to tell him how wonderful he was.

'Do you wanna hear a crazy story?' he asked while we waited for the food.

'Sure!' I replied, sipping on my wine. I assumed he'd tell me a crazy story of how he'd been arrested or ended up in jail one night; how he'd been chased down by a lion on a safari or something just as riveting.

'So when I was younger, an ex-girlfriend dragged me into a field and fucked me into the mud,' he said. 'I was covered in it from head to toe.'

I sat there, perplexed. Why was this first-date conversation? I didn't laugh, which clearly made him feel as though he had to go further.

'She kept riding me and riding me,' he said. 'My dick was covered in mud. It was everywhere.'

'Out of curiosity,' I asked, 'what makes you think it's acceptable to tell me this?'

He glared at me from across the table, as though I'd accused him of a horrific crime.

'What do you mean?' he replied. 'Why do you care? It happened before you were born.'

'I just don't understand why you'd tell me about your sex life.'

I didn't raise my voice in the slightest. I was calm and collected. I had a new-found confidence within me; a new part of me that was unwilling to feel uncomfortable just to make a man feel better.

But while calm, I still asked him the question with conviction. Why did he think it was OK to share this with me? What made him think I'd like to hear about who he'd slept with, regardless of when it was?

'Wow!' he said, surprised, and when I mean surprised, I mean fiercely defensive and taken aback.

'Why are you being so weird about it? I can talk to [insert mutual friend's name here] and she doesn't get weird about me telling her these things.'

'Do you see me as just a friend, then?' I asked.

'No.'

'So why would you think it was OK to share stories like that on a date?' I asked. 'You asked me whether I'd slept with women and whether I had threesomes, and now you're telling me about being fucked in mud. If you see me as just a sex object, then just say that.'

'Wow,' he repeated. 'I thought you were cool.'

The waiter came and placed the plates on the table. We sat in silence.

Once the waiter left, he looked up at me.

'I'm not gonna lie,' he said. 'It kind of turns me on when you tell me off.'

I didn't speak to this man again. A few weeks later, he messaged me out of nowhere to tell me he missed me, bizarre considering we'd ended on such strange terms and barely knew each other.

Later, the man went to our mutual friend and told her a completely fabricated version of events: that I had become 'aggressive' and 'jealous' over dinner when he'd told me 'about an ex-girlfriend'. While I laughed out of shock at this blatant, self-preserving lie, I was impressed with my response. I didn't care. I didn't give one ounce of a fuck. I didn't care whether he liked me or not. If he wanted to turn me into the bad guy to defend his behaviour, let him. Let him tell people a different version of the story. Let him tell people that I was aggressive and jealous and a prude. Because while buying me an expensive dress may have worked on the previous version of me or made me feel as though I owed him the opportunity to speak to me however he wanted, it wasn't going to fly with the new me going forward.

I was proud of myself and how I'd reacted to the situation. I was proud of the woman I was becoming. Had this occurred a year, even a few months prior, I'm sure my reaction would've been completely different. The likelihood is that I would've sat back, smiled, possibly laughed and continued to date him, despite how he'd made me feel, hoping that if I did appear cool, or chilled, or OK with him telling me about his sex life, that he'd want me. And only once he'd made me feel truly shit enough about myself, whether weeks or months later, would I finally try to step back and let go of him.

I used to believe self-respect came from how I dressed or from not sleeping with someone too early. Now, I saw it came from saying no, saying that I didn't like being spoken to in that way. I was learning that setting boundaries and telling men what made me uncomfortable was an act of self-love and respect.

Self-love saved me. I had been waiting on my Prince Charming to come and save me, to rescue me from my insecurities and give my life meaning. The truth is, I had the answer all along.

Love had always been there. I had it in abundance. I had just been directing it in the wrong places. I had it in bucketfuls and never realised that I'd been deserving of it all along. I'd seen love as something to accomplish; something that could be mine, if only I performed or suffered enough for it. I'd focused so hard on the performance of love, that I'd wilfully ignored the greatest love of all: the *love* I had for myself, the *life* I had for myself.

When we think about self-love, we often focus on surface-level acts. While having a bath, putting on a face mask or speaking positively about ourselves can be important steps as part of our healing journey, we must go deeper, we must listen to our hearts. When we sit with ourselves and what our hearts need, we connect with our truest, most vulnerable selves.

Self-love can appear in many forms. It can appear in self-care, by nourishing your mind, body and soul. It can appear via self-expression, in being your authentic self, without worrying what others think of you, and in speaking your truth. It can come from self-compassion, in learning to take the pressure off yourself. It can come from self-respect, from knowing your worth and your standards. And it can come from self-acceptance, in choosing to love yourself unconditionally, even the parts you don't particularly like. All of this is within your body. Self-love is there, living in your flesh. You just have to believe that you are worthy of the love you keep giving to everybody else and that your body is more than just an object.

It can show up when you say no, setting firm and healthy boundaries and in being OK with people disliking you. It can show up in embracing the lines etched on your skin, the proof of the journeys lived, and in turning down cosmetic procedures that aim to make you look younger. It can show up by actively refusing to chase beauty standards set by men who are attracted to teenagers. It can show up by learning to love your squishy stomach, in embracing the happiness, and not the guilt, from ordering French fries and a burger when you go out to dinner instead of a salad; when you push past the fear of posting an unedited selfie and showcase the unretouched body that you wish you'd seen as a teenager, instead of trying to morph your body into something it's not. It can show up in accepting your cellulite – not necessarily loving that the skin on your thighs isn't super smooth but in understanding your legs have far more use than simply looking good. It can show up by embracing your uneven breasts, by accepting that ageing is inevitable. It can show up in realising that you don't need to show your skin in order to be loved: that the type of person who loves you only for your sex appeal or what you can offer them sexually, isn't a person worthy of you to begin with.

Self-love can show up by walking away from dates that make you uncomfortable; in refusing to feel bad for standing up for yourself if a man is rude or inappropriate. It can show up in knowing when a relationship is over; by allowing yourself to be sad over a break-up but realising that it doesn't reflect on you as a person. It can show up by being selective in who you sleep with. It can show up in knowing that no relationship is worth rejecting yourself for; in knowing that you are worthy of kindness, of love, of support and if you are not receiving what you deserve, by walking away with your head held high.

Self-love can show up in asking for a raise at work. It can show up from cutting toxic people from your life. It can mean being OK, but not entirely happy, with being alone. It can arise from rebelling against the negative voices in your head that convince you of your worthlessness; in *choosing* to focus on the positive. It means accepting yourself, even when life is messy, scary and uncertain. Self-love can come from listening to your heart. Why be afraid of fully loving yourself?

Self-love doesn't always mean easy. It doesn't always mean instant gratification or peace. It can be slow, painful and uncomfortable. It can often feel lonely. It will require a lot of internal work, in sitting with bad memories and feelings, feelings that we often choose to bury. But once you learn to sit with these feelings, slowly you will realise just how incredible and valuable you are.

You can join the millions of women who are choosing to say no to a life of objectification, of male servitude, of people-pleasing, of performance, of insecurity, of feeling worthless. You can speak up for yourself and others; call people out on their behaviour; walk away from people who make you feel less than. We can choose to adopt practices that allow us more freedom.

You can never go wrong when you choose to love yourself. There is never any love wasted when you pour it into you.

Love can be what you decide to make of it. Love can be putting yourself to bed at night after a long day, when you're tired and your knees are aching. Love can be soothing yourself with a hot drink, in telling yourself you will be OK. Love can carry you, as much as you choose to carry it.

So, choose differently. Choose a different kind of love. Choose yourself.

Decentering men may be your greatest act of self-love.

whole.

I often fantasise about the type of woman I could've been or the life I could've led had men not shaped every moment of it. I suppose it begs the question: how can I fully embrace my identity when I've been dominated by so many external ideas of who I am or who I'm supposed to be?

What might life look like under the female gaze? I wonder what kind of media I'd have consumed if we saw the world from a female perspective? How women, and men, might've been presented in TV, film and advertisements and the influence that would have had on women in every aspect of their lives. I question the careers I might have aspired to, whether I would've had a career in modelling at all. I imagine the way my body might've looked if beauty expectations were defined *by* women, *for* women and what those expectations – if any – might've been. I dream about the opportunities and routes I would have taken had I the true freedom to do, say, act, dress or behave as I wished.

Who might I have *truly* been, if the actions and behaviour of men hadn't influenced me in every area of my life?

If, for example, I hadn't been molested as a child, would I have battled such debilitating anxiety? Would I have felt happier about or more comfortable embracing my changing form as a teenager, instead of feeling ashamed, scared and trapped in a body that didn't yet feel like my own?

If I hadn't been sexually assaulted as a teenager, would I have still sexualised myself in the ways I chose afterwards? Would I have continually chased men that made me feel terrible about myself as a means of feeling validated or loved?

If I hadn't grown up in a world that encouraged women to look beautiful for men, what would my beauty regimen have looked like? Would I have taken a more relaxed, softer and kinder approach to the way I viewed myself and my body, instead of worrying about whether or not I looked pretty or sexy on the surface?

If I hadn't listened to the numerous comments said over the years about my body and the ways in which I should change it, would I have felt pretty as I was? Would I have seen myself as attractive without needing to be told by other people?

What would sex be like if I was fully able to relax and seek satisfaction for myself, if my body wasn't expected to be lasered and preened to perfection, like women we see in porn? Would I have spent my twenties and early thirties performing sex or would it have been a more collaborative experience?

Who am I, if I am not the woman society tells me I am?
Who am I, if I am not the person I feel that I should be?
Who am I, if I'm not an object?
Who am I, beyond my body?

At the beginning of this book, I spoke about personal choices, about how many of the choices we make as women are not entirely our own. But even in a world that is stacked against us, we *can* make choices, choices that will better us for the remaining time we have on this planet.

You can choose to romanticise your life. You can choose to be happy. Do things that bring you back to your body, which recenter you in the here and now, instead of the future. Make your space at home cosy and beautiful, even if it's just placing some supermarket flowers in a jar or covering your bed in a fluffy blanket. Listen to podcasts and fill your brain with information about a new subject. Call a friend you haven't spoken to in a long time. Go for a walk, even if it's just around the block. Read books that transport you to a different world. Look up at the sky and stargaze on a clear night. Wear outfits that make you feel comfortable and confident, not that make you look what you think is most sexy.

Clinging to our sexual appeal is not power. It is submission. Why would you possibly want the male gaze to dictate your worth? Your role is not to keep someone entertained or turned on sexually so that a person doesn't abandon you. It is important that in our quest to find love we learn to love ourselves first.

Decentering men gives us the space to discover our desires as our own. It allows us to create room for healthier relationships, helping to build lives that are full and meaningful, regardless of whether a man is in it. It's about understanding that women, too, have a place on this earth and a vast history worth telling.

The only way to experience real joy, health and happiness is to live inside your body, no matter what it looks like. Tell yourself how great you are. Eventually, you'll believe it. Sit in yourself and feel your body. Breathe deeply and feel the air filling your lungs. Place your hand on your heart and feel your heartbeat. Our bodies provide us with so many experiences: the ability to hold our children, to think of new ideas, to be in love. It was always more than how it looked.

I love this quote by body neutrality activist Lexie Kite, co-author of *More Than a Body*: 'Your body is an instrument, not an ornament.'

By that, she means we should change our perception of ourselves as a decorative, pretty ornament and accept and come back home to our body, no matter how it looks. Your body is an instrument for your use, your experience, your life.

This is the only body you're ever going to have. And if you live floating on the outside of it, constantly trying to change it or beautify yourself, controlling your body according to how you think other people might judge when they look at you, your energy, your life, is being sucked out of you.

What does it mean to be whole?

In the past, I looked to outside sources to make me feel complete. My worth was based on how others viewed and treated me. The power lay with them, in their words, actions and behaviour. My body could only be validated if a man found me attractive or sexy. I viewed myself as a series of body parts and not as someone complete in who I am.

In my journey of decentering men and reclaiming my body, I realised that no relationship can fill periods of darkness. You will never feel whole if you constantly rely on beauty, men or a romantic relationship to complete you. Wholeness comes from learning to be alone and becoming comfortable with it, in learning to be content sitting in your silence. It comes from understanding yourself, embracing your imperfections, pursuing your true purpose and passions, practising self-compassion and forgiveness and letting go of the need to be perfect.

I feel whole when people tell me I am smart instead of hot, when people comment on how fun or funny I am, when they acknowledge the times I've been kind or caring to somebody else, when I've made someone feel good in *their* body. I feel a deep sense of fulfilment when people comment on my talents as a writer, which creates a warmth inside me that burns far longer and brighter than when people comment on my appearance, and it's a feeling that seems to shine from within. I've come to realise that my appearance is the least interesting thing about me and that is wonderful. And when my looks *do* eventually fade, I know that these traits, talents and characteristics will remain with me regardless.

Women focusing on themselves is the greatest threat to the patriarchy. When women center men, they are likely living in a chaotic state, unsure of their own worth and power, pouring their labour and emotional energy into the wrong cup. Imagine how powerful you could be if you poured that love into yourself?

Being whole means nourishing yourself physically, emotionally and mentally. It can come from finding fulfilment in your career, your social life with like-minded people, your hobbies, spending time in nature, reading, listening to music and pursuing other passions. It can come from staying true to your values and making choices that align with your core beliefs. It can come from setting boundaries, rejecting comparison and believing in life's numerous opportunities beyond being someone's partner.

There is a transformation that comes from embracing your body in its entirety. Healing towards wholeness has allowed me to accept every part of my body, flaws and all. By focusing on yourself, in time your fractured heart will mend. You will release bitterness from your soul. Your mind will become clearer and focused on more important things.

The more women choose to decenter men and live a life free of self-observation and objectification, the more it will force men to change and do the inner work. It will force men to be self-sufficient, to be better people and, hopefully, to view us as equals.

When we are treated in an objectified and degrading way, it can lead us to question what it means to be a woman. Every time I learn to trust my gut without questioning myself, every time I use my voice to stand up for what I believe in, every time I stand up to a man who makes me feel uncomfortable within my skin, every time I choose to wear what I want rather than clothing that tightens, smooths or shrinks my body, I feel as though the broken parts of myself are slowly coming back together; that I am slowly rebuilding myself and reclaiming my objectified body as my own.

Are you ready to do the same?

notes

preface

Doctor Caroline Heldman has studied: 2014 TED Talk, 'The Sexy Lie'
A 2006 study examined self-objectification: Szymanski, D.M. & Henning, S.L. (2007) 'The Role of Self-objectification in Women's Depression: A Test of Objectification Theory', *Sex Roles*, 56, 45–53. doi: 10.1007/s11199-006-9147-3
A further study found correlation: Szymanski, D., Gupta, A., Carr, E. & Stewart, D. (2009) 'Internalized Misogyny as a Moderator of the Link Between Sexist Events and Women's Psychological Distress', *Sex Roles*, 61, 101–9. doi: 10.1007/s11199-009-9611-y
Research shows how our emotions: Levenson, R.W. (2003) 'Blood, Sweat, and Fears: The Autonomic Architecture of Emotion', *Annals of the New York Academy of Sciences*, 1000, 348–66. doi: 10.1196/annals.1280.016; Kövecses, Z. (2000) *Metaphor and Emotion: Language, Culture, and Body in Human Feeling* (Cambridge University Press)
In 2024, Home Secretary Yvette Cooper: Catt, H. & Rose, C. (2024) 'Misogyny to be treated as extremism by UK government', BBC, available at: www.bbc.co.uk/news/articles/c15gnolq7p50
The Femicide Census shows: The Femicide Census, 'Femicide Census 2022', available at: www.femicidecensus.org/wp-content/uploads/2025/09/2022-Femicide-Census-Report.pdf
A 2025 report from the National Audit Office: National Audit Office (2025) 'Tackling violence against women and girls', available at: www.nao.org.uk/reports/tackling-violence-against-women-and-girls

vagina.

As a baby, I obviously had no idea: World Health Organization (2021) 'Devastatingly Pervasive: 1 in 3 Women Globally Experience Violence', available at: www.who.int/news/item/09-03-2021-devastatingly-pervasive-1-in-3-women-globally-experience-violence
I had no idea that every ten minutes: UN Women (2024) 'Five Essential

Facts to Know About Femicide', available at: www.unwomen.org/en/articles/explainer/five-essential-facts-to-know-about-femicide

Had I been born in, say: UN News (2023) 'Afghanistan now "most repressive country" for women, Security Council hears', United Nations, available at: https://news.un.org/en/story/2023/03/1134352

The UN estimates that every two hours: World Health Organization (2023) 'A Woman Dies Every Two Minutes Due to Pregnancy or Childbirth: UN Agencies', available at: www.who.int/news/item/23-02-2023-a-woman-dies-every-two-minutes-due-to-pregnancy-or-childbirth--un-agencies

According to the charity Girls Not Brides: Mayor, S. (2004) 'Pregnancy and childbirth are leading causes of death in teenage girls in developing countries', *BMJ*, 15;328(7449):1152. doi: 10.1136/bmj.328.7449.1152-a.

If I were born in Sierra Leone: Action Aid (2025) 'Female Genital Mutilation (FGM)', available at: www.actionaid.org.uk/our-work/vawg/female-genital-mutilation

In 2024, the National Police Chiefs': End Violence Against Women Coalition (2024) 'VAWG Is a National Emergency, Say Police Chiefs', available at: www.endviolenceagainstwomen.org.uk/vawg-is-a-national-emergency-say-police-chiefs

A 2018 report by the FBI: Federal Bureau of Investigation (2018) '2018 Crime in the United States', Table 42, available at: https://ucr.fbi.gov/crime-in-the-u.s/2018/crime-in-the-u.s.-2018/tables/table-42

In 2023, a report by the International Society: Ortega-Sánchez, I., Lucha-López M.O., Monti-Ballano, S. (2025) 'Motivational Factors for Labiaplasty: A Systematic Review of Medical Research', *Journal of Clinical Medicine*, 14(8):2686. doi: 10.3390/jcm14082686

A study by YouGov: Waldersee, V. (2019) 'Half of Brits don't know where the vagina is - and it's not just the men', YouGov, available at: www.yougov.co.uk/health/articles/22596-half-brits-dont-know-where-vagina-and-its-not-just

A 2019 Eve Appeal and YouGov report: Watkins, E. (2019) 'Less Than A Fifth Of Parents Use The Word "Vagina" When Talking To Their Kids About Vaginas', Grazia, available at: www.graziadaily.co.uk/life/in-the-news/a-fifth-of-parents-use-vagina-for-female-genitals-with-daughters/

Studies show that refusing to call: Rees, J. (2023) 'Women's health: Body part names taboo a risk to health', BBC, available at: www.bbc.co.uk/news/uk-wales-65122134

The Rape Culture Pyramid: 11th Principle: Consent!, created by Jaime Chandra & Cervix (2018), available at: https://www.11thprincipleconsent.org/consent-propaganda/rape-culture-pyramid

breasts.

Boob jobs continue to be: International Society of Aesthetic Plastic Surgery (2023) 'Global Survey 2022: Full report and press release', available at: www.isaps.org/discover/about-isaps/global-statistics/global-survey-2022-full-report-and-press-releases

In environments characterised by: Uppuleti, J. (2023) 'The Dalit mothers who were forced to become wet nurses', Al Jazeera, available at: www.aljazeera.com/features/longform/2023/3/8/the-dalit-mothers-who-were-forced-to-become-wet-nurses; Corey, R. (2022) 'The controversial history of wet nursing and what the "informal", "underground" practice looks like today', Yahoo! Life, available at: www.yahoo.com/lifestyle/wet-nursing-history-190132701.html

A study in 2011 by the *British Journal of Psychology*: Horvath M.A., Hegarty, P., Tyler, S., Mansfield S. (2012) '"Lights on at the end of the party": are lads' mags mainstreaming dangerous sexism?', *British Journal of Psychology*, 103(4):454-71. doi: 10.1111/j.2044-8295.2011.02086.x

In a UK study, 39 per cent: Laville, S. (2016) 'Most boys think online pornography is realistic, finds study', the *Guardian*, available at: www.theguardian.com/culture/2016/jun/15/majority-boys-online-pornography-realistic-middlesex-university-study

Monroe had been a victim: Buchthal, S. & Comment, B. (eds) (2010) *Fragments: Poems, Intimate Notes, Letters by Marilyn Monroe* (Farrar, Straus & Giroux)

In *Right-Wing Women*: Dworkin, A. (1983, 2025) *Right-Wing Women* (Penguin Classics)

One of the most famous: Hilton, P. (2023) *Paris: The Memoir* (Dey Street Books)

Statistics show that disabled women: Mailhot Amborski, A., Bussières, E.L., Vaillancourt-Morel, M.P., Joyal, C.C. (2022) 'Sexual Violence Against Persons With Disabilities: A Meta-Analysis', *Trauma Violence Abuse*, 23(4):1330-1343. doi: 10.1177/1524838021995975; The Nia Project (2020) 'Double Oppression: Violence Against Disabled Women: A resource pack for practitioners', available at: www.niaendingviolence.org.uk/wp-content/uploads/2020/02/double-oppression-violence-against-disabled-women.pdf

skin.

A study on Italian women: Campos-Vazquez, R.M. & Gonzalez, E. (2020) 'Obesity and hiring discrimination', *Economics & Human Biology*, 37. doi: doi.org/10.1016/j.ehb.2020.100850

Studies show that those who look less white: Forth, J., Theodoropoulos, N., Bryson, A. (2021) 'The Role of the Workplace in Ethnic Wage Differentials', IZA Discussion paper: 14697, Institute of Labor Economics (IZA), Bonn

I googled this specific brand: Olsen, C.A., Olsen Law Offices, APC, 'Complications Leading to the Yasmin and Yaz Lawsuit', available at: www.olsenlawapc.com/personal-injury/product-liability/yasmin-yaz; Anapol Weiss (2024) 'Depo-Provera Lawsuit Settlements 2024', available at: https://www.anapolweiss.com/blog/depo-provera-lawsuit-settlements-2024-most-recent-in-a-long-line-of-litigation-against-unsafe-birth-control-products

It is estimated that more than 99 per cent: Herzig, R.M. (2015) *Plucked: A History of Hair Removal* (New York University Press)

However, the machines were dangerous: Ibid.

Barclays say that the global: Gilchrist, K. (2023) 'Obesity drug industry could be worth $200 billion within the decade, says Barclays, as market valuations grow', CNBC, available at: www.cnbc.com/2023/04/28/obesity-drugs-to-be-worth-200-billion-in-next-10-years-barclays-says.html

But rather than the majority: Institute of Medicine (US) Subcommittee on Military Weight Management (2004) 'Weight Management: State of the Science and Opportunities for Military Programs', *National Academies Press*, 4, Weight-Loss and Maintenance Strategies

stomach.

But rather than the majority: Wing, R.R. & Phelan, S. (2005) 'Long-term weight loss management', *The American Journal of Clinical Nutrition*, 82(1). doi: 10.1093/ajcn/82.1.222S

The *Guardian* also reported that: Siddique, H. (2019) 'One in eight UK adults have suicidal thoughts over body image – poll', *Guardian*, available at: www.theguardian.com/lifeandstyle/2019/may/13/body-image-survey-one-in-eight-uk-adults-suicidal-thoughts

A shocking study by researchers: Hruschka, D.J., Brewis, A.A., Wutich, A. & Morin, B. (2011) 'Shared norms and their explanation for the social clustering of obesity', *American Journal of Public Health*, 101, Suppl 1, S295–300. doi: 10.2105/AJPH.2010.300053

Studies show that by the age: PA News Agency (2019) 'Four-year-olds view overweight people negatively – study', *South Wales Argus*, available at: www.southwalesargus.co.uk/news/national/17607141.four-year-olds-view-overweight-people-negatively-study/

Scientifically, studies show that Black women: Gasperino, J. (1996) 'Ethnic differences in body composition and their relation to health and disease in women', *Ethnicity & Health*, 1(4):337-47. doi: 10.1080/13557858.1996.9961803

thighs.

For many Black women: Holmes, C.M. (2016) 'The Colonial Roots of the Racial Fetishization of Black Women', *Black & Gold*, 2, available at: https://openworks.wooster.edu/blackandgold/vol2/iss1/2

BBLs, where fat is transferred: Pazmiño, P. & Garcia, O. (2023) 'Brazilian Butt Lift-Associated Mortality: The South Florida Experience', *Aesthetic Surgery Journal*, 3;43(2):162–78. doi: 10.1093/asj/sjac224

The International Society Of Aesthetic Plastic Surgery's: International Society of Aesthetic Plastic Surgery (2022) 'ISAPS International Survey on Aesthetic/Cosmetic Procedures, Performed in 2022', available at: www.isaps.org/media/aoqfm4h3/isaps-global-survey_2022.pdf

And, despite the dangers: Applegate, Z. & Burchell, H. (2023) 'Brazilian butt-lift surgery: What are the risks and why is it so popular?', BBC, available at: www.bbc.co.uk/news/uk-england-norfolk-66798236

Although it is estimated that 80–90 per cent: Gabriel, A., Chan, V., Caldarella, M., Wayne, T. & O'Rorke, E. (2023) 'Cellulite: Current Understanding and Treatment', *Aesthetic Surgery Journal Open Forum*, 5. doi: 10.1093/asjof/ojado50

brain.

The mental health charity Mind: Butt, S., Randall, E., Morris, S., Appleby, L., Hassiotis, A., John, A., McCabe, R. & McManus, S. (2025) 'Suicidal thoughts, suicide attempts and non-suicidal self-harm', *Adult Psychiatric Morbidity Survey: Survey of Mental Health and Wellbeing, England, 2023/4*, NHS England, available at: https://digital.nhs.uk/data-and-information/publications/statistical/adult-psychiatric-morbidity-survey/survey-of-mental-health-and-wellbeing-england-2023-24/suicidal-thoughts-suicide-attempts-and-self-harm

heart.

Studies show that Gen Z women: Ipsos (2025) 'International Women's Day 2025', available at: www.kcl.ac.uk/giwl/assets/iwd-2025-survey.pdf

references

Bates, Laura, *Men Who Hate Women* (Simon & Schuster, 2021)
de Beauvoir, Simone, *The Second Sex* (Alfred A. Knopf, 1953)
Federici, Silvia, *Caliban and the Witch* (Autonomedia, 2017)
Greer, Germaine, *The Female Eunuch* (MacGibbon & Kee, 1970)
Herzig, Rebecca M., *Plucked: A History of Hair Removal* (New York University Press, 2015)
Hilton, Paris, *Paris: the Memoir* (Dey Street Books, 2023)
Holmes, Rachel, *The Hottentot Venus: The Life and Death of Saartjie Baartman* (Bloomsbury Paperbacks, 2016)
hooks, bell, *Black Looks: Race and Representation* (South End Press, 1999)
Jackson, Lottie, *See Me Rolling* (Penguin, 2024)
Kite, Lexie and Lindsay, *More Than a Body* (Harvest, 2021)
Smolak, Linda and Levine, Michael P. (eds), *Wiley Handbook of Eating Disorders* (John Wiley & Sons, 2015)
Strings, Sabrina, *Fearing the Black Body: The Racial Origins of Fat Phobia* (NYU Press, 2019)
Walter, Natasha, *Living Dolls* (Virago, 2009)
Wolf, Naomi, *The Beauty Myth* (Chatto & Windus, 1990)
Wollstonecraft, Mary, *A Vindication of the Rights of Woman* (Penguin Classics, 2004)

Further reading

If you enjoyed this book, I encourage you to read the writing of these amazing female writers.

Ashley, Beth, *Sluts* (Penguin, 2025)
Bravo, Reah, *Complicit* (Gallery Books, 2024)
Cheetham, Jo, *Killjoy* (Picador, 2023)
Gay, Roxane, *Hunger* (Harper, 2017)
hooks, bell, *The Will to Change* (Washington Square Press, 2025)
Levy, Ariel, *Female Chauvinist Pigs* (Free Press, 2006)
Ratajkowski, Emily, *My Body* (Quercus, 2021)
Taylor, Dr Jessica, *Sexy but Psycho* (Constable, 2022)

Katz, Dr Jackson, *Every Man* (Penguin Life, 2025) (one of the few books written by a man that discusses how men can combat extreme misogyny)

acknowledgements

This book has only been made possible because of the help, hard work and dedication of a tribe of wonderful women: agents, publishers, designers and contributors, and I must first acknowledge them and their unwavering support in helping bring *Flesh* to life.

To Sabhbh Curran and Cathryn Summerhayes at Curtis Brown: I truly lucked out with you being my literary agents and appreciate you not only believing in my writing but in also pushing me to be the best writer I can be. What a wonderful way to start our chapter together. Thank you for everything!

To Beth Eynon and Katie Ogunsakin, my editors at Trapeze: thank you for believing in this book, its premise, for taking it on and for the constant words of encouragement – especially when I've been anxious about my own capabilities! It has been an absolute joy working with you both. I am honoured to have *Flesh* sit alongside books by your other fabulous female writers and am grateful to have had such smart women championing me all the way.

To the rest of the team at Trapeze and Orion, who have worked diligently on the book cover design, the copy-editing and legalities, again, thank you for your help: Jess Hart, Georgia Goodall, Hannah Cox, Sarah Lundy, Holly Wilson and Louise Richardson. It truly takes a team to make this happen and I am lucky to have had your time, energy and support.

Above all, I want to thank the women who have contributed or shared their experiences with me as part of this book, but also the women who continue to share their stories *outside* of these pages: the uncomfortable, the heartbreaking, the dark, the depressing, the scary. Each time you speak up for yourself and share your truth, you provide solace and support for fellow women, allowing us to be seen beyond our physical bodies. It is women like you who are helping bring women's issues to light and holding misogynists and the patriarchy accountable, who are allowing our voices to be heard and trying to make life better for the future generations of girls and women.